Whatever Possessed the President?

WITHDRAWN

By Robert Wood

Metropolis against Itself

Suburbia: Its People and Their Politics

1400 Governments: The Political Economy of the New York
Metropolitan Region

The Necessary Majority: Middle America and the Urban Crisis

With others

Schoolmen and Politics: A Study of State Aid to Education in
the Northeast

Politics and Government in the United States

Remedial Law: When Courts Become Administrators

WHATEVER POSSESSED THE PRESIDENT?

Academic

Experts

and

Presidential

Policy,

1960–1988

Robert C. Wood

Amherst

THE UNIVERSITY OF MASSACHUSETTS PRESS

Copyright © 1993 by
The University of Massachusetts Press

Printed in the United States of America

LC 92–41985

ISBN 0–87023–862–0 (cloth); 863–9 (pbk)

Designed by David Ford

Set in ITC Bookman Light by Keystone Typesetting, Inc.

Printed and bound by Thomson-Shore, Inc.

Library of Congress Cataloging-in-Publication Data
Wood, Robert Coldwell, 1923–
    Whatever possessed the president? : academic experts and
presidential policy, 1960–1988 / Robert C. Wood.
        p.   cm.
    Includes bibliographical references and index.
    iSBN 0–87023–862–0 (alk. paper). —
ISBN 0–87023–863–9 (pbk, : alk. paper)
    1. Presidents—United States—Decision making.
2. Presidents—United States—Staff.   3. Government
consultants—United States.   4. Political consultants—
United States.   5. Policy scientists—United States.
6. Social scientists in government—United States.   I. Title.
JK518.W66   1993
353.07′72—dc20   92–41985
                                                CIP

British Library Cataloguing in Publication data are available.

This book is published with the support and cooperation of the
University of Massachusetts at Boston.

Once again, to

Peggy,

Franny,

Maggie,

Frank—

and now to

Tom,

Ben,

and

Meg—

with thanks

for your patience

and with love

CONTENTS

Preface   xi

Introduction: Talking Presidents   3

1

Helping Presidents Talk: The Basic Model   8

Who Shapes the Action?   8

Who Shapes the Action? The Presidential Policy Process Writ
   Large   9

The Intervening Elites: Political Self-Starters   11

The Intervening Elites: Resourceful Administrators   15

The Intervening Elites: Ambivalent Academics   20

Challenges and Constraints: Outriders   26

Challenges and Constraints: Gatekeepers   29

2

The Glory Years Begin   33

The Coming of Age of the Social Sciences   33

The Sketchy Heritage   42

The Academic Advisory Committee of 1959   46

The Republicans Respond   54

Transition Breakthrough   56

Policy in Camelot   59

3

Flood Tide: Experts and the Great Society   67

Coping with the Legacy   71

Kingpins of the Great Society   73

The Process Rationalized   78

One Bridge Too Far   81

Coonskins on the Wall   84

4

Cracks in the System   89

The Nixon Transition   89

The Campaign Ritual: Cambridge Perseveres   91

Institutionalizing the Experts   93

Rockefeller to the Rescue   95

Big Names and Little Deeds   99

Disciplining the Policy Process   102

The Ford Interregnum   105

Experts in Limbo   109

5

The System Disassembles   115

Carter and a Conventional Beginning   117

Short Circuit: Jordan vs. Watson   121

The Domestic Policy Staff: The Triumph of Lawyering   124

Bootlegging New Policy: Two Last Flings   130

The Policy President: All by Himself   135

6

Takeover: The Reagan Recess   139

The Quick Consensus   139

Second Thoughts on the Consensus   140

Experts at Work: Supply-Side Made Simple   147

Experts at Work: The New New Federalism   151

Experts at Work: The Triumph of Urban Enterprise   156

The Revolution on Hold   159

7

The New Order   162

The University Disassembles   162

New and Hostile Horizons   166

The Rise of the Think Tanks   169

The Future of Policy Experts   174

Notes   179

Index   199

PREFACE

Over the space of the last forty-two years I have worked for four American presidents and watched with considerable professional interest the performance of all nine. My first introduction to the presidency was in 1950 with the Truman administration as a junior staff member in the Bureau of the Budget (now the Office of Management and Budget) of the Executive Office of the President. My principal assignments were to develop administrative measures designed to prevent crime and corruption in the executive branch and to provide timely assistance in communities striken by floods, hurricanes, and other natural disasters. I was not entirely successful in either endeavor. But I learned a lot.

I continued my work for two years of the Eisenhower administration where I still explored instances of crime and corruption and tried to mediate between the Federal Bureau of Investigation and the Secret Service with respect to their jurisdictional boundaries. I came back to the office as a member of the Academic Advisory Committee for John Kennedy and his Preinaugural Task Force on Housing. I chaired the first two task forces on Urban and Metropolitan Problems for President Lyndon Johnson and then served as Undersecretary and Secretary of Housing and Urban Development from 1966 to 1969. So, I have worked in and near the White House, in the land of long knives, across two decades.

Thereafter, from several academic posts, I have observed President Johnson's successors. Occasionally I have served as a temporary or part-time adviser in the Nixon, Carter, and Bush administrations. But for the most part, in recent years I have moved from the playing field of politics and government to the academic bleachers.

Nine years ago Wesleyan University and the Henry R. Luce Foundation provided me the explicit opportunity to explore the interaction of academic experts, presidents, and the presidential office in shaping policy. The Henry Luce Chair in Democratic Institutions and the Social Order was designed by the Wesleyan faculty to focus on this relationship. Successive waves of students stood ready to do the number-crunching essentials in identifying the academic experts, their backgrounds, and the extent of their involvement. I thank both faculty and students, although they carry no responsibility for the content or conclusions of the book.

I especially thank Jane Fountain, now assistant professor at Harvard's John F. Kennedy School of Government, who served as research associate overseeing the principal data assembly and interpretation while a graduate student in political science at Yale. She designed our computer programs that identified and characterized 339 principal academic advisers in the Kennedy, Johnson, and Nixon administrations to be supplemented by separate studies of the Ford, Carter, and Reagan years. She directed the student inquiries and validated the results. A baker's dozen or more Wesleyan students helped us assemble these profiles, but Lawrence (Muzzy) Rosenblatt, Susan Toothacker, Neal Blicher, Alice Carter, James Dearborn, Jennifer Neel, Isabel Miller, and Lisa Cerbone Gorman deserve special thanks. They showed that committed undergraduates can be as good researchers as their graduate student counterparts—and often with more enthusiasm and imagination.

To my friends at the presidential libraries—in particular Megan Desnoyers at the Kennedy Library, Nancy Kegan Smith at the Johnson Library, and Joan Lee Howard at the Alexandria, Virginia, warehouse that still holds the most important papers of the Nixon administration—special thanks. Special thanks as well to Martin Anderson of the Hoover Institution who opened his personal files on both the Nixon and the Reagan administrations and began a welcomed correspondence that I hope long endures.

Ten academic colleagues reviewed and critiqued the manuscript and decisively affected its final form: Martin C. Anderson, Hoover Institution; Robert Armstrong, then president, The Henry Luce Foundation, Inc.; William J. Barber, Wesleyan University; Jane Fountain, John F. Kennedy School of Government; Cynthia Horan of Wesleyan University; John H. Kessel, Ohio State University; Philip Pomper, Wesleyan University; Donald L. Robinson, Smith College; Peter Schauffler, Committee on the Constitutional System; and Harold Wolman, Wayne State University. I prevailed on Nan Robinson to do the impeccably professional and honest task of genuine editing.

The University of Massachusetts Press has once again provided support and guidance. Paul Wright, Bruce Wilcox, and Pam Wilkinson have, as before, made the book much better than the manuscript. They have been pleasantly aggressive in their editing, and I am grateful.

At the center of this endeavor—pulling it all together, seeing through the successive drafts, ensuring accuracy and quality, commenting with critical discernment, retaining composure and cheerful encouragement—was Jane Tozer of Wesleyan. Of all the university's resources, her presence as manager of my professional affairs is the best.

Finally, the family. Down through the years, Margaret Byers Wood has been a loving partner, a good friend, and a constructive critic as I painfully scribble out my thoughts. Three splendid young people—Frances, Maggie, and Frank—from childhood to grown-up time have been friendly, loyal but forthright observers of my career and they are now joined by son-in-law Tom Hassan and grandchildren Ben and Meg. They have always supported my choices—even if they have not always been sanguine about them.

I thank them all. I have enjoyed recollecting the forty-two years, undertaking to analyze them as I have experienced them and others have observed and evaluated them. In these ways I have tried to trace the not-always-happy relationships among presidents and academics with the knowledge, sympathy, and, I hope, objectivity to which the role of a participant-observer is well suited.

I hope the reader will enjoy the recollections, analyses, and judgments, too.

Robert Wood
Little Compton, Rhode Island
July 14, 1992

Whatever Possessed the President?

INTRODUCTION:
TALKING PRESIDENTS

Politics is talk, or to put the matter more exactly the
activity of politics ("politicking") is talking . . . the
transmission from intelligence to intelligence of
ideas . . . the special characteristics of political ideas
being continuously about the pursuit and use of
power.—H. Mark Roelofs[1]

If politics is talk—and political talk-
ing requires ideas about the pursuit and use of power—where do the
ideas come from? More precisely, who offers ideas in politics, through
what forms of talk, and at what time in the political process? Most crit-
ically, here in the United States, who talks to its most powerful politician,
the president, in what tongues, and on what occasions?

Like all modern democratic politicians, striving to win and govern in an
information-rich, media-saturated, nonauthoritarian "Persuasive Society," a president requires ideas because he gains the office and exercises
its powers, as Roelofs says, by "talking people into obedience." If he must
talk, he must have ideas, for he must have something to say. They are, in
the terms of the trade, the hard currency of politics. If we are to know what
"possesses" a president, where he got "such an idea," what led him to do
"such a thing," we need to know, in the language of a cub reporter, who,
what, where, when, why, and how.

The three principal talkers to presidents in our pluralistic political
process are elites. They are *fellow politicians;* they are *resourceful professional administrators* permanently established in the national government; and they are *policy experts,* once almost always recruited from the
academic community, now increasingly found in the halfway houses of
policy research, think tanks. They are "intervening elites" in the presidential arena by reason of election or political support.

Two types of "outriders" circle the intervening elites: *political philosophers,* who offer general-purpose ideologies about how the world works
and how it can be made better, and *image makers,* pollsters and media

3

specialists who attach themselves to the politically active. Outriders of both types are bent on transforming typical pedestrian personalities into charismatic ones. *Gatekeepers* also arise at "choke points" to control the flow of talk on the campaign trail and in the White House. But the three intervening elites—fellow politicians, bureaucrats, and academic experts—are the principal ones able to talk regularly to presidential candidates and presidents.

The talk these elites use also comes in threes. Conventionally, the modes are known as rhetoric, ideology, and knowledge. Those who actually craft the president's talk—his speeches, his State of the Union address, his special messages, his Oval Office fireside chats—often distinguish this triad more colloquially. They call them "blue smoke," "dreamboats," and "reality time." Essentially, rhetoric or "blue smoke" is talk that appeals by metaphor and narrative to the instincts, base or noble, of those to be persuaded—most often, the voters. This "smoke" evokes symbols, stirs memories, and produces images. It often veers into demagoguery, and it can be nonsensical in the exact sense of the word. That is, it is not usually responsive to the actual public problems and issues of the times.

Ideology, or "dreamboats," is that tapestry of broad generalities and grand designs—sometimes loosely woven, sometimes laboriously constructed—that depicts the world and societies as they might be. It consists, as Philip Pomper best puts it, of "developed doctrines containing ideas of evils to be combatted and goods to be pursued in a secular context . . . instruments created, discovered and used by different men with different purposes."[2] Typically visionary, embracing ultimate questions, ideological talk is usually subjective, but it is born of sophisticated dialectical discourse. It speaks particularly to the true believer in the American way.

The third kind of talk, "reality time," actually conveys knowledge—the conclusions and inferences drawn from observation, experimentation, and discoveries in bounded fields of inquiry. It is the talk, most naturally, of scholars who incrementally and painstakingly balance propositions capable of independent substantiation by others. They employ every intellectual means they can muster—deduction, induction, observation, experimentation, demonstration—and their talk is, in the American vernacular, data-rich and overwhelmingly pragmatic. It is concerned with what works. It is the professional language of natural and social scientists.

All three elites use all three kinds of talk but in different proportions. The languages are never "pure." Like the three rings in the old Ballantine logo, they overlap. Disentangling conviction from observation of recurrent patterns of behavior—"what is supposed to be" in contrast to "what is"—

is always difficult. Where faith and commitment to values leave off and positivistic "truth" begins bedevils every formulation of policy, presidential or otherwise. Who the talker is, however, and what kind of talk prevails is critical to devising "workable" policy.

The comparative influence of these elites and the mix of talk wax and wane according to the stages of presidential politics. In the primary and general campaigns for election, the political elite and their image-making outriders hold sway, and ideas rich in rhetoric and ideology surface. "Pop" social scientists are in charge. After the election, in that desperately short, holiday-packed ten weeks of transition, the "knowledgeables" are likely to take brief command. Transition task forces heavily dependent on academic experts and former administrators are the order of the day, and although their constraints in time and their compulsion to be different from the preceding administration are severe, the purple prose of the campaign recedes.

After the inauguration, the "dominant" elite and kind of talk shift once again. The task of governing has begun, and, as Richard Goodwin reflected at the end of the 1960 campaign, "politics is to governing as a cartoon is to an etching." The administrative elite reasserts its influence, and the talk, though it continues to be knowledgeable, is institutionally biased by the particular department or agency the administrator represents. On any given issue, in the words of the outstanding federal civil servant Rufus Miles, "Where you stand . . . depends on where you sit."

The political campaigners and the outriders attached to them continue to be present, principally in the White House but scattered as well throughout the executive branch in cabinet and subcabinet posts. As time slips by, the need to do something that works becomes anxiously compelling. So both the career civil servant insiders and the academic think-tank experts have their crack at the action.

A sketch of three elites, three discourses, and three phases of presidential process omits the central actor: ideas do indeed come from the experience, conviction, and/or knowledge of the president himself. Thus, Harvard-tutored John Kennedy came to a commitment on hunger and poverty after the West Virginia primary campaign showed him "the truly needy." Lyndon Johnson recalled his teaching of Mexican students in Southwest Texas in insisting on a new federal role in education. Richard Nixon's personal indignation at welfare cheaters triggered his Family Assistance Plan. Jimmy Carter conceived of the energy crisis as a moral crusade and, dressed in a turtleneck sweater, he undertook to persuade a skeptical public of a common imperative. A strong sense of outrage at injustice, an enduring compassion for human suffering, a visceral resentment of regulation and discipline lying deep within a presidential psyche, shaped in childhood, scarcely capable of articulation, can be the inspiration for a New Frontier, a Great Society, a New American Revolution, or "Morning Again in America."

Yet the presidency remains a "plural," "collective" office. Few major presidential initiatives originate purely within the presidential brain. The office has become too institutionalized now to allow the chief executive to be sole author of almost anything.[3] The presidential campaign process is too laden with sweeping ideological generalizations and rhetorical promises to permit a specific "pure" idea spontaneously to surface even if it comes from the candidate himself. Moreover, Bush's "reading lips" on taxes, Reagan's pledge to get government off the peoples' backs, Nixon's promise to bring peace to Vietnam are not the products of the candidate's individual rumination. They are "collective" policy positions. They emerge as incumbent presidents or candidates assemble their advisers on the campaign trail, respond to situational crises or specify priorities, and then receive proposals and options from a wide array of sources.

This study undertakes to trace this ever-present struggle between the ideas of the president and those of the three elites, and the mix of rhetorical, ideological, and knowledgeable talk in the campaign, transition, and governing stages of the presidency. It does so in the arena of domestic policy beginning with John Kennedy, the first president born in the twentieth century, and it focuses particularly on the ideas of academic experts. How have these experts fared from one administration to another? How do they insert themselves into the presidential policy process? Are they rewarded? Do they come to possess political power on their own when their ideas prevail and persuade the president? Or do they remain hired guns, "instrumental intelligentsia," in Pomper's words, lackeys in the premier American political arena?

This inquiry starts with the campaign of 1959 and the Academic Advisory Committee established by John Kennedy. It continues by examining the scientists and scholars—men and women who, as the late speaker Sam Rayburn once observed, "never won an election or met a payroll"— whom Lyndon Johnson brought together in the era of the Great Society. It goes on to describe the temporary rebuff that Richard Nixon gave the experts in the 1970s when he declined to resolve the controversy over the Family Assistance Program between economist Arthur Burns and sociologist Daniel Patrick Moynihan. Growing out of that debate came the institutionalization of scholarly knowledge and advice in the Domestic Policy councils from Nixon to Carter, although in the end, ironically, that process was "lawyered" more than it was "professored."

Finally, attention falls on the Reagan administration. Despite the high profile of ideology and the superlative use of rhetoric, knowledgeable talk continued and shaped the most successful elements of the president's program. At the end, this study assesses the role of the emerging think tanks, which now institutionalize a strange mix of rational analysis and ideology and increasingly exclude university academics.

This account and analysis are limited to domestic policy-making during these six administrations, partly because the role of academic experts in foreign affairs and national defense during this period is reasonably well known. Indeed, established scholars dominated the field from 1960 to 1980—in succession McGeorge Bundy, Walt Rostow, Henry Kissinger, and Zbigniew Brzezinski. They have played substantial roles in intelligence, communications, weapons systems, and defense strategy, and they still do. Although they have not been reticent in accounting for their times, the secrecy that security policy imposes impedes the full exploration of their role in foreign and security affairs. Their occasional revelations only permit partial glimpses of the full iceberg, and the next round belongs to the longer-range evaluations of historians.

This study excludes as well any analysis of the substantial contributions and influence of natural scientists in domestic affairs. As with foreign affairs and defense, there is a considerable literature on the role of scientists, particularly the Office of the President's Science Advisor and his Science Advisory Committee. Again, there are problems in access and clearance even on domestic issues. So "hard" scientists—biologists, chemists, physicists—are touched upon only tangentially in such areas as telecommunications, medical research, and the technological potential of new forms of transportation and urban infrastructure, where the engineering profession seems increasingly influential. My concern is essentially with social scientists—economists, psychologists, political scientists, sociologists—and experts in specialized policy fields—human resources, housing, education, health, environmental affairs.

In short, this book describes a political system of domestic brain trusts linked to presidential palace guards themselves linked to presidents as candidates and officeholders, responding to pressures other sectors of a larger system have placed upon them. It is an account of an intervening elite in competition with other elites, sometimes prevailing and sometimes not.

I tell the story from the perspective of a direct participant in the Kennedy and Johnson administrations, as a close observer in the Ford and Carter eras, and as a retreaded scholar working through the records of presidential libraries and systematic interviews with other participants.

How knowledge vied with ideology—with rhetoric in occasional support of both sides—forms the greater part of the account that follows. How knowledge might prevail is the final chapter.

1

HELPING PRESIDENTS TALK:
THE BASIC MODEL

Who Shapes the Action?

When a newcomer to America asks how national policy is initiated, all eyes turn to the president. It is conventional wisdom, for the most part true, that the presidency is, in David Truman's felicitous phrase, the "mainspring" of the national governing system.[1]

To be sure, the Congress and the courts on occasion jump-start a response to a perceived public need or resolve a long-standing public dispute. The One Hundredth Congress seized the horns of the immigration and drug dilemmas when a laid-back Reagan administration was disinclined to act. The Supreme Court had the first word on school desegregation in the 1950s with the landmark *Brown v. the Board of Education* cases. More recently, the Court came to two decisions with respect to capital punishment, and it has had a further word on abortion that is likely to be decisive for a generation. The comparative activity of the three institutions varies according to the policy disposition of respective administrations: domestically, presidential initiatives were down with Nixon and Ford; up again with Carter. The budget deficits of the 1980s tended to squelch initiatives from either the executive or the legislative branch.

Nonetheless, day in and day out the modern "plural" presidency initiates the overwhelming majority of national policies. Presidents have done so sporadically since the Republic was established, particularly in times of crisis, war, or depression. Since Franklin Roosevelt, the presidency as an institution has come consistently to be the departure point for deciding the magnitude of national resources devoted to public purposes and the priorities among those purposes.

The tempo of presidential initiative varies with disposition of the incumbent, be he passive or active, positive or negative.[2] When a president is passive, as Eisenhower seems to have been, the public agenda is light, and the pace of public affairs is slow. But the president's position remains controlling. So Lyndon Johnson, as Senate majority leader, discovered to his discomfort when he undertook to present his own national agenda in 1957, only to have it stalled by Eisenhower's opposition. When a president is inclined to be active and positive, the pace of the policy process takes a quantum jump, and it can suffer "overload." So Jimmy Carter found out in his first year as president, when he sent proposal after proposal to the Congress in such a steady stream that the institution balked. Sheer energy and quantitative output does not guarantee presidential success in a divided government. Nonetheless, the president, passive or active, prudent or impulsive, remains the chief initiator of public policy.

The institutionalization of policy initiative in the presidency expresses itself in the State of the Union message and subsequent presidential addresses dealing with specific problems or concerns as they may be perceived by the Congress, the Washington community, the media, and the public at large. Since at least the New Deal era, all these audiences now expect the State of the Union message to outline the broad goals of an administration and to be elaborated in specific messages, executive orders, and announcements of presidential appointments. If the reception is mixed or negative, and if the president really cares, he "goes public" in press conferences and direct public appeals. So the policy ball starts, for the most part, in the president's court. He serves first.[3]

Who Shapes the Action? The Presidential Policy Process Writ Large

The central actors in presidential policy-making—politicians, administrators, and substantive experts—provide most of the ideas for most of the policy in the various phases of the process. They do so in talk that is rhetorical, ideological, knowledgeable, or some combination thereof. It is essential to recognize, however, that they introduce their ideas and choose their form of talk in a broad political environment. Conventionally that environment is described as pluralistic. Alternatively, in simplified Marxist terms, it is depicted as a single all-powerful elite, a national version of a worldwide capitalistic ruling class.

In sparse outline, the pluralist theory in contemporary political science holds that the "public interest" is forged from convergence of and compromise among special interests in order to build a majority coalition in any given political arena. In the typical American version of the model, businesses large and small contend against labor (organized and unorganized), agriculture (region by region and crop by crop), consumers (old folks and young), and veterans. In recent years, single-issue groups and "networks" targeting environmental concerns, housing, or other specific issues have complicated the pattern.[4]

As the textbook reasoning goes, all three major branches of government, in their own distinctive processes, strive to accommodate these interests. The president typically purports to be the sole representative of the "public will"; the senator or representative responds principally to her or his "constituency"; the Court "interprets" the law. In actuality, each institution is highly sensitive to the presentations of lobbies, political action committees, and "public interest" groups (which steadily increase in number) ever present in the national Capitol building. The result, so the pluralism theory runs, is policy that is never totally responsive to the problems it purportedly addresses but is framed instead so that those groups affected can "live with" the results. Indeed, the programs that emerge from the clash of competing interests can range from highly logical to monstrously irrational: the first Carter proposals reacting to the energy crisis or the lengthy laundry lists found in every omnibus housing bill fall in the latter category. Incremental, not optimal, advancement is the way of life and the genuine goal in pluralistic politics.

Contemporary textbook analysis contrasts pluralist theory with rule by an all-powerful elite, by a worldwide capitalist class—the regime. One formulation of American elitism identifies the Trilateral Commission organized by David Rockefeller in the seventies and kindred associations of interlocking elites—the Council on Foreign Relations, the Committee for Economic Development, for instance—as the prime instruments by which capitalism holds sway in the United States, Europe, and Asia. Politicians are puppets, and academics are hired guns paid to provide the ideology that justifies this hidden power behind the facade of democratic institutions.[5]

The theory of intervening elites is a less sweeping, more parsimonious concept of elitism. The politicians who regularly function in the presidential arena, the senior professional administrators in the top echelons of the executive branch, and the policy experts drawn from universities at first and now more frequently from think tanks are elites, to be sure. They conform to the traditional definition in social science—a fairly numerous, recurrent political species that possesses particularized skills, resources, and symbols of political value, certified by some gateway procedure, and empathic to fellow members. But intervening elites are strongly competitive, one against another; they do not compose an all-embracing, single class.

It is also important to emphasize that each elite has its coterie of interest groups seeking to influence and persuade. They are recipients of pressures unleashed by the pluralistic subcultures outside the presidency. Because they interact with some regularity in the discharge of their functions, they are occasionally mistaken for a single elite—or seen as being under the control of the "capitalist class." Yet each displays group attributes sufficient to distinguish it from the others. All exhibit considerable autonomy, and, most important, all function to examine, evaluate, modify, accept, or reject the propositions that politically active segments of the public advocate.

The Intervening Elites: Political Self-Starters

Clearly central to presidential policy-making are the politicians active in the campaign or present in the Washington community. Most frequently lawyers by profession, they are present by virtue of being elected to office (governors, mayors, senators, and representatives, friendly or unfriendly) or of having helped the president win election (a more select subset of the elected officials, plus the campaign operatives). They are also often cabinet and subcabinet members, the one thousand or so presidential appointees publicly sworn at least to be loyal to the president.

The most valuable service the political elite makes to a president or candidate is its capacity to predict "what will play in Peoria." From its hands-on, common-sense perspective comes a judgment about what ideas are likely to attract or alienate voters. That function may be time honored, but the attributes of the political elite today are far different from the conventional stereotypes. Until this generation at least, the popular image of the politician was the disreputable ward heeler, the slightly sleazy representative, the pompous senator on the take, and the president who somehow rose above it all to statesmanship. Two characteristics predominated: the politician was part of a partisan organization and usually worked his or her way up the ladder slowly, and the president, by virtue of his office, was the leader of a party, half beholden to it, sometimes able to bend it to his own vision. Party organization and party discipline were never as strong as current advocates for party resurgence remember. But they were there—an influential factor in nominating or electing a president.

That image of the politician is far from present-day reality. Today the ties of party loyalty lie lightly upon political activists. The dictates of monolithic community power structures, the big mules of business, the bosses, are few and relatively inconsequential to campaign or to governing. What is extraordinary about the present American political process is—given money and the ability to use it through the mass media, a most important qualification but not yet quite controlling—how easy it is for almost any young aspirant to enter the electoral arena, and how difficult it then becomes to succeed.

American politics, even at the presidential level, is a process of easy in and easy out, and the exit via primary and caucus results can be extraordinarily cruel. Consider the twenty-three candidates for the Democratic and Republican presidential nominations in 1984 and 1988 in alphabetical order (remembering that Reagan was unchallenged by any other Republican in 1984): Applegate, Askew, Babbitt, Bush, Cranston, Dole, DuPont, Dukakis, Duke, Gephart, Glenn, Gore, Haig, Hart, Hollins, Jackson, Kemp, LaRouche, McGovern, Mondale, Robertson, Simon, Traficant. What a diverse and improbable cast to try out in the exhausting succession of state primary elections! Calculating the odds and the minimal financial costs, one is tempted to ask what could have possessed them other than massive egos, rose-colored spectacles, and idiosyncratic agendas.

In addition to being self-starters, those who participate in successful campaigns have other distinctive attributes. In contrast to the seedy image of American politicians in the past and cynically extended by media commentary today, the fact is that political recruitment, especially at the national level, draws primarily from a pool of people who would, possibly to his delight, conform to John Adams's criteria of "the rich, the able, and the well-born." "Middle-aged, married, business or professional careers, with a comfortable income and some standing in the community based on long residence or organizational contacts there" was the composite picture I painted of national political figures in the Kennedy era.[6]

The advent of more women and minority officeholders has not substantially altered this picture. What has changed dramatically are the rapidly escalating financial requirements of campaigns, and this change has yielded more senators wealthy in their own right. Further, for both House and Senate, there is now a premium on congressional incumbency. Those who are already in public office receive contributions of political action committees by virtue of their seniority in committee assignments. Given these contributions, they are more likely to stay in.[7]

Added to initiative, education, and comfortable economic status is a distinctive personality structure drawn naturally to power, inclined toward dominance, socially mobile, oriented toward self-realization, and possessing at least on occasion idealistic values. The interplay of personality and politics has been a subject of systematic investigation for half a century since Harold Lasswell explored the impact of infantile and early childhood experience in shaping a political disposition. Subsequently Fred Greenstein and James David Barber have focused on presidential character and personality directly. In these formulations, successful politicians play "hardball"—or, more precisely, they make choices while experiencing two different concepts of "self," largely unrelated.[8]

One of these personality concepts is, in Lloyd Etheridge's words, "a 'lower' depleted insecure self, disposed to feel inadequate and ashamed. Coexisting is a second 'grandiose' self, with drives for great accomplishments and psychic recognition." Found together, the dual tracks yield a personality prone to be excessively ambitious, weak in ethics, cold, condescending, aggressive, bureaucratic, deficient in love, defective in humor, disposed to "slightly drunken" thought. What is most troubling about hardball politicians—for whom winning, whatever the issue and whatever the cost, is all-important—is their propensity to block rational thinking with emotionally organized thought, which admits simultaneously the dramatic sensibilities of overconfidence, ambition, fear, and ethical weakness. The American irony is that the prototypical political elite is one that succeeds by virtue of the very psychological traits usually regarded as nonvirtuous in American culture. These traits are also the least reasonable.

Key elements of our political environment encourage and exaggerate these attributes in the hardball politician. The decline of the party and its discipline is one factor (although historically, the extent of party control of nominations for public office in the United States and of the financing and conduct of campaigns has often been overemphasized). A second is the growing independence and/or apathy of the voter; two others are the erratic character of primaries and caucuses and the unpredictable role of the media in making news. These all combine to heighten the uncertainty of campaign strategies.[9]

So candidates run scared, except in the safest of districts. Periodic polls fluctuate widely and therefore compound uncertainty. Accordingly, candidates learn to keep their cool, project rationality, and restrain sharp comment or risk defeat—as Robert Dole learned to his sorrow when he snapped out that Bush "lied" in the 1988 New Hampshire Republican presidential primary. They must also exhibit a decorum and probity in private life—as Gary Hart learned in Miami—which until Watergate was territory considered largely out-of-bounds by the press. These constraints serve to put the political personality under considerable stress.

The stress is intensified during campaigns as outriders, media consultants, and pollsters vie with policy advisers in structuring the candidate's campaign image. The consensus of the campaign staff is usually that the image must be "reasonable" and that the candidate must appear "sincere." How the image is projected, however, is always a matter of considerable controversy, which the candidate must resolve or abdicate control over the campaign. Beset by Etheridge's internally conflicting "selves," forced to portray themselves as reasonable, pure, and earnest, driven to the point of exhaustion by the twin technologies of television and the jet airplane, modern politicians are further burdened by the need to build their own campaign organizations and finance them. With little or no party context—no real party platform, little party organization beyond personal "handlers"—they are catapulted into office, pressed for time, and almost always on public display. Little wonder, then, that when they become engaged in governing, the principle of marginal attention—a compulsion to shift from one issue and constituency to another with great frequency and little apparent comprehension of the stakes involved—applies. Marginal attention becomes a major attribute, not only because of the personality construct and the press of time, but also because of the sheer complexity of the issues on the modern public agenda.

Over the years, at least since Walter Lippmann, scholars and commentators alike have documented the awesome compulsion of politicians to oversimplify complex issues because they all too often lack the time either to understand the problems that underlie the issue or to parse the alternatives thoughtfully.[10] So, in the sixties, Lady Bird Johnson's strong commitment to the preservation and enhancement of our natural environment—policy-making involving substantial knowledge of biology, engineering, and sociology—was translated for political consumption into "beautification." The enormously intricate and quantitatively subtle strategies involved in fashioning a reliable defense against a nuclear first strike emerged as "Starwars." The triad of approaches to contain and ultimately conquer the AIDS epidemic, in which specialists have painstakingly assessed the respective roles of research, education, and treatment, became a twenty-second television spot advocating safe sex.[11]

In sum, the modern politician, as a member of a presidential elite, is for the most part intelligent, well educated, and financially secure—game-oriented, in Harold Lasswell's words, not gain-oriented. Yet such is the nature of the public issues politicians face and the pressure-cooker environment in which they work that the attention they give to a specific issue is almost always marginal, distracted, incomplete. Thus, their formulation of the issue is likely to be simplistic to the point that it distorts, misshapes, and twists the policy solution to grotesque formulations. Good, doable ideas left entirely to professional politicians with all the good intentions in the world will emerge at best so grossly transformed as to become the roughest approximations of feasible policy.

Modern, ambitious politicians working at the national level can command considerable respect even if their good will is sometimes obscured by troubling messiah complexes. The naiveté they exhibit regarding public problems, the frivolity of most of what they do in campaigns, and the shallowness of their public comprehension are therefore worrisome, at least to the student of democratic government. Nonetheless, their role is the crucial one because without politicians' espousal and defense no cause would be adopted or endure. And their special talent, as John Kingdon has pointed out, is sensing when an idea's "time has come."[12] No idea, no matter how sensible, can be realized in public action at the presidential level without their judgment. Given both their compulsions and their skills, the president and the politicians engaged with his endeavors are the first members of a possible alliance that now and again comes together to make a government work.

The Intervening Elites: Resourceful Administrators

The second and very permanent elite of presidential policymakers consists of the Senior Executive Service, top-level civil servants in the Executive Office of the President, the cabinet departments, and the major agencies of the executive branch. Some seven thousand seasoned professionals are in the service now, and another nine hundred at the so-called super-grade level (GS 16–18) occupy strategic positions year in and year out. These largely career executives work directly with about five hundred presidential appointments and their six hundred political staffers. The political appointees require Senate confirmation, and they hold titular direction and oversight over the executive establishment. Still, they come and go. The professionals have staying power and thus influence policy just by being "there," administration after administration. The senior service executives average seventeen to twenty-five years on the job compared to the scarcely two years that presidential appointees achieve.

Their role is critical to the capacity of the government to function and to the success of presidential administrations. In 1989, the National Commission on the Public Service, led by Paul Volcker, characterized the corps as "the repositories of organizational memory. They have built up personal intelligence and communications networks over many years through dealing with the same organizations, people, and issues. Perhaps more importantly, career executives are the professional line managers . . . They are in charge of mission accomplishment and service delivery." While the proliferation of political appointees in the service has been dramatic (up 13 percent from 582 to 658 in the 1980s) and this "administrative overbrush" has discouraged careerists (more than half left the service in the same period), it remains a coherent, cohesive body. So Senator John Glenn observed in 1987: "it knows how to grease the wheels of government and make them turn."[13]

Like its political counterpart, the professional administrative elite is upwardly mobile within its own ranks and has been for the past thirty years. Its members "cluster" according to educational speciality and to some degree geographical region in the departments and programs that fit their professional interests. Military leaders tend to come in disproportionate numbers from the South and Midwest. The foreign service still heavily relies on the Northeast and to a lesser extent the far West. Military academies and land-grant public universities educate most of the officer corps. Private universities and colleges on the East and West coasts provide the lion's share of foreign service and intelligence officers, although this concentration has thinned over the generation just passed.

Surveying the service in 1991, Fesler and Kettl concluded, "The American higher public service is a representative, fragmented, open elite." It is an elite, they argue, because of the influential positions its members hold, the salaries they command, and the high educational degrees they have attained. "It is not a close-knit group of people who, by formal organization, shared values, or informal understandings, act in a unified fashion . . . [it is] built variously on educational and professional specializations, single agency attachments and distinctive, congressionally established career services. Finally, the Service is not a closed group of careerists who entered in their twenties and thereafter had their promotional opportunities protected against competition."[14]

More than in other professional services such as the British and French, American administrators tend to spend most of their careers in a single department or agency. Although the Carter administration made a major effort in the Civil Service Reform Act of 1978 to establish a special class of general-purpose executives, disposed and equipped to move from one department to another as the need arose, to date this reform has had limited impact.

Across the upper echelons of the civil service, the networks that rise above departmental and agency provincialism and command allegiance are those of profession (law, accounting, medicine, espionage, and military, for example) and school tie. The schools need not be old or Ivy, although these still are important credentials for professional staffs in the justice and state departments and in the Central Intelligence Agency. For other departments and agencies, the Maxwell School at Syracuse University, and the public policy and management schools at the universities of Michigan, Texas, Massachusetts, and California provide important alumni groups to augment formal search and advancement procedures. These ties that bind give colleagues word of important new posts and vacancies before the official job descriptions appear.

The psychological attributes of the seven thousand senior career executives differ substantially from those of the political elite. The power drive is there, but it is more restrained, almost covert, often denied, cloaked under the pretense that all decisions and actions are authorized by existing law and initiated by the dictates of pure reason.[15] Triple, indeed quadruple, alliances exist with the congressional committees and subcommittees, interest groups, clienteles, customers, courts, and judges that oversee administrative behavior, but these common bonds are rarely if ever formally acknowledged. The networks are, in a professional sense, bootleg operations—and an administrator openly caught developing political power relations with Congress or clientele is likely to be treated severely by his or her political superior: newly appointed Secretary of Defense Richard B. Cheney disciplined generals who paid unauthorized visits to Congress early in 1989. Still, bureau chiefs can become "untouchables." J. Edgar Hoover and Admiral Hyman Rickover are the most obvious examples of professionals who successfully defied presidential oversight in one administration after another.

This secretive disposition to power of senior administrators is tied to certain other key personal attributes. Longevity in the service typically arises from experience in a single organization with a recurrent pattern of events, which somewhat naturally yields an expectation that things will continue as they have before. When a new presidential administration arrives, the seasoned bureaucrat often likens himself to the Indians greeting Columbus as he discovered America. "It may be new to him," they observe, "but we've been here all our lives."

Knowing that the new, innovative, but inexperienced politician who is now secretary or administrator is anxious to achieve radical change in a short time through "slightly drunken thinking," the senior civil servant will counsel gradualism and indirection and will seldom, if ever, exhibit overt insubordination or even clumsy foot-dragging. In dealing with political superiors or outsiders within and outside government, the senior administrator's approach is not to stand pat, heels dug in or head in the sand. Remembering that, whether a policy rises or falls, there is always next year, the civil servant is rather committed to incremental program development and step-by-step implementation. Change is advanced by envelopment and flank attacks, by the rejection of every frontal assault.

Typically, senior administrators, prudent in approach, are sticklers for details. Honest and cautious, reluctant to gamble, they take the long view. "Old walruses," as they call themselves, gauge program prospects beyond the goals of a single presidential administration. They rely on enduring, nonpartisan, interdepartmental, and interagency relationships among career officers like themselves. The hallmark of the senior administrator is commitment to the institution, not to the individual temporarily in command.

The complex relationship between administrator and political appointee is often marked by respect but rarely, if ever, by trust. Elliot Richardson, who has headed four cabinet departments, pinpointed the issue: "The trouble is that all too many political appointees . . . suspect . . . that senior civil servants lie awake at night scheming to sabotage the president's agenda and devising plans to promote their own." Even respect often comes after the fact, as a Reagan cabinet member confessed at the end of his term. "I had always felt that government people were not motivated . . . Well, I was dead wrong . . . There is a tremendous cadre of professionals highly motivated, not by financial incentives but to serve their country. It's as simple as that."[16] The overwhelming professional instinct is to preserve things as they are, adjusted only to fully documented changes in circumstance and clear demonstration of new needs.

These consistent and persistent attributes of senior civil servants lead many observers to mistrust them as a class and to lump them under the derogatory title of bureaucrat. Scorned especially by academics and journalists fond of quoting Weber and drawing a false analogy to the German establishment, their behavior is "averaged out." That is, a given office or role is viewed as so routinized that the particular person placed in a particular post is judged irrelevant. Thus individuals become interchangeable in bureaucracies, disposable like plastic cups. They are cogs in a wheel, and bureaucratic behavior is uniform, predictable, molded by massive, impersonal pressures and processes. "Administrators," James March has argued, "are vital as a class, but not as individuals . . . What makes an organization function well is the density of administrative competence . . . When an organization is working well, variations in outcomes will be due largely to variables unrelated to variations in attributes of top leaders."[17]

On closer inspection, the quick write-off of senior civil servants as robots replicated on an assembly line appears a dubious proposition. What is significant in the post–World War II cadres of senior administrators, especially in the policy analysis staffs that emerged in the 1970s, is their initiative, creativity, and energy. Surveying the careers and accomplishments of a baker's dozen of top-flight permanent public chief executive officers, Jameson Doig and Erwin Hargrove recently identified and coined them as "entrepreneurial" public executives.[18] These are the relatively rare administrators who identify new programs, motivate and energize internal constituencies, and discover and co-opt external constituencies while they sharply upgrade organizational capabilities and integrity.

They have capacity to reason systematically ("uncommon rationality," as Doig and Hargrove put it) and the talent to assess intuitively the opportunities an emerging historical situation offers; the will to conquer and to make a difference also comes into play. Where these attributes are present, the senior administrator indeed becomes resourceful and steps out from the crowd of his fellows. Then skills in coalition-building or in using rhetoric and symbols come to the fore and are recognized and rewarded.

These unusual public executives do not appear everywhere by magic. They are found principally in four organizational settings—autonomous programs often featuring high technology; new programs just getting underway; multiagency, multigovernment undertakings; and oversight agencies with governmentwide responsibility.

First, entrepreneurial administrators often work in an organization that has achieved considerable autonomy within our fragmented governmental system—a Forest Service, a Federal Bureau of Investigation, an Army Corps of Engineers. The autonomy can be enhanced if the agency is blessed with a new user-friendly technology that generates a special supportive public. Such was the case with Admiral Rickover and the nuclear submarine and James Webb and the Apollo spacecraft.

A second environment conducive to attracting "entrepreneurial" administrators are new and novel public programs where their experience and skills are valuable and their will to make a difference encourages them to abandon professional caution and take a chance. These are not necessarily high-technology programs in the defense department, or NASA in its early years. In the 1960s, the Department of Housing and Urban Development's Model Cities, the Office of Economic Opportunity, and the Peace Corps all attracted outstanding civil servants. Positive, innovative government has lured them since David Lilienthal led the New Deal's "socialist experiment," the TVA, and it is represented in contemporary times by Nancy Hanks's creative enhancement of the prestige and the budget of the National Endowment for the Arts. Here, civil servants can attain visibility and public appreciation. Their satisfaction is often enhanced by a lifeline to permanent civil service status, which still allows a return to another assignment if the current one proves too risky and controversial.

A third setting for truly exceptional men and women to emerge from the ranks of the seven thousand senior executives are programs with no clear boundary lines that require orchestrating different agencies and levels of government. The institutional circumstances in such programs are the reverse of those that prevail in autonomous agencies. Entrepreneurial administrators often flourish in domestic programs that require the participation of state and local government or the common efforts of a number of departments and agencies and that feature the involvement of the private sector in what is now known as "partnership." In modern American public policy-making and execution, these attributes are on the rise. Few organizations continue to have self-contained missions and exclusive command of their own turf. A web of intricate relationships—contracts, interagency memoranda of understanding, intergovernmental grant programs—bind public and private organizations together in such great undertakings in almost every important domestic endeavor. It is to these policies and programs—multiagency, multigovernmental, both public and private in character—that the special elite of public administrators are often drawn to work in close concert with other intervening elites.

Finally, since the Second World War, the oversight agencies of the Executive Office of the President and the Comptroller General have been incubators for the most distinguished and durable professional entrepreneurs. Roger Jones, John Macy, Elmer Staats, Harold Seidman, Alan Dean, and Dwight Ink were key participants in major decisions that shaped the New Frontier, built the Great Society, and fashioned Nixon's New American Revolution. Macy was for a time the principal headhunter for Johnson's presidential appointees; Seidman and Dean were critical in housing and transportation policy-making; Jones and Staats ensured a powerful role for the Bureau of the Budget in determining "the program of the President"; and Staats went on as comptroller general to transform a staid and orthodox General Accounting Office into an imaginative and occasionally crusading program evaluation instrument for the Congress. Working usually in deputy positions and always under some sort of powerful political oversight, these and a few score other men and women carried out the critical switching-station role of turning simplistic and often contradictory policies into workable programs that the street-level bureaucracy could carry out.

The Intervening Elites: Ambivalent Academics

The third elite—the credentialed experts first found predominantly in university settings but in recent years more and more in the burgeoning staffs of think tanks—is different in attributes and role than the politician and administrator elites. For openers, the criteria for elite status are more elusive: the archetypal policy expert is not captured by such clear-cut, quantitatively specific criteria as elections and civil service status. Traditionally "certified" by virtue of a doctoral degree and subsequent tenure, these professional hurdles are desirable but never sufficient conditions for "experthood." Social science experts slip in and out of the policy process, sometimes cherished in one administration, then scorned in another. Their influence turns heavily on personal relations with members of the other, more permanent elites and on the shape of the public agenda. Yet although its profile is more fuzzy at the edges, the third elite has been powerful for the last thirty years in the social sciences, for fifty years—since World War II—in the natural sciences.*

John F. Kennedy advanced the unorthodox concept of a tax cut designed to stimulate economic growth on the advice of Keynesian economists who triumphed over conventional Treasury Department thinking. Johnson proclaimed a Great Society backstopped by ideas from sociologists about empowering the poor. Richard Nixon sought welfare reform by choosing between conflicting notions of income maintenance and job creation advanced by a sociologist and an economist. Gerald Ford, in his brief tenure, sought to end inflation without real recourse to economists and failed. Jimmy Carter, largely on his own initiative, tried with an "in-house" version of welfare reform and a similarly constructed national energy policy, and also failed. Ronald Reagan stayed the course with tax reductions and deregulation as advocated by credentialed California-based conservative economists. Expert policy influence, then, has been considerable and generally continual.

For the presidential administrations from Kennedy to Bush, academic experts came overwhelmingly from seventy leading research universities offering doctoral degrees in substantial number and generously supported by government research grants. Their aggregate social science fac-

---

*My colleague John Kessel, in a letter to me of November 7, 1991, has reminded me of the importance of distinguishing between "politicized" social science experts based in the Academy and attracted to policy issues and research scientists who do not offer policy advice. Kessel emphasizes that there are distinctive academic cultures in which behavioralism in the social sciences (as distinguished from behaviorism as a prime concept of psychology) found deeper roots in the Midwest than on either coast. Kessel agrees that policy scientists in the years this book examines tended to congregate on the coasts, but he documents convincingly the Midwest's superior research reputation and commitment to sophisticated quantitative techniques of analysis in the rise of behavioralism. Except for the discipline of economics and a sprinkling of social science departments at such coastal institutions as Yale and M.I.T., the technical competence on both coasts remains extremely limited. As Kessel puts it, "Big-Ten research social scientists are more concerned with securing a project funded by the National Science Foundation, while Cambridge academics find much more excitement about getting a letter published in The New York Times." Accordingly, the third elite needs to be understood as a subspecies of social scientists and considerably restricted in number compared to the entire faculty complement in these disciplines. In Kessel's analysis, then, Harvard's self-image as the center of the academic universe is true only in the limited sense that a lot of social scientists with "pronounced policy interests" are in Cambridge.

ulty profiles confirm their scholarly disposition—that is, their far greater commitment to research than to teaching. Fifty percent of their faculties spend a quarter of their time on research. Eighty percent have published at two-year intervals. Ninety percent teach less than ten hours a week. By contrast, only 10 percent of the American college and university faculty on the whole do research, 69 percent have never published a book, and 53 percent have published nothing at all.[19]

Of the seventy research universities, nine currently have endowments whose 1991 market value exceeds one billion dollars. Their senior faculty salaries now average seventy thousand dollars. While these seventy universities constitute the principal pool for expert advice, the policy experts cluster in these nine. For the policy-oriented domestic social sciences, the university faculty pool is about seven thousand, roughly the same size as the administrative elite.

Those of the academic elite disposed to offer policy number about one thousand. From Kennedy through Reagan, they came overwhelmingly from the most wealthy and well-known universities on the two coasts—New England to the Middle Atlantic, and California—and occasionally from Michigan, Minnesota, and Chicago. Some come and go with changing administrations. Others endure as semipublic figures: the late Edward Mason, John Kenneth Galbraith, Richard Neustadt, and Nathan Glazer of Harvard; Paul Samuelson and Lester Thurow of M.I.T.; Eli Ginsberg and Bernard Barber of Columbia; Milton Friedman of Chicago; Martin Anderson and George Shultz from the Hoover Institution and Stanford; and, from various locations, Alan Campbell, Richard Nathan, and Daniel Patrick Moynihan.[20]

Whether their names are household words or they appear regularly on television, academic experts turn up by the several hundreds in presidential campaigns, transition teams, and administration appointments. They review, write, or "check out" presidential messages and legislative proposals, and they share common attributes of lifestyle and professional behavior. Though their sites shifted in the 1980s from university to think tank and from the two coasts to Washington itself, the credentials of these academics and their capacity to move from one setting to another remained fairly constant. As Carol Weiss concluded in 1990, the "uneasy partnership" between social science and government "endures." "Research," she writes, "has become a regular component of policy discussion in the U.S. Government. Its influence has survived the Reagan Administration, budgetary cutbacks and self-doubts in the social sciences."[21] Indeed, its presence has become a taken-for-granted element on the policy scene. Heralding in 1989 the effectiveness of the "policy community" to "push and haul their way to policy," Bernard Barber summarized eight cases in which mostly "quiet" but effective social science shaped policy. "All our respondents believe in the effectiveness of empirical social research. But not all by itself and not under all conditions . . . No matter what the knowledge base on any problem, not everything is possible at any given time."[22]

In their everyday professional lives, academics are preoccupied for the most part with empirical research, patterned as closely as possible on that of the natural sciences but juggling fact and value, induction and deduction, as the phenomena under study require. This elite broke sharply in the post–World War II decade from the dialectic of moral philosophy that had spawned their disciplines in favor of "a public, explicit, common fund of propositions . . . for use by all who can learn." Social scientists employ two modes of inquiry—statistics and psychology—unknown to the ancients. Overwhelmingly, they are considered "behavioralists"—that is, committed to the modern conception of knowledge, "a common fund of propositions, explicitly formulated, empirically tested, and objectively validated . . . a public treasury."*

This post–World War II university-based, research-oriented professionalism carries with it an aura of meritocracy, an emphasis on the intelligence, energy, and imagination that epitomize good scholarship. The university professor, whether oriented to research or policy, now ranks in the five professions held in highest public esteem, substantially above the lawyer and banker. Those disposed to policy constitute "a new breed of

---

*Daniel Lerner, *Evidence and Inference* (Glencoe, Ill.: The Free Press, 1958), 7. In the introduction to this volume, Lerner (a collaborator with Lasswell) offers what in my judgment is the clearest statement of the behavioralist approach as it emerged in the early postwar period. Lerner attempts to distinguish political science from the dialectic "knowledge derived evidence which is 'secret.'" On this point Lerner wrote that dialectic decisively parts company from science which must be public not private, explicit not "secret," and available in a common fund "for use by all who can learn." Over the years, Herbert A. Simon has continued to serve as a central authority, following Lasswell and Lerner, on the reshaping of the social sciences by "a celebration not of reason but of real human behavior." Since 1947, with the publication of *Administrative Behavior*, through his Nobel Prize address, "Reason in Human Affairs," to his autobiography, *Models of My Life*, interspersed with distinguished journal articles, Simon has insisted on distinguishing between the "bounded rationality" in social settings that encompass values, emotions, stupidities, and ignorance, and the neoclassic orthodoxy that still enthrones the pure reason of economic rationality, currently represented by game theory and public choice. His letter in the *Chronicle of Higher Education* January 15, 1992, 33, is the best contemporary statement of the behavioralist approach "replacing legalism and traditional theorizing with empirical evidence and theory based on evidence."

professors" who move easily between the academic world, business, and government; in the words of Ernest Lynton and Sandra Elman, "knowledge transfer is too critical now. It can no longer trickle down."[23]

Not only do contemporary academic experts at elite universities enjoy public prestige and compensation equivalent to the other professions, but their family backgrounds today have higher status than do those of their counterpart elites. Less decisively WASP in composition than fifty years ago, there is increasing and growing Jewish and Catholic representation to balance mainstream Protestantism. Present-day university professors are more likely to be offspring of well-to-do professional and business people than are successful politicians or public administrators. Sons and daughters of blue-collar farm and working families are comparatively rare in the "best" institutions of American higher education. Younger academics in the great universities more often come from privileged backgrounds, even though they have "earned" their positions through a meritorious record of research accomplishments.[24]

Esteemed by the general public, judged by professional academic performance rather than by social status—but at the same time possessed of select family background—university experts are a far cry from the familiar Mr. Chips image of the revered but ineffectual college professor enduring genteel poverty. Nonetheless, this cohesive, professional community of university faculty scholars is divided by at least two internal attributes. First, the personalities attracted to serious research are not typically endowed with the extroverted bonhomie of the successful politician or the rule-driven caution of the senior administrator. Second, the ethos of research scholars is in conflict with the utility of their inquiry to immediate popular concerns and often depreciates the work of policy-oriented colleagues.

Ever since Max Weber analyzed the professions of science and politics early in the century, academic scientists have been portrayed as committed with single-minded intensity to the pursuit of truth. However idealistic and exaggerated this portrait may be, the career success of university academics does not depend heavily on harmonious human relations. Qualities of empathy, gregariousness, warmth, and charm do not figure (at least formally) in evaluations for promotion or tenure. The typical academic is preoccupied with work and pursues avocations of an individualistic, not a team, nature. Egos are strong, but they are more likely to express themselves in the satisfaction of objective research accomplishments than in affiliating with or manipulating others.

Added to this disposition to play the loner is an ethical constraint special to the academic culture—a commitment to the pursuit of knowledge in a manner fundamentally unconcerned with practical application.

It is at rock bottom nonutilitarian. Sheer curiosity, so the operative folklore runs, should drive the research endeavor, a characteristic that is especially alien to the pragmatic American creed.

These two traits work to reduce sharply the number of university academics disposed to take the political world seriously: about one in seven join the subculture of the policy-oriented academic elite. Clearly, they compose only a small subspecies of the general class of "intellectuals," as the term has come into vogue in the United States since the 1930s. Academic experts may share with journalists, commentators, artists, and philosophers at large a preoccupation with ideas and their articulation; occasionally they can join the discourse and debate of the broader "intellectual community," in the media or on campus, about the great issues of the time. By and large, however, the experts who make up the third elite are not, to use Russell Jacoby's phrase, "the independent intellectuals," "the city Bohemians," the free lancers, present-day descendants of the habitués of Greenwich Village or the Parisian Left Bank earlier in this century. They constitute only a small part of the "intellectual class" devoted to molding public moods and opinions through talk, writing, publishing, and other means.[25]

However small a subset, expert scholars in universities and think tanks carry considerable political clout. Since World War II, they have been prime sources of new public ideas in education, welfare, housing, poverty, transportation, and health from their conception to law and implementation. To be sure, their collective influence can be ephemeral, for it depends heavily on the disposition of the two other intervening elites to listen to them. Their own academic community also questions the legitimacy of their public involvement. Further, their discoveries, inventions, and observations are often distorted through political oversimplification and erroneous interpretations in the media and elsewhere. Nonetheless, they are active proposers of policy on which governmental responses to public needs depend. They constitute a major pool for presidential appointments to cabinet and subcabinet posts, commissions, and task forces, averaging about two hundred of the roughly one thousand political appointments in each of the past six administrations. They fill the lists of congressional expert witnesses, and they are the talking heads for television and op-ed newspaper and magazine columns. They are consistent players in the national political game.

Political common sense can judge whether the remedies scholarly advisers offer are palatable, and popular common sense can say whether they address the most urgent issues and thus justify the political pain and suffering involved in turning them into legislation. Yet without the expert adviser, workable responses to crucial collective problems seldom appear.

Their first proposals may not work at all and may have to be reformulated again and again. But where inherited knowledge and tradition have little to say and ideologies sweep the issues up in an inapplicable theory, academic expert knowledge is the best and most realistic point of departure in policy-making.

Challenges and Constraints: Outriders

A sketch of the American political arena as an overlay of three intervening elites on a pluralist system of competing interest groups and the public at large is, of course, too simple. Other actors are involved. Other scribblers, not only university professors, write.

A truly comprehensive depiction of how the American political system produces and processes ideas into public programs has to include the other talkers: the ideologues searching for neat and comprehensive answers and the ancient orators in their modern garb as consultants and image makers. The model has to encompass the three branches of the national government as well as the fifty state and ninety thousand local governments. The demands of communication need to be specified, in particular the institutional gatekeepers through which all ideas must pass—White House staffs, gubernatorial and mayoral deputies, legislative assistants, and court dockets triggered by contesting parties.

Besides the three elites, then, the two other principal talkers, media brokers and ideologues, are political actors in the presidential show, competitors for attention in shaping presidential talk. They do not constitute genuine elites for they rarely, if ever, provide policy ideas for governance. Too often, in fact, the outriders offer noise rather than signals.

The modern-day rhetorician—the consultant, image maker, symbol manipulator—is now present in campaign and in governance, in political strategizing and in speech writing. Almost always dominant at campaign time, these outriders articulate "basic values," as George Bush's organization did in 1988, so that talk of flags, prison furloughs, and the Pledge of Allegiance drowned out substantive discussion of deficits, defense, and health. Outriders are in the business of generating symbols and encouraging ambiguity. Campaign rhetoric appeals to fear and distrust and distorts the opponent's views. It is talk that excites emotions in order to prevail, like the presidential debates themselves, and it is only tangentially responsive to America's "real concerns." But that talk, those symbols in place of ideas, is often effective, and frequently it suffices to determine the election.

The archetype of the senior campaign staffer is still the organizer of people who canvass, telephone, provide audiences at rallies, dispatch advance men, and arrange for the press conference on the airport tarmac that can make the six o'clock television news. Accompanying the organizer is the pollster, tracking day by day the candidate's standing in an increasingly cynical and fragmented electorate, assembling focus groups, and interpreting responses. Finally, the media expert who buys advertising time appears. Often possessing a skilled and insightful lay appreciation of social psychology and political science, such advisers as Robert Goodman (for the Republicans) and Robert Squier (for the Democrats) identify one or two simplified themes on which the campaign rises or falls.[26]

Some systematic knowledge about the craft of rhetoric is beginning to emerge on a national level, although it still is heavy with anecdotal information about specific individuals. One can still count on one's fingers and toes the most prominent and successful national consultants since Larry O'Brien and Joe Napolitan came into prominence in the 1960 Kennedy presidential campaign: Patrick Caddell, John Martilla, John Sasso, Ann Lewis, Lee Atwater, John Sears, David Garth, Roger Niles, Robert Teeters, Walter DeVries, Matt Reese, Cliff White, Ted Van Dyke, and Richard Wirthlin head the list. Yet the ranks of "hands-on pols" working with "pop" social scientists multiply. The American Association of Political Consultants (AAPC) has grown exponentially since it was established in 1967. By 1989, the association had eight hundred members and represented four hundred firms. Twelve thousand people were making part or most of their livings as paid consultants in political campaigns. Between 1984 and 1988 alone, candidates paid consultants six billion dollars.[27]

Despite their explosive growth in numbers, consultants are an unstable, volatile, and diverse group. Once drawn principally from government, journalism, or advertising, "now they come from just about anywhere," as DeVries has observed, "many . . . very young, many . . . inexperienced." DeVries has calculated that 42 percent of the AAPC membership have been at their craft for less than two years and that there is "a tremendous turnover in consultants . . . In a typical profession, 15 or 20 years just gets one going; but, in campaign consulting, few last that long." Indeed, Mark Petracca estimates that 50 percent of all present consulting firms began after 1980.[28]

There are some signs of stability within the calling, but they parallel more closely those of the entertainment industry than those of parties or interest groups. AAPC now awards "Pollies," its own version of Hollywood's Oscars, and it has established a Hall of Fame. Its credo, as hall of famer Joe Napolitan has counseled, is "decide what you want the voter to feel or how you want him to react. Decide what you must do to make him react the way you want. Do it." Or, as Benjamin Ginsberg has said, consultants pack a new form of political weaponry: "RIP"—standing for "revelation, investigation, and prosecution." Political consultants enjoy a symbolic relation to the media—providing information in exchange for absolution from blame in a losing campaign—but the boundaries of the consultant universe are difficult to establish. "Anyone can be a consultant," DeVries has argued. "All you have to do is *say* that you are one and then you are. There really are no licenses, no regulations, and no standards that one must meet." For all their image-making skills, and their evident power to weaken, if not destroy, the two-party system, the modern rhetoricians are no elite. No elections, no merit system, no degrees earn them credentials.[29]

As campaign consultants, modern-day rhetoricians come and go. Not only are consultants wills-o'-the-wisp in features and endurance; they also fade when the time for governing arrives—or at most, as in the Reagan administration, they serve the president on a second track of photo opportunities, ceremonial occasions, and stand-up appearances. Pat Caddell tried mightily in the Carter administration to exercise genuine influence, but when he succeeded, as he did in the "malaise speech" Carter gave in the midst of the gasoline crisis and after his Camp David assembly of wise owls, the operative results were disastrous. Michael Deaver and Lyn Nofziger enjoyed greater and longer-lasting influence in the first Reagan term, but the images they created and the symbols they evoked were rarely associated with the policy issues of the day.

Ideologues, the other outriders, have, of course, been present all along in American political life. The Left and the Right—in Louis Hartz's words, "the impulse for equality and the impulse for individualism"—have appeared in doctrinaire form since Jefferson vied with Hamilton over whether America's future was agrarian or industrial.[30] But in America, both Left and Right are contained within the loosely constructed generalities of liberalism, which stands in contrast to established regime and inherited station. They are both infected with American pragmatism.

In this century, ideological doctrine, in the sense of a logically consistent, comprehensive justification of a political order, has had tough sledding in national campaigns, let alone in government. Advocacy of capitalism, American style, almost goes without saying. Both parties embrace its "true features" and try to present the opposition as deserting the cause. But sharply contesting ideologies do not fare well. The Socialist party reached high-water mark in the late 1920s and early 1930s. Genuinely fascist movements never took hold even in the Depression-ridden thirties. Presidential candidates touched with an ideological brush—George McGovern is the latest example—fare badly.[31]

In fact, no presidential program ever carried the ideological tag of pure capitalism until Ronald Reagan's. Indeed, the Reagan administrations stand in danger of being misinterpreted when they are treated primarily as ideological triumphs. It is true that in contrast to Carter's policy perspectives—technocratic, analytical, and incremental—Reagan's reassertion of American-style capitalism was close to overwhelming in the campaigns and often a guiding star in governing. It is also true that the neoconservatives of *The National Review* and the Public Interest and Heritage foundations could appear to be what Sidney Blumenthal, in his 1986 *The Rise of the Center-Establishment,* termed a "counter-elite" to the "liberal thinkers" of the sixties who dominated the national scene until the end of the decade. Yet, specific program by specific program, the neoconservatives rarely prevailed. In foreign affairs, the "Evil Empire" of their rhetoric fell of its own weight—although admittedly pushed a bit by American diplomacy and the defense buildup. In domestic matters, except for tax cuts, congressional commitment to constituencies managed a standoff to the neoconservative challenge.

Challenges and Constraints: Gatekeepers

Rhetoricians and ideologues vie with the intervening elites for attention as major domestic policy issues are defined and solutions proposed. The ideas of the policy experts in welfare reform, housing for the homeless, drug control, AIDS, catastrophic health insurance, and farm assistance must find their way through the blue smoke of the consultants and the dreamboats of the ideologues. The last channel through which they must pass is the gatekeeper—the personal adviser who is attached to the final decision-maker and thus decides who the president hears.

However varied in personality, number, and authority, the White House staff fulfills the ancient function of the ruler's court. Lewis Dexter pinpointed the role when he wrote, "The conception of court politics provides a counterpoint or modification of Weber's classic discussion of bureaucracy. In any large-scale organization there is, at least, a strong tendency (possibly an inevitable one) for the top officer to be surrounded by a set of advisers, surrogates, agents, official and personal servants, flunkies, handymen, technical aides, and so forth, who constitute what in bureaucratic language is often called a 'staff.' But the *personal* staff . . . of a top executive, a king, a president, a company chairman, and so on, often operates and *is expected to operate* in direct opposition to what are generally regarded as bureaucratic norms."[32]

Having identified the staff as both agents and filters for the chief executive, Dexter then specified the critical role of the gatekeeper. Kings, presidents, and governors need personal staffs because they "must necessarily have surplus resources available to handle emergencies, crises and threats—contingency funds, the ability to make appointments outside normal bureaucratic requirements—plus, of course, the capacity to give prestige to those whom they single out for positions of trust and confidence."[33] And from that personal staff usually emerges a confidante, "confessor, soothsayer, astrologer, magician, valet, doctor, mistress or paramour, to whom the insecure monarch or president or executive can explain his worries and concerns, by whom he can be reassured."[34]

Matthew Holden, Jr., is even more specific in his treatment of White House staff as a modern version of the king's court. The modern presidency, Holden has argued, is "the Twenty-Person Government." Although presidential motivation is always a decisive factor, "presidents work amidst a tripartite entourage: friends and peers, ambitious younger people, and migratory technocrats . . . [they] want zealous servants more than they want candid friends." But, Holden has added, "the friends and peers really do not belong, and soon must disappear from everyday decision-making. That leaves the ambitious younger people and the technocrats." Since Lincoln, the entourage has been much younger than the president (seven out of ten are at least ten years younger), and its members' tacit "bargain" with the president is that they extend his "reach" while he enhances their influence by granting them access to the center.[35]

Holden has emphasized that the bargain is "inherently unstable," for the temptation among staff to speak for themselves in the name of the president is strong, as is the inclination of some presidents to delegate psychologically demanding decisions that "literally give them headaches." Court politics, being unstable, ambiguous, and professionally risky, is intensely competitive. Advisers struggle for the president's mind. Loyalty to his subsequent wishes is the price. Speaking *for* the president is the staffer's glory. *Mis*-speaking—if detected—assures shame, humiliation, and downfall.

In this arena of court politics and with this entourage—the twenty people in the White House and executive office, whose names and faces the president actually knows—barriers appear to ideas from whatever source, couched in whatever language. Variously organized—as a hierarchy with an all-powerful chief of staff or as a hub with a relatively open door for several coequal staff members—the three elites come to the gatekeepers seeking policy consensus on one issue after another. Rhetoricians and ideologues in various guises contend at this point as well. The stage is awe inspiring, the atmosphere electric, the key communications for most part verbal. Nonetheless, policy ideas pass through the White House choke points unless the expert has a special standing with the president, or unless a president reads.[36] John Kenneth Galbraith had that standing with Kennedy, and, by reading, Kennedy discovered Dean Rusk as a potential secretary of state and Michael Harrington's focus on poverty as a major condition of American life. A reading, listening, reaching-out president intent on change and innovation, like Kennedy and Johnson, can transform a White House staff into a vast search-and-discover operation. Staff visit campuses, flatter experts, and plead for effective ways to resolve present or emerging issues. Alternatively, an introspective, insecure president such as Nixon can bar the door to all but a chief of staff as abrupt and laconic as Haldeman.

What is crucial, however, as Dexter and Holden make plain, is the disposition and skill of the White House gatekeepers, the particular members of the entourage who make "idea-management" their special concern. Diplomacy, understanding, and ability to translate ideas into politically palatable policy are absolutely critical attributes for these White House aides. Sorensen and Schlesinger for Kennedy; McPherson, Moyers, Califano, and Cater for Johnson; Ehrlichman for Nixon; Eizenstat for Carter; Baker, Meese, and Regan for Reagan were prime gatekeepers whose sense of timing—when to present an idea to the president, how to respond to his insistent request for information—often made the difference in whether an idea found a place on the national agenda, and, if it did, whether or not it became law.

In sum, the political requirement that modern governments "do something" to keep the system in rough equilibrium against the onslaughts of a volatile environment is constant. Regional conflicts, depressions, inflation, riots, epidemics, public discontents over countless indignities are ceaseless, the everyday bill of fare. This constant turmoil places a premium on ideas about how to cope with the immediate economic, social, technological, and ecological issues. Political elites, expected to resolve these issues and beset by an array of narrowly focused interest groups, depend on an administrative elite—bureaucracies—to help assure that policies actually are put in place and work at the street level. Both depend on experts who can generate ideas capable of garnering support from a coalition of interests and of reasonably effective execution.

Outriders contend in the production of ideas—rhetorical messengers of old themes and conventional knowledge, ideological purveyors of grand designs and scenarios that explain human behavior for all time. And the bridge from idea to policy is a fragile structure, heavily dependent on the skill and sympathy of the gatekeepers. Most of all, the successful transformation of an idea into a workable program depends on the personality, disposition, and legislative and executive abilities of the decision-maker, in this instance the president.

As the process of creating presidential talk unfolds, different modes of language are paramount at different stages. In the campaigns, rhetoric and a simplified version of capitalistic ideology hold sway. In the transition from campaign to administration, under constraints of time and partisan advocacy, substantive knowledge is at a premium. That need to find what "works" intensifies as the time for governing arrives, although the perspectives of the three elites will continue to vary sharply.

If, after some time, national boundaries are not protected, jobs do not materialize, the ignorant are not taught, the poor are not cared for, the criminal neither constrained nor rehabilitated, the mentally ill not removed from nor returned safely to the community, the government will not endure. Presidential talk has to consist of more than "wish lists," desirable objectives, admirable goals. It must affect events. Some ideas must work. Some talk must be real.

Herbert Hoover discovered this reality in the America of the Great Depression. Lyndon Johnson and Jimmy Carter came up against it in Vietnam and Iran. Nixon was revealed as naive in the energy crisis, as Reagan was in his embrace of an unrestrained capitalist ideology as major parts of the banking system tumbled down. For politicians seeking to stay in office, political talk turns finally to ideas that natural and social scientists provide. They persevere in the mixed process and mixed talk that for the last thirty years have shaped the program of the president—and in large measure, therefore, the public agenda of the nation. The questions are: How did academic experts and their ideas fare as one of the intervening elites—1959 to 1989? What is their present status and future prospects in policy-making? How good were their ideas?

2

THE GLORY YEARS BEGIN

Writing in 1967 at the flood tide of the Great Society and close to the pinnacle of his own literary career, Pulitzer Prize winner Theodore H. White proclaimed the emergence of "a new power system in American life," nothing less than a "new priesthood of action-intellectuals." In a three-part series featured prominently in *Life*, White claimed that this new academic elite was "unique to this country and this time." In the same breathless prose that had marked his best-selling quadrennial series *The Making of A President*, White declared that over the past decade "this brotherhood of scholars" had become "the most provocative and propelling influence on all American government and politics. Their ideas are the drivewheels of The Great Society: shaping our defenses, guiding our foreign policy, redesigning our cities, reorganizing our schools, deciding what our dollar is worth."

White argued that American public officials had turned "with almost primitive faith" to these action-intellectuals, "the men who believe they understand what change is doing, and who suggest that they can chart the future. For such intellectuals now is a Golden Age, and America is the place. Never have ideas been sought more hungrily or tested against reality more quickly. From White House to city hall, scholars stalk the corridors of American power." White added, "All paths start from the dynamics of modern knowledge. Learning today accumulates at such an accelerated rate that no one can keep up with it . . . Between idea-producers and government stretches a gulf and across this gulf the action-intellectuals throw up a bridge."[1]

The Coming of Age of the Social Sciences

Although it took a decade for the academic community to catch up with White's profile (in Alvin Gouldner's concept of a "New Class"),[2] the plain fact was that from 1950 to 1970, both the social sciences and the natural

33

sciences in the United States were on a roll. The natural "hard" sciences had been heavily engaged in public policy since World War II when the atomic bomb, radar, penicillin, and blood plasma demonstrated their spectacular utility. But social sciences, "the soft sciences," also proved important. Sociologists and psychologists produced personnel testing and classification systems for the military and devised new approaches dubbed "psychological warfare." The "Jockey Committee" of young economists in the Office of Strategic Services picked the targets in Europe for the U.S. Strategic Air Command. Political scientists organized and directed the government of occupied Japan and Germany.

After the war, Washington in effect accepted the Keynesian rationale for government intervention in a capitalistic economy and assumed that obligation by establishing the Council of Economic Advisors. Building on the beachhead of the 1922 Bureau of Agricultural Economics and on the cadre of economists assembled by the New Deal, the CEA began, in William Barber's words, as an "exercise in scientific harmony" under its first chairman, Edwin C. Nourse. (Subsequently, it functioned more as "inside" consultant and advocate.) However disposed, the economists were the first "institutionally recognized social scientists"; they are still the only social science recipients of the Nobel Prize.[3]

But political science was not neglected in the immediate postwar years. Its most relevant specialty was public administration, and its Washington "act" was "reorganization" of departments, agencies, and the entire executive branch. The "wisdom" of political science dominated the reorganization plans structured by two Hoover Commissions on the Organization of the Executive Branch, the bases of the administrative reforms of both Presidents Truman and Eisenhower.[4]

By the time White wrote, social and natural scientists alike were convinced of two things. First, their disciplines could systematically and substantially widen the sphere of empirically established knowledge and restrict accordingly the role of opinion, folklore, superstition, and "common sense." Second, given this rapidly expanding base of knowledge, the disciplines, behavioral as well as natural, could help politicians and public officials resolve long-standing public problems that heretofore had been considered intractable. Until the second half of this century, boom-and-bust business cycles, poverty, illiteracy, ill health, and racial intolerance had been treated largely as conditions to be endured. Now, given the knowledge and techniques of the behavioral sciences, they were, in the view of the action-intellectual, problems to be solved.[5]

The conviction that "our time has come" rang through professional journals, scholarly press books, and the public pronouncements of academic experts. The newly established Ford Foundation explicitly embraced and generously underwrote the behavioral sciences. The potential of the empirically oriented, experimental, positivist approach captured social science disciplines long committed to philosophical speculation and historical metaphor, and they were exuberant in their newfound methodology and discoveries. The approach soon crystallized in the annual presidential addresses of the academic professional associations of the decade.

In his 1961 "Reflections on a Discipline," for example, American Political Science Association president Emmette Redford of the University of Texas reviewed the intellectual debate that was then transforming his discipline. Historically, political science had been a branch of moral philosophy, rooted in tradition, concerned with values—how the state *should* behave—and committed to devising the ideologically "best" forms of government. Now postwar American political science erupted, in Redford's words, "to reflect an unprecedented intellectual ferment . . . a search for reality," and had "produced a group within our midst called behavioralists." The behavioralist, according to Redford, focused on people acting politically rather than on the formal, deductively determined properties of political institutions and philosophies. The modern political scientist seeks the "preciseness and empirical testing characteristic of exact science . . . He uses contemporary data. He or she finds common grounds of interest with psychologists, sociologists, and cultural anthropologists."[6]

By the next decade the commitment to behavioralism appeared more explicit and solidly rooted in American political tradition. Speaking in the bicentennial year of 1976, APSA president Austin Ranney of the University of Wisconsin asserted that the republic's founding fathers were consciously "scientists." They recognized, he argued, that they had embarked on a "noble experiment" and were convinced that they had at hand the "basic principles for engineering the new political institutions."

"Engineering" and "experimenting," Ranney stressed, characterized the founders' thinking—empirical, inductive, systematic, experiential, and explanatory, not mystic. "That 'divine' science" of John Adams "launched a faith in political and social engineering that has persisted ever since as one of the main elements of American culture." Always prepared for revision, acknowledging imperfect understanding but prepared to make another reasonable guess as to what might work, Ranney not only reaffirmed the "science" and "engineering" in political science; he anchored it in the most revered period of American history.[7]

Actually, for all its honorable American tradition, political science was a Johnny-come-lately to the behavioral scene. By the end of World War II, and thereafter for at least a generation, the Keynesian consensus as to how an economy could run at near full-employment levels and with only a little inflation—and how it might be managed by the national govern-ment—held sway. A massive statistical data base of painstakingly con-structed national accounts allowed the economist to build quantitative models of economic behavior and to predict changes in economic ac-tivities with increasing precision.

Similarly, sociology pioneered in public opinion survey research even before World War II and continued its mastery of the sampling and statisti-cal methodology in that field. By the sixties, the discipline was comfort-able in describing itself as committed to "the discovery, description, and analysis of *social inventions for solving human problems.*" Looking back in his 1981 presidential address to the profession's past, William Foote Whyte argued that the research strategies that had worked since World War II had been deliberate inventions that encouraged or persuaded peo-ple to change attitudes and behavior. Social inventions, he declared, are what the discipline should be about.[8] Psychology's claim to utility in policy-making was even older. Psychologists had tested military re-cruits for specific jobs requiring specific abilities since World War I. The Stanford-Binet Intelligence Test and the Scholastic Achievement Test (SAT) have been in continuous use since the mid-1920s.

Official and semi-official governmental reports at the end of the sixties reaffirmed the academic community's proclaimed breakthroughs. Three in particular—the 1968 report of Advisory Committee on Government Programs in the Behavioral Sciences of the National Research Council, the 1969 joint report of the National Academy of Sciences and the Social Science Research Council, and the 1969 report of the Special Commission of the National Science Foundation—were influential endorsements, all agreeing that social science had arrived. The last report, *The Behavioral and Social Sciences: Outlook and Needs,* was especially optimistic about the future role of academic advice:

> The activities of social scientists are inviting because their problems are so obviously important to man; the fields pose difficulties because the substan-tive problems of human behavior and human institutions are enormously complex and the objects of inquiry do not remain unchanged while they are being studied. But methods have been found to make scientific investiga-tions possible, and to arrive at reasonably firm conclusions, subject always to the self-correcting and changing character that all sciences share.
>
> . . . Opinion in federal, state, and local governments and in the nation generally about social science has changed in a favorable direction in the past half-dozen years or so. Social scientists are in increasing demand as consultants to public and private organizations. More and more of them are asked to leave their university positions and take employment in govern-ment, corporations, community service organizations, hospitals, schools, and many other settings. Economics, psychology, sociology, political sci-

ence, and their sister social sciences are getting increasing attention in the mass media and in public discussion.[9]

Persuaded as to both the academic respectability and the policy utility of social science, the special commissions and committees let loose a barrage of recommendations largely based on what their members perceived to have been accomplished in the New Frontier and Great Society programs. Each major executive department or agency should establish a planning and analytical unit staffed by behavioral scientists. The scope of university research supported by the National Science Foundation and the National Institutes of Health should be broadened explicitly to include social science research grants. So should the perspective of the presidential Office of Science and Technology and the President's Science Advisory Committee. In general, more staff, more fellowships, more research grants—in short, more money—and more access to power were in order.

The Advisory Committee on Government Programs in the Behavioral Sciences of the National Research Council put forth the most ambitious proposal. It called for a National Institute for Advanced Research and Public Policy in Washington to undertake a long-range analysis of public policies and problems. (Although this particular proposal never found support, a more focused counterpart, the Urban Institute, was created in 1969 and initially funded by President Johnson.) The later National Science Foundation and the National Academy of Sciences/Social Science Research Council reports echoed the National Research Council recommendations and expanded upon them. They called for the construction of "social indicators" to parallel those already routine in economics, an annual "social" report, a national data system, and a much heavier investment in graduate schools of applied behavioral science. In the Nixon administration, Raymond Bauer, on leave from Harvard Business School, would begin this process.[10]

For all the formal consensus that the social sciences had arrived, there were blips on the screen even in the sixties that signaled future trouble for the behavioralists. In fact, the specific impetus for the National Research Council's report was the so-called Project Camelot Affair, the "other" Camelot of the Kennedy administration. Project Camelot was a 1965 research venture sponsored by the Army to explore the "potential for conflict in national societies." Pollsters dispatched to do survey research in several Latin American countries came to realize the implications of using the information to ensure political control of those presently in power. Yet what the behavioralists viewed as a potentially major contribution to a theory of social change seemed to Latin American journalists and politicians to be covert "establishment" planning, an exercise for counterinsurgency operations, a new form of espionage. The political outcry accordingly became intense. That the U.S. Army sponsored the research exacerbated this response. Diplomatic protests continued, and an embarrassed White House canceled the project.[11]

The lesson that Project Camelot drove home was that social science data can talk back, generate perceptions, and arrive at conclusions researchers or sponsors do not anticipate. As survey research came of age in the late sixties and in the seventies, social scientists learned this lesson again and again in opinion studies of Vietnam villages, inner-city neighborhoods, and election campaigns.

It was not just the sensitivity of social science research when it delved into intimate personal and political matters that represented a cloud on the horizon. Many influential scholars in the natural sciences remained skeptical of the assertions of objectivity and methodological rigor of their colleagues in the social sciences. In part, this skepticism reflected natural scientists' ignorance of, and naiveté in, public affairs. It also reflected the inability of the social sciences to demonstrate the effectiveness of their work and the quality of their methods. Human social problems turned out to be sticky and their resolution difficult to demonstrate persuasively.

Thus, the inner sanctum of American science, the National Academy of Sciences (chartered in 1863 and ranked second only to the Nobel Prize in prestige) was then and remains still wary of the true worth of the social sciences. Only grudgingly and under pressure has the NAS accepted the most distinguished behavioral science scholars as members. It did not formally acknowledge any soft discipline until 1899, when an anthropology section was established. It served, according to observers, as a sort of "garbage can" to permit the election of not only anthropologists and archaeologists but economists, psychologists, philosophers, zoologists, and medical librarians as well. Sporadically in the next twenty-five years, annual meetings of the academy discussed the position it should take on the social sciences and the humanities. Not until the growing political power of social scientists in the New Deal and Fair Deal eras became evident did NAS move to piecemeal accommodation.[12]

In 1948, NAS created a separate section for psychologists, and in 1949 an academy reorganization explicitly established the biological and behavioral sciences as one of the main "classes" of members. In 1971, a growing recognition that public policy problems had major behavioral components led to a new section within that class for the "social, economic, and political sciences."

NAS elected its first sociologist and economist to membership in the 1960s, but the enthusiasm of other members for their election was by no means universal. More particularly, it seems, the academy accommodated social science experts whose research the government needed and would finance. So, searching for support for academy research, natural scientists swallowed their reservations and accepted, but did not embrace, their behavioral colleagues.

The media also expressed some caution, not so much about the scholarly worth and rigor of social science but rather about whether it could unlock Pandora's box and make Huxley's Brave New World a reality. Earlier journalists had characterized academics as "pedantic, irritating, tactless, self-satisfied bores," ineffectual and clumsy. But in the sixties, they questioned whether social scientists truly possessed effective social solutions. Theodore White again said it most succinctly: "Today, with utmost difficulty, government is groping to find guidance from a third category of scholars—social scientists, nominated by history to explain how communities shall master the changes provoked by the physical scientists . . . And it is here that controversy blisters. Do social scientists know enough to guide us to the very different world we must live in tomorrow. Do they offer wisdom as well as knowledge?"

In the end, White backed off. "The action-intellectuals," he concluded, "have no certain answers for tomorrow . . . To measure something does not mean to understand it . . . Their studies and surveys, however imperfect, are only road maps of the future showing the hazy contours of a new landscape. It is vital work—so long as the mapmakers do not confuse themselves with tour directors. How Americans shall move across the panorama they describe and what structures shall be erected . . . There is work for other men."[13]

Nonetheless, despite setbacks such as Project Camelot, the misgivings of natural scientists, occasional media skepticism, and White's ultimately dour conclusions, for behavioralists in the sixties, the times remained golden. True, the king's advisers had changed. No longer did they evoke an image of one placed close to the ruler by reason of wisdom derived from long experience and trust. Far less did it conjure up the mystic interpreter of dreams, portents, and oracles, the provider of proverbs and fables and manuals of princely rule. As Herbert Goldhamer, longtime Rand scientist and thoughtful observer of the contemporary think tank, explained, "Today the expert is characterized less by his experience than by his education and degrees, that is by his book and school training. This higher degree of training and professionalization has favored the development of a guild or corporate spirit among experts and sets them off more sharply from the man of common sense than was the case when the expert was primarily a man of practical experience."[14]

Goldhamer went on to describe, with more precision than White, what White sensed about the "new" behavioral sciences. True, there had been precursors—in Herbert Hoover's 1929 President's Research Committee on Social Trends, which set the stage for the flurry of proposals from FDR's various brain trusts. But Goldhamer makes a critical distinction between these advisers and their successors of the 1960s and 1970s.

> The contrast between the analytic and intuitive minds has been perhaps sharper than at any previous time. This was from the extraordinary development on the analytic side of the disciplines, devices, and organizations dedicated to the fullest exploitation of the rational powers of the human mind. Mathematical disciplines no longer remained—as they had previously—largely an inspiration toward a certain outlook that had relatively little effect on day-to-day politics. Mathematics and statistics, game theory and decision theory, military and political gaming, simulation, cost-benefit analysis and program budgeting, organization theory, econometric and other areas of mathematical modeling, operation research, management science, policy science, psephology (the "science" of polling), theoretical developments in the social sciences generally and quantification on a grand scale . . . achieved substantial success in claiming the attention of political and administrative leaders.[15]

This receptivity among political and administrative leaders was the final component in the success of social scientists in the sixties. Not only were the disciplines achieving far greater analytical and interpretive powers, but the political arena was anxious to receive the ideas the new research produced. Policymakers too believed in the "plasticity of problems." The gatekeepers of the sixties, as well as their political chiefs, were in fact committed to the analytical search for options and accordingly distrustful of historical metaphors.

More specifically, both Kennedy and Johnson were intent upon surpassing the politics of distribution—that is, deciding what shares of public subsidies and public regulation to assign to the broad interest groups of business, labor, agriculture, and consumers. Instead, the two presidents sought to play the politics of innovation, relying on the new ideas, inventions, and options that the behaviorists provided to solve the problems they regarded as "plastic." So poverty seemed capable of elimination. Heart disease, cancer, and stroke were health hazards that could be abolished. Mutually assured destruction (MAD), as defense secretary Robert McNamara's whiz kids conceived it, could banish war as an acceptable alternative in the diplomatic relations among the great powers.[16]

John Gardner, preeminent among the leaders of the "third" not-for-profit sector in the United States, President of the Carnegie Foundation, and Secretary of Health, Education, and Welfare during the Johnson administration, emphasizes the critical importance of a receptive political culture this way:

There are two categories of successful social scientists as policy experts. The social scientist turned administrator is one, and this is rare because two skills in one skull are required. The second is the expert talking to the policy-maker, and here the prevailing political culture is the vital factor. The policy-maker must be sophisticated about dealing with experts and vice versa.

The expert needs to understand that his contribution will be mixed inevitably with other considerations, and with that understanding a communion of interests emerges. This is a rare and fragile situation which was obtained in the Kennedy and Johnson years when the two quite different kinds of groups understood each other. The relationship broke down in the Nixon administration when neither side could understand one another, like a marriage breaking down.

Dividing experts into two groups, "those who accept real active responsibility and those who do not," Gardner concluded that "the latter simply has not grown up."[17]

Gardner's judgment is harsh, and indeed scholars who chose not to become politically involved in the sixties resented the "action-intellectuals." The distinguished political scientist Edward C. Banfield observed, "It's a national tragedy that people in decision-making roles turn over to intellectuals or computers the right to make their decisions. And it's bad for scholarship, too . . . A good professor is a bastard perverse enough to think what he thinks about is important, not what government thinks is important."[18] But Banfield was a lonely voice in the sixties. In the seventies, apparently on the theory that one joins a trend one cannot defeat, he headed a Nixon task force and served as a White House consultant. For the overwhelming majority engaged in New Frontier-Great Society policy-making, however, those who gave advice and those who received it understood and respected one another.

So the new social scientists, the behavioralists, climbed aboard the national policy-making machinery. They believed themselves equipped with a capital stock of reliable knowledge, unappreciated for the most part in the Eisenhower years, and capable of making substantial progress in solving public problems, a goal that had heretofore eluded political leaders.*

---

*As John Kessel has pointed out, the Eisenhower administration had its share of experts in both domestic and foreign affairs. In the political aftermath of Sputnik, James Killian and George Kistiakowsky mobilized the "hard science" community in a reinvigorated presidential Science Advisory Committee and a new presidential Office of Science Advisor. Domestically, Robert Merriam, Malcolm Moos of Johns Hopkins, and the president's brother Milton were either academics or sympathetic to academic counsel. Yet behavioralists such as the Ford Foundation was then sponsoring were not appearing in Washington in any great number in the fifties. In my own time in the Eisenhower executive office, physical "planners" and "institutionalists" were generally in vogue. (Kessel, letter to author, October 24, 1991.)

In important ways, the new experts held, human behavior could be constructively modified—especially with the very young, the mentally ill, the indigent unskilled for productive work, and the minorities heretofore ideologically written off as inherently inferior.

The action-intellectuals found a political culture largely receptive to their concepts. There were skeptics—in politics, in the media, in the natural sciences. But these voices were for the most part muted. The third intervening elite had arrived, jostling its way through image makers and ideologues to join hands with the political and administrative elites making policy and executing it.

Few decades faced the future with greater promise and confidence than the sixties. Economically and militarily, the United States was Number One. American supremacy had been troubled but not fundamentally challenged by the Korean War. Here were the new policy sciences, with new ideas and politicians ready to try them out as part of their pledge to get the nation moving again. Here were administrators confident that their skills, honed in the massive efforts of World War II, could now be applied to long-neglected domestic ills. What a combination! Glory years indeed.

The Sketchy Heritage

It is neither fair nor accurate to characterize the arrival of the behavioralists on the policy scene as something entirely new in American politics. Later softening the hyperbole to which he had given way in the opening paragraphs of the *Life* series, White devoted two-thirds of his second article to establishing the fact that the founding fathers were "a remarkable assembly of intellects" and that "the best scientific thought of the day colored the making of the American system." He anticipated Austin Ranney's characterization of the constitution-makers as practitioners of empirically based, experiment-prone political science, consistent in approach if not in methodology with modern behavioralism.

Whether or not the expert lineage in fact stretches back to revolutionary activists, it was clearly present at the turn of this century in the commitment of land-grant public universities to formulating ideas for public policy. Alongside dedication to education and research came the explicit commitment to "service." Originally, the focus fell on the improvement of agricultural practices and production through the transfer mechanism of the "county agent," part university staffer, part government officer. But in a number of universities, and particularly in Wisconsin, the service concept spilled over into economic and political affairs.

Where and when progressive politics flourished, as they did in the La Follette years in Wisconsin beginning about 1900, the call for reform ideas was insistent. The rise of progressivism coincided with the arrival from Germany of a new school of economic thought, statistically oriented and conceptually inclined toward state intervention in regulating and on occasion operating private enterprise. To the outrage of the Ivy League laissez-faire economists, the Wisconsin school led by John Commons advocated regulation of utilities, railroads, and other monopolies. They called for major tax and election reforms and backed all their proposals with impressive arrays of quantitative data. The "Wisconsin" influence increased in close correlation with the rise of the Progressive movement. When a receptive Theodore Roosevelt entered the White House, it attained national respectability.

The arrival of the Wisconsin economists on the political scene came near the end of a thirty-year post–Civil War evolution of the social sciences from a largely undifferentiated assembly of scholars loosely grouped under the nomenclature of philosophy or political economy. Led by the economists, the new disciplines organized one professional association after another as they groped to escape an almost suffocating ideology of laissez-faire economics and its companion Protestant ethic. Mary O'Furner documents how the steady drip-drip of reality in the form of business cycles, farm failures, and homesteading tragedies finally broke through laissez-faire ideology to present real problems that must be solved.[19] And Edward Silva and Sheila Slaughter show how academics in effect struck a bargain with the capitalist powers of America—accepting a "transaction" whereby the experts would advance "moderate" reform rather than challenge the "system."[20]

Whatever the motivations or limitations of the emerging social sciences, their influence did not last long in the first half of the twentieth century. Even the presence of an academic—Woodrow Wilson—as president did not suffice. Except for the economists engaged in the economic mobilization efforts of World War II and the academics carrying out background research for the American position in the postwar Versailles Conference, the expert role waned with the loss of Progressive fortunes and the return to normalcy in the 1920s. Herbert Hoover did establish a Commission on Social Trends, and there were stirrings at state and local levels of "efficiency" studies by certified "academics," as in New York City's Bureau of Public Administration. Nonetheless, it remained for Franklin Roosevelt and the New Deal to reestablish the link between scholars and politicians, and to expand it to active service in campaigns and elections.

John Kenneth Galbraith, whose status as Democratic presidential adviser extraordinaire is unrivaled in influence and duration, regards the New Deal experience as "seminal" in structuring a more or less permanent partnership between the university and the political arena. "FDR," he has observed, "had the closest associations with academic thinkers of any American president before or since at a breathless, intense time. Harvard actually came to think of itself as the government. Washington officials journeyed to Harvard to learn about Keynes. To participate in government was a badge of honor in academic circles. It was not viewed as a departure from genuine academic life."[21]

Whether the 1930s were in fact the pinnacle of academic influence or only the forerunner of the more systematic pattern of relations after the 1960 election is questionable.[22] Clearly, however, academics emerged on the national scene in the thirties. White identified the cast of the most prominent university actors who provided ideas during the 1932 campaign—Raymond C. Moley, Adolf A. Berle, Jr., Rexford G. Tugwell. The tilt was not so much to "pure" academics, except for the economists (who were indeed ill prepared to offer much policy advice), as it was to the law schools, especially Harvard. James Landis, James Rowe, Thurman Arnold, and Jerome Frank came out of an activist law tradition, epitomized by the new empiricism of Louis Brandeis. In techniques of analysis and mode of reasoning, they were also a far different breed of cat from their arts and sciences colleagues.[23]

Despite the Brandeis era, the ideological Left came subsequently to conclude that the university people FDR gathered around him were "hired heads," committed to saving capitalism rather than overthrowing it. The Left's attack castigated an earlier generation of political scientists for concentrating on municipal reform to overthrow immigrant bosses and perfecting colonial administration in Puerto Rico and the Philippines in the service of the American "empire." Neo-Marxists judge the Roosevelt brain trust to have been unprincipled defenders of American capitalism, however much their ideas and programs offended Wall Street at the time.[24]

The radical ideological attack on the sciences was short-lived. By the 1940s, under Hitler's threat, the defense of America became an overt, acknowledged, overriding purpose for natural and social scientists alike. The overwhelmingly important assignment went to the natural sciences in new weaponry and new medicine, but there were also important tasks for the "soft side" in the Offices of Strategic Services, War Information, and Price Administration. Here young social scientists came to terms with their business and industrial counterparts, who also volunteered to come to Washington and also learned how the capital worked. White highlighted this contribution early in his analysis when he traced the influence of Harvard economist Edward Mason and his young assistants on American strategic bombing policy and later on the country's economic assistance and resource conservation policies. Even to White, the network begun in World War II and continued thereafter had the aspect of a cartel. Do the action-intellectuals, he wondered, constitute "truly a community of scholars or a new kind of political machine?"[25]

What emerged from the war were important institutional arrangements through which university academics could serve policymakers. For the natural sciences, the National Science Foundation, the National Institutes of Health, and the Pentagon (spearheaded by the Office of Naval Research) came to provide a constant and substantial flow of dollars in support of basic and applied research. Ultimately this would spill over— though never in large amounts—to the social sciences. The economists found a secure niche in the Council of Economic Advisors. And after the natural scientists endured the trial of Robert Oppenheimer on security charges, Sputnik provoked the creation of the President's Science Advisory Committee, with James Killian, then president of M.I.T., as the first science adviser within the White House.

Yet down through these years of the New Deal, the Fair Deal, and the Eisenhower administration, American academic influence in government proved to be a "sometime" thing.[26] It was, above all, heavily dependent on the disposition of political incumbents and the accident of political events. When a large number of participants, politicians, and administrators consider themselves men of ideas—Gardner's two skills in one skull—the three elites are easy to unite. When the political and administrative actors are indifferent, complacent, or, even worse, captured by ideological fervor, the going is rough regardless of the size of the stockpile of ideas or the professional status of academic experts. If presidents have no inclination to pay attention, even institutional legitimacy cannot ensure that ideas break through, are understood, and then are acted upon.

With this uneven record of influence, up to 1960 the strongest link between the three elites was forged in the Depression, when desperation sanctioned new approaches, and in wartime, when defense needs mandated them. Whatever spillovers occurred in domestic affairs, such as the contributions of radar to civilian air safety, were accidental by-products. The economists were not called on to intervene systematically in the business cycle. The psychologists, sociologists, and political scientists were abandoned after their wartime contribution. Policy lessons were ignored, even when Samuel Stouffer's *The American Soldier* joined the *Strategic Bombing Survey* to demonstrate precisely the successes and failures of the massive wartime deployment of men and technology.[27] Throughout the late forties and entire fifties, except for the technological breakthrough of hard scientists in defense and space, little substantial policy innovation occurred. Social science experts lapsed into their traditional role as outside kibitzers and critics of the existing regime. It remained for new political actors to call the experts back into service. The first of these was John Kennedy.

The Academic Advisory Committee of 1959

Kennedy had at least three good reasons for seeking to involve university scholars in politics once again. First, unlike the 1932 election where Hoover's unpopularity ran so wide and so deep that, in Theodore White's words, Roosevelt would have won "had he been advised by Aimee Semple McPherson or Karl Marx," the 1960 election promised to be razor-edge close. As Theodore Sorensen has put it, "JFK believed intellectuals were a small but influential component of the Democratic party. In particular, he needed their support to counteract the negative public image created by his ambivalence to McCarthyism, his religion, his father, and his brother."[28]

Second, to gain the Democratic nomination, Kennedy had to push aside the titular party leader and still potential presidential candidate, Adlai Stevenson. And Stevenson, even after two defeats, remained the darling of the academics—"the thinking man's candidate." During Stevenson's earlier two campaigns, Galbraith, Arthur Schlesinger, Jr., and John Barlow Martin had set up shop as speech writers at the Stevenson farm in Libertyville, Illinois. Now Galbraith co-chaired the Democratic National Advisory Committee with Thomas Finletter, former secretary of the Air Force, established in 1956 after earlier Democratic government officials discovered that Stevenson was "no good on issues and that Democratic positions had to be staffed out."[29]

The advisory committee was anathema to Democratic congressional leaders. Senate Majority Leader Lyndon Johnson was busy preparing his own State of the Union Message, and Speaker Sam Rayburn regarded advice from outside the halls of Congress as coming from "foreigners." But the committee proved to be an effective way to organize networks of academics who were inclined to support the party. By the late 1950s, Seymour Lipset reported, such academics constituted a sizeable majority of the Social Science guild, especially among the newly arrived behavioralists.[30]

To ensnare the latter, the net Galbraith and Finletter cast was broad and loose. "We selected people," Galbraith has recalled, "with the criteria of (1) earned right of access because of former well-recognized work, (2) the capacity to make a good contribution, (3) having time on their hands, either because they were out of office or were academics."[31]

Divided into the two broad sectors of foreign affairs and domestic issues, the advisory committee spawned a series of subordinate panels, organized as two rough pyramids reporting to the central committee. The panels were usually a mixture of past academic policymakers and professors newly enticed to the task. The combination proved fruitful, and a series of policy and program proposals emerged in the late fifties to be stockpiled for the coming presidential campaign.

What was critical, of course, so far as Kennedy's prospects were concerned, were the commitments of the committee's leaders. Those thought to be most influential with editorial writers, columnists, and commentators were, specifically, Galbraith, a fellow Harvard economist Seymour Harris, and Harvard historian Arthur Schlesinger, Jr. If these three could be persuaded to leave Stevenson and bring some of their colleagues with them, an important shift in the political winds would occur. Conceivably, the entire Democratic Party advisory network could be delivered over with only a few defectors.

Beyond the political compulsion of a close election and a still potentially formidable competitor in Stevenson, Kennedy had another reason for courting academics. Nineteen sixty was the year of the first primary-dominated campaign, and the nomination would no longer be decided by party leaders, big city bosses, or state committees in smoke-filled rooms. Sixteen states had broken away from nominating conventions to select delegates by caucus or direct primaries. One consequence of the new system was the extension of the campaign period to exhausting lengths and the need to crisscross the country to establish a candidacy state by state. A second followed from the first—an insistent, relentless demand for ideas, something plausible to say, some defensible position to take on every conceivable issue from agricultural price supports to subsidies for a municipal zoo.

The vacuum-cleaner sweep for ideas that the primary- and caucus-driven campaign schedule imposed became standard operating procedure in all future campaigns. Peter Edelman, "idea" person for Robert and Ted Kennedy, Walter Mondale, and (to a lesser extent) Michael Dukakis, describes the process and the prime attributes of the primary-oriented campaign best:

> As the year goes on and the campaign becomes national, with one primary after another, we clearly—just really—were eaten alive by the voracious demand for new subjects. You simply could not get away solely with national releases on the same old subjects and just repeating them . . . When you look at the speeches in the campaign, the prepared texts, there was only one major foreign policy speech . . . one nuclear speech . . . on the domestic side a "national impact program" . . . So it ended up being a combination of rehashes and a system of doing a major new position paper a week . . . one on welfare, one on the economy, one on the cities, and so on. Those things got

press attention because if you put them out on the Wednesday before the following Sunday and gave reporters a chance to digest them, you would get good coverage and you'd get it in some papers around the country as well as in the East.*

Edelman goes on to describe the "slippery" process of coordinating research, speech writing, and scheduling that Kennedy would introduce in the primaries, a situation previous presidential candidates had hardly faced. Campaigning from the front porch was never feasible after the 1920s, but it was in 1960 that the primary floodgates truly opened.

"It's got to be a two-way street," Edelman observes, "because the new politics . . . eschews the classic kind of baby-kissing politics, but on the other hand, it believes strongly in going to the people. Its problem is over the hoked-up stuff, whether on television or alive."

Accordingly, as a campaign drags on for the issue person, "What do I know about that he can use?" becomes "Who do we know who can do this for us?" and then "Who do we know that knows somebody who can . . . ?" and finally, in Edelman's words, "It's a question of finding the person who was able, that didn't cost you any money, if possible . . . It was really a very modest kind of effort."[32] In the early primaries, then, when visibility is everything and money is hard to come by, ideas must come on the cheap. Enter the academic expert psychologically drawn to politics, full of ideas, flattered to be asked.

It was in this context, fresh from his bid for the vice presidency in the 1956 convention, that John Kennedy began his search for ideas. Over and beyond the compelling political considerations that sparked the search was the young senator's natural disposition to be open to ideas and intellectuals. As Sorensen has recalled, "Kennedy loved to read. He was intellectually curious and comfortable with academics." "Look at the letters they write to the *New York Times* . . . Why don't they write to me?"[33]

---

*Peter Edelman, Oral History Transcript, Robert Kennedy Project, John F. Kennedy Presidential Library, 27–28 (hereafter cited as JFK Library). The specific campaign Edelman describes in these paragraphs was Robert Kennedy's in 1968. The principal features of the process were put in place in 1960, and the L Street boiler room where Archibald Cox worked on policy became a standard fixture thereafter. Theodore White's *The Making of the President* series, from 1960 through 1972, has particularized the personalities and circumstances of idea-gathering, but the pattern remains constant. White's publishers were successively, Pocket Books, Athenaeum, and Bantam Books of New York, and each volume appeared in the year after election. A specific 1988 reaffirmation of the pressure-cooker introduction of policy ideas in a presidential campaign is David Blumenthal, "Health Policy on the High Wire: Thirteen Days with a Presidential Campaign," *Journal of Health Politics, Policy, and Law* 17, 2 (Summer 1992): 353–73.

So it was in the mid-fifties that Kennedy dispatched Sorensen to Massachusetts. For the young Nebraskan, the commonwealth was unfamiliar territory, so much so that he mistook the four colleges then clustered around the town of Amherst as the intellectual center of the state. (He later called Harvard Yard an ordinary "campus" when he drafted an article for the senator.) His early academic friendships were with Earl Latham at Amherst College and James MacGregor Burns at Williams, both political scientists. It was from Latham that the explicit suggestion of an academic advisory committee came—Sorensen recommended it, Kennedy agreed, and in 1958 Latham began the task of putting such a collection together.[34]

Latham worked, of course, at the considerable disadvantage of being from western Massachusetts, far away in image more than in miles from the Cambridge citadels of Harvard and M.I.T. But he arranged to summer in Cambridge and by late 1958 had persuaded Deidre Henderson, a staff assistant to Henry Kissinger, then director of Harvard's Center for International Affairs, to serve as liaison between the academics and Sorensen. Intelligent, discrete, energetic, and ambitious, Henderson proved a happy choice. A graduate of Wells College in Upstate New York with family friends who knew Kennedy from Harvard College days, she asked Kennedy directly about the wisdom of leaving Kissinger, and, once reassured that at least "a" job would continue after the campaign, Henderson set up shop to attract Harvard and M.I.T. professors to the Kennedy cause. Her pattern has since often been copied but never equaled.[35]

Henderson's strategy proved especially attractive to academics who had labored for Stevenson. His practice had been to commission major speeches on major topics, often with impossibly short deadlines. A professor would abandon every other assignment, work frantically to translate new and exciting ideas into passable political prose, and then discover, after the fact and only after persistent inquiry, that Stevenson had ruthlessly excised nine-tenths of the draft with his blue pencil. If a single paragraph remained unscathed, the academic could count him- or herself lucky.[36]

Henderson's style was the opposite. She researched the background and accomplishments of the professor before she arranged a contract, which would come in the form of a letter from the senator that usually noted with approbation an obscure article the professor greatly admired himself but that had been rarely read except perhaps by fellow scholars. The letter would then introduce Henderson and ask if the professor could spend some of his or her "valuable time" with her. Henderson then phoned and arranged an appointment on a topic that was the professor's speciality. After the meeting, during which Henderson took copious notes, she drafted a speech or position paper and sent it to the professor for revision. These changes would be scrupulously noted, the draft mailed off, the speech delivered, and almost immediately a thank-you letter from the candidate with a copy of the speech as delivered would arrive on campus. It made for a very pleasant faculty club luncheon topic and display.

One by one, Henderson assembled potential members of the Kennedy Academic Advisory Committee throughout the spring of 1959 until thirty-seven scholars from Harvard, M.I.T., and a scattering of other Boston universities were identified as "inclined to join." Henderson tracked the extent of work (memoranda, draft speeches, telephone calls, conversations) of each one.

As the campaign pace intensified, Latham bowed out as chair. Sorensen first asked Mark deWolfe Howe, a distinguished Harvard law professor, to take over, but Howe demurred, citing "five hundred blue books and other heavy academic burdens." Sorensen then persuaded Howe's colleague Archibald Cox, whom Howe had recommended to undertake the assignment, and Cox in turn recruited Abram Chayes, another law school colleague, to serve as his deputy. In the end, more than thirty professors nationally known in academic circles were on board.[37]

There were a few holdouts, or, more accurately, "floaters," candidly waiting to see whether Stevenson and/or Humphrey were going to run. Contrary to the memories of some advisory committee members, Galbraith recalls that he declared for Kennedy as early as 1957 when Stevenson formally announced that he would not stand again for the presidency. He had known Kennedy for some years and had originally advised him on agricultural policy. Whether or not he renewed this pledge in 1959 before some of the primaries is not clear. Certainly any endorsement was not very visible, and Galbraith's support remained one of Latham's concerns through 1958.

So did the commitment of Arthur Schlesinger, Jr. The Kennedy-Schlesinger relationship had endured, typically in occasional dinners at Boston's Locke Ober Restaurant, since Kennedy's first congressional campaign in 1946. But Schlesinger, a "wise owl" like Galbraith, remembers holding out longer. In fact, he found himself considerably embarrassed when in May 1960, with Stevenson an overnight guest in his house, the morning newspaper carried an advertisement in which his name appeared with other academics endorsing JFK.

Richard Neustadt was also a holdout. The absence of an endorsement from him was a serious gap because Neustadt was a veteran of the Truman White House as well as a recognized academic. He had earlier written a widely respected dissertation on the patterns of presidential policy-making; the manuscript based on that research, *Presidential Power*, destined to be a classic, was then at the printer. Already a "bridge" person between academics and Washington policymakers, shuttling easily between the capital and eastern campuses, Neustadt held back until the eve of the Democratic National Convention in Los Angeles in June 1960. While there, he wrote to his colleague at Columbia, David Truman, that the Kennedy people were "a bunch of bastards—hard, cold, and smart, but *our* bastards." Of JFK himself he observed, "FDR was not only power-sensitive and thought-hungry, his personality radiated warmth. This guy strikes me as very cool—and where's his Eleanor? Well, I'd rather have a second-generation rich bastard than a lower-middle class one on the make and a Democrat rather than a Republican. I'm a sucker for competence . . . I can't wait to see what happens when Khrushchev and Jack confront each other after the election."[38]

Though Neustadt would remain aloof until after the convention, he would be very influential in the transition period when Sorensen and other members of the campaign staff would assume incorrectly that he was a "close family friend."[39] Indeed, Neustadt's reserve and hesitation reflected the feelings of a number of the Cambridge academics, who not only perceived the image problems Sorensen had noted but balancing this concern, after having followed Stevenson loyally through two defeats, did not want to lose again. Cross-pressured, they were cautious.

Sorensen and Henderson persevered. On June 13, 1959, Sorensen wrote Henderson that he would like those who had joined Cox and Chayes to write position papers by Labor Day with top priority being given to new ideas and "specific recommendations." By then, Henderson had signed on economists Arthur Smithies, Carl Kaysen, Jim Dusenberg, John Meyers, and Walt Rostow. I was there with fellow political scientists Samuel Beer, Samuel Huntington, and Lucian Pye. John Howard, M.I.T. planner, and Charles Schottland, social welfare expert from Brandeis, were declared supporters. Henderson could count on at least twenty academics as "dependable" or "very helpful."

The advisory committee went public on December 12, 1959, at a gathering at the Continental Hotel in Cambridge. The *Boston Globe* reported the Kennedy organization had brought together "intellectual heavyweights of national stature . . . who hated to desert Adlai" but were "the better pick of HHH and Adlai's political stables," all assembled "by pretty Deidre Henderson, an Earl Latham protégé."

The Continental Hotel meeting was a loose, semisocial occasion. The real meeting came on January 24, 1960, at the Harvard Club on Commonwealth Avenue in Boston. Henderson had asked her hardest workers if they "could possibly give up a Sunday teatime" to meet the senator. Wild horses could not have kept the invitees away—if only to learn who else had been invited. The senator appeared, the conversation was witty and superficial, tea was served, and the assembled academics were captive and committed for the duration.

The Cambridge advisory committee proved to be both unique and of limited substantive value. Sorensen tried to set up similar groups in his native state at the University of Nebraska and to call on the birthplace of the brain trust in the Progressive Era, the University of Wisconsin. Letters from his original academic contacts discouraged him. At Nebraska, professors again complained about the heavy press of blue books and posed the cautious question whether the senator "was of the Catholic persuasion." Wisconsin had already signed up for Humphrey. Sorensen gave up, content to go with Cambridge.[40]

But Cambridge—by all accounts, including Sorensen's, Neustadt's, Schlesinger's, and Galbraith's—did not help out much during the campaign itself. Cox did go to Washington in the summer of 1960 to run an L Street "boiler room" speech-writing effort with a mixture of academics and writers including Yale economist Arthur Okun, *Washington Post* columnist Joe Kraft, and James Sundquist, senior staff associate for Senator Joseph Clark of Pennsylvania. His efforts, however, did not seem to match the skills Richard Goodwin was showing on the campaign trail (Sorensen had discovered Goodwin on a congressional committee staff investigating TV quiz shows). Sorensen recalls the limited usefulness of the academics Henderson and he had found and those whom "wise owl" figures (notably Galbraith and Schlesinger) had recommended. They were, to be sure, a source of ideas, and they reacted to or confirmed the ideas of others. However, as the national general campaign got underway, they did not work out well as speech writers. When Neustadt asked Sorensen "what the Cambridge group was up to," Sorensen answered, "They prepare position papers preparatory to my speech writing, and then I throw them in the waste basket." As "a campaign vehicle," Sorensen admitted, "the group was a bust."[41]

Neustadt himself concluded that the brain trust was peripheral to the campaign. It "legitimized" liberal support, perhaps, but in no sense did it guide the candidate's thinking. "Most of the brain trusters submitted things only when asked," he observed. One exception was Walt Rostow, who peppered Sorensen with proposals undaunted by the absence of a response. But as time went on, Cox's frustration grew to the point that he demanded a meeting with the committee on the campaign trail. Disagreements and disappointments were papered over at a mutually unsatisfactory conference in Minneapolis. The committee did not dissolve, but the impact of its ideas on campaign speeches and statements was negligible.

The academics' impact on the media, however, was not. The *Boston Globe* ran the first of its series of expert articles in December 1959. An account of the Continental Hotel gathering, the story was later picked up by national publications. The *Washington Post* ran two series on "Professors and Policies" in early August 1960. So did the *Wall Street Journal*. When the *New York Times* weighed in later that month, JFK became firmly identified as the intellectual's choice. Indeed, so strong did the connection between ideas and Kennedy's campaign take hold that after his inauguration such influential columnists as Joseph Alsop would charge that the president had "too many intellectuals." Alsop joined other commentators in calling for "human judgments by visible, responsible officials."

Mel Elfin, Washington bureau chief for *Newsweek* from the Kennedy to the Reagan years, put down the media's highly visible and generally favorable treatment of the academics in the sixties as "a psychological compulsion to embrace intellectuals comparable to that which Lyndon Johnson displayed in his effort to top Camelot." Not only did print journalists and television commentators accept the assertion that "JFK's heart rested with the intellectuals," according to Elfin, but they themselves yearned for academic approbation. "The old-style media type, 'no drunks or floaters' that used to appear in want ads for reporters had disappeared. Now media types were moving toward professionalism . . . reporters were college graduates who were now comfortable with domes . . . they believed they could hold their own with eggheads."[42]

In Elfin's view, print journalists were even more eager to seek out academic experts because television had co-opted the old-style "who, what, where, why, when, and how" reporting. Newspapers and magazines were forced to become interpretive. "While the TV did not have to explain, the rule that Henry Luce first imposed for *Time* magazine was that every story must have one word that forced a reader to go to the dictionary. You did not have to explain who Walt Whitman was in the story." Elfin continues, "JFK created a sense of history and intellectual perspective. In this context the media led you to believe that social scientists had something to say and that it had to have 'smarts' and be the broker of ideas. Intellectuals were fashionable, and ideas were trendy."[43]

A strong measure of irony attaches to the experience of the advisory committee. Its position papers, draft speeches, memoranda, and phone calls contributed next to nothing to shaping the campaign's policy agenda. Indeed, when ideas such as "The Missile Gap" found their way into the candidate's speeches, they often turned out to be factually wrong. What did make news was not the ideas of the academics, but the academics themselves, certainly to the satisfaction of many of them. Those who invested a considerable amount of time and effort, such as Cox, ended up frustrated and angry, but those with a marginal investment found large dividends in publicity.

In the end, Henderson patched things up for almost all the professors with extraordinary diplomacy. In September 1960, a party at the Chayes house in Cambridge honoring Chester Bowles thanked the people as Chayes said "who have contributed so generously of their time and ideas thus far in the Kennedy campaign . . . with no view to reward or self-aggrandizement." To top it off, Henderson arranged inauguration tickets for a long series of events for thirty-four who "truly worked" and carried out the charge of the committee. As she had reported to Kennedy a year earlier, many had signed on because "their satisfaction seems to be in knowing that they can channel their ideas to someone who can appreciate their value." Now perhaps that was still indeed reward enough, even if the ideas went mostly unused. But the inaugural tickets certainly helped, too, and a large contingent of academics and spouses traveled south to Washington to dance at the ball on that snow-swept evening.

The Republicans Respond

About the same time Sorensen began to round up academic experts in Massachusetts, the Republicans launched a comparable effort. The party had suffered a particularly galling defeat in the 1958 congressional elections, while the Democrats had scored their largest gain since 1946. The next meeting of the National Republican Committee in January 1959, a soul-searching review of campaign shortcomings, promised more appealing programs.

Accordingly, President Eisenhower agreed to a recommendation by NRC chairman Meade Alcorn to establish a forty-member Republican Committee on Program and Progress. Charles Percy, who had become president of Bell and Howell at twenty-nine, chaired the committee, which included party congressional leaders Charles Halleck and Everett Dirksen. As Joseph Monsen and Mark Cannon wrote, eight members of the committee "carried the titles of Dr. or Professor," the most prominent being political scientist Malcolm Moos of Johns Hopkins and economist Gabriel Hauge. Its end product was the "progressive . . . long-range problem solving" Percy Report. Fifty thousand copies of the report were distributed in the hope of "attracting intellectuals."[44]

Alcorn also launched a more specifically focused effort early in 1959 when he convened a political science advisory committee to counteract the prevailing liberal sentiment within the profession—about three to one. A battery of suggestions emerged from the meeting, most prominently the recommendation that the party become engaged in the meetings and activities of the American Political Science Association.[45]

Alcorn's successor, Thurston Morton, continued to work with the committee, which offered to draft a brochure titled, "Operation Social Scientists." The committee assembled comprehensive lists of social scientists, discipline by discipline, worked to create a closer liaison with professional associations, and began to compile a directory of "pro-Republican professors" which by 1963 included 12,500 names. A permanent Arts and Sciences Division was organized in the Republican National Committee and by 1960, ten state party committees had followed suit. The advisory committee also urged Morton to encourage "articulate Republican intellectuals, e.g., 'Kistiakowsky, Flemming, Derthick, Milton Eisenhower, Killian, and John Hannah' to address more conventions" and to advertise successful congressional elections in which social scientists had been active.

Yet there is little evidence that the committee or many academic experts supported Richard Nixon in the 1960 election. The usual newspaper endorsements of university and college professors appeared, and the committee prepared an occasional policy memorandum. But Nixon as vice president "had" his policy positions and could summon up memoranda and analyses from within the executive branch. His problem was to secure the open and unquestionable support of Eisenhower—which, although it would come eventually, would turn out to be too late to help Nixon's candidacy. Spokesmen for the Republican-oriented academic community at large, Killian and Kistiakowsky, held back. Although Lon Fuller of the Harvard Law School led a Scholars for Nixon Association, the three-to-one Democratic preference among academics prevailed.

Reviewing Republican efforts to engage social scientists in 1960, Monsen and Cannon ruefully concluded, "The nomination of Barry Goldwater . . . in 1964 lost to the Republican party much intellectual support which they [sic] had been laboriously establishing. . . . The major factor that attracts academicians . . . is the nomination of candidates that they can identify with and who will respect them as well. Too often both the Republican candidate and the intellectuals as a group are suspicious of each other." Cannon pinpointed Kennedy's appeal in these respects, based on "both a liberal program and appeal as a writer and intellectual himself."[46] So, despite the formal advisory structure and the good intentions of national committee chairs, no genuinely comparable assembly of academics appeared to support Nixon in 1959 and 1960. Kennedy had captured the big leaguers, at least in the eastern division. When he squeaked through the election as Daley delivered Chicago, the academics won as well. Cambridge was on its way to Washington.

Transition Breakthrough

Although victory was sweet to Cambridge, in plain fact the Kennedy academics had demonstrated notoriety more than utility in the 1960 campaign. In their detractors' words, they were "used" to lure liberals away from Stevenson and Humphrey, the true keepers of the liberal flame. In the ten transition weeks between election day and the inaugural, however, they played sharply different roles. In essence, three separate tracks opened up for the Cambridge group, both for those formally a part of the committee and for those whose affiliation was loose.

Richard Neustadt had a lead role in this "interregnum."[47] Neustadt represented the premier disinterested transition adviser—the "fast track"— the explicit practitioner of the self-denial ordinance. He announced early on, loudly and clearly, that he would not accept a post in the new administration.

Already an adviser to Senator Henry Jackson, then chairman of the Democratic National Committee, Neustadt had prepared a memorandum on transition matters at Jackson's request. Neustadt's advice was separate both from the research the Brookings Institute had commenced on its own initiative and from the paper Kennedy had asked Clark Clifford, Neustadt's senior White House colleague in the Truman administration, to prepare. Neustadt continued at work on the subject and delivered a second version of the memorandum, "intimate, direct, crisp," to Kennedy on the *Caroline* en route from Toledo to Chicago, where he met Sorensen for the first time. Neustadt found the senator, with whom he was barely acquainted, to be especially impressed with the appendix on FDR.[48]

Neustadt enjoyed early name recognition when Kennedy announced (and mispronounced) his name at the first early morning postelection press conference in Hyannis as a coequal transition adviser with Clark Clifford. He would continue throughout the Kennedy administration to take one special assignment after another—and Kennedy's staff continued to receive him warmly on the incorrect assumption that he was an "old friend" of the president.

Arthur Schlesinger, Jr., a genuine old friend (though not an especially close one) who had also remained aloof from the advisory committee, represented a second track of academic influence. An academic amenable to taking a position in the administration, Schlesinger experienced "some friction with Sorensen and [Adam] Yarmolinsky (one of the principal headhunters in the administration) and so communicated directly with Jacqueline Kennedy on a range of matters. After the election there seemed to be a presumption among Cambridge academics that he would be appointed to the White House." But this appointment did not crystallize until Kennedy attended a Harvard Board of Overseers meeting in January 1961 and stayed at Schlesinger's house. Schlesinger recalls Kennedy saying, "'Bobby tells me you are going to the White House. Phone Ralph Dugan.' Dugan asks, 'Sworn in for what?' That was the way arrangements went."[49]

Kenneth Galbraith's role on the second track was perhaps even more indirect. He was active in nominating and commenting on cabinet and subcabinet choices, like Walter Heller and Orville Freeman. Like Neustadt, he visited the Kennedy postelection family headquarters, the house in Palm Beach. In the end, as the jostling for positions in the new administration intensified, Galbraith accepted the position as ambassador to India enthusiastically as he had a long-standing interest in that country. His perception (subsequently confirmed by Brauer) was that Kennedy was relieved that Galbraith did not opt to take the chair of the Council of Economic Advisors or a domestic cabinet post where his "controversial writings" were likely to have been a political embarrassment.[50]

Most of the academics in the campaign entourage, however, ended up during the transition on a third track—as members of the twenty-nine unpaid preinaugural task forces asked to set agendas in major policy areas such as education, housing, agriculture, and economics. Meeting in hurried and informal circumstances in airport motels and New York and Washington offices, the task forces proved surprisingly successful. Academics were paired with practical politicians, congressional staff members, and business people active in the particular policy area; their analyses and recommendations frequently were right on target.

Overall, academics made up 53 percent of the membership of the task forces. Forty-nine percent of the academics came from Ivy League universities; almost half of this Ivy group were from Harvard or M.I.T. By contrast, only 8 percent of the task forces' nonacademic members possessed Harvard or M.I.T. undergraduate degrees; 12 percent had graduate degrees from these schools. Clearly, task force recruiters reached beyond their original network, for the issue now was governing, not campaigning. Sorensen found the task force reports "very important, much more so than [in] the campaign, and critical in drafting the legislative messages in the first three months when we sent up a message a week."

Kennedy's brother-in-law Sargent Shriver organized the recruiters who pulled together the task forces, which profited (unlike the committee that preceded them) by having a specific focus and a deadline. They also had a relatively blank check, for the recruiters "never talked about the substantive program for which we were attempting to line up the talent."[51] The reason recruiters were silent about the task forces' agendas was of course that Kennedy had in fact emerged from the campaign without a domestic legislative program. The field was wide open.

Five years earlier, Neustadt had traced the postwar evolution of presidential legislative messages, including the economic message newly required by the 1946 Employment Act as well as the traditional State of the Union and budget messages. What began in 1947 as a request from Truman to department and agency heads for proposals for his messages emerged in 1960 as an institutionalized pattern of interaction between the line departments and the Executive Office of the President, principally the Bureau of the Budget. Through these major messages, the EOP defined annually the president's program. More important, it identified proposals that were in its formal language as conveyed to the Congress "not in accord with the program of the president"—a clear signal to the White House and the Congress that a loose cannon stood on the executive branch's deck.

Neustadt observed that the development of both departmental and presidential programs quickly became "habitual." "Repetition," he wrote, "robbed these programs in varying degrees of interest or excitement in high places . . . [and encouraged] habit forming ways of working with the White House." Professional civil servants in the Bureau of the Budget became accustomed "to the role of 'institutional' exponent in interchange with the White House 'politicians.'" Eisenhower accepted and refined the process Truman began and so enhanced the professional's power in the executive office and in the top echelons of the major departments. Early in 1954, he surprised and in the end pleased the Congress when he presented some sixty-five proposals for new legislation—"a massive affair" generated almost entirely by the request for departmental proposals, budget bureau review, and the process of White House reaction Truman had initiated.[52]

By the time Kennedy was elected, the decade-old "custom" depended heavily on the skill, objectivity, and judgment of the senior budget staff. It was understandably conscious of budgetary impact, institutional in outlook, and more likely to be responsive to the presidency than to a given president. In the end, except for the occasional bright idea that came unpredictably from an individual staff member or emerged from a legislative conference, the budget staff depended on what departments and agencies recommended, often at the prodding of interest groups.

The Kennedy task forces broke the monopoly of the executive branch agencies on program ideas. In 1960 and 1961 with the encouragement of the new Director of the Budget, David Bell, then a Harvard administrator, the bureau's permanent staff welcomed the flood of reports because it provided ammunition to fire back at departments. Anticipating an internal power struggle with Kenneth O'Donnell, Sorensen, as Carl Brauer has put it, "grabbed hold of the special counsel's position as Clifford and Neustadt had envisioned it," and, working closely with budget bureau professionals, he translated many of the recommendations for the president's messages. The substance of the task force reports gave both Sorensen and budget bureau senior staff a leg up in a White House arena which, in Schlesinger's words, was "a ruthless scramble for access and power."[53] Or, as Sorensen himself somewhat ruefully observed, "A group of able and aggressive individuals all dependent on one man could not be wholly free from competitive feelings or scornful references to each other's political and intellectual backgrounds."[54] Kennedy's political and administrative elites had found the first serious and tangible benefit of alliance with the academic elite.

So the Cambridge academics, or a good number of them, redeemed themselves in the ten-week interregnum. They continued to demonstrate their utility in the six months that followed the election of 1960. They may have been largely window dressing in the campaign, and their utility in mobilizing liberal Democrats rapidly decreased after the election. But they became part of the national process by which ideas are translated into a presidential program, messages are sent on to the Congress, and some proposals ultimately emerge as law. Postwar pressures of a mature economy and world leadership had forced Truman and Eisenhower to rationalize the way ideas were assembled and packaged. The task force mechanism allowed a strategic and innovative intervention at the vital juncture of executive office and White House staffs. It challenged the capacity of departments and agencies to propose policy without serious competition. In 1961, academics had a place in the fierce competition for attention and approval that always exists in the presidential "land of the long knives." It remained to be seen how well they would fare.

Policy in Camelot

Conventional wisdom these days discounts heavily John Kennedy's long-run impact on American government and especially on domestic policy. He was, it is said, preoccupied with foreign policy, his attention progressively consumed by Cuba, the Berlin Wall, the test ban negotiations, the forays into Vietnam, the Peace Corps, the Alliance for Progress, the space probe, and "putting a man on the moon." Furthermore, when he turned his attention to domestic matters, his efforts were complicated by Democratic congressional losses in the 1960 election, and the resulting political uneasiness—if not hostility—in both House and Senate. Procedural battles in the House Rules Committee, the inherited "Eisenhower deficit," and clear southern opposition to any real move to secure civil rights legislation thinned the domestic agenda. Finally, and inevitably, the president's assassination eliminated the possibility of midcourse corrections and changes in a second term. So the common judgment is to dismiss the Kennedy "One Thousand Days" as inconclusive and unproved.

Actually, Kennedy's domestic policy initiatives conformed with typical postwar experience—that is, three-quarters of his legislative requests came in his first six months in office. More important, Congress supported almost 75 percent of these initiatives in his first year, a higher rate of approval than any of his successors except Johnson achieved.[55] Kennedy's chief domestic focus was aid to education, followed by area redevelopment and unemployment. He achieved substantial if not dramatic legislation in housing subsidies, compensatory education programs, and antirecession measures. Moreover, the pipeline proposals steadily built up as his popularity rating remained high (59 percent the month before his death).

Although the Kennedy administration seemed to shunt aside deliberately such major proposals as civil rights (and the creation of a new Department of Housing and Urban Development, defeated largely because of civil rights considerations), academic advisers nonetheless found the time intoxicating. James Sundquist, a senior member of Senator Joseph Clark's staff, noted the "rush of experts to be 'brain trusts' for the New Frontier. . . . The Senate senior staff was decimated as the best brains of Capitol Hill went over." Sundquist had worked in Cox's L Street boiler room and had watched the Cox-Sorensen battles at close range. Accordingly, he "expected a call from the White House, but it never came. With the experts in the executive branch, the power of the Hill stopped. I felt demoted."[56]

Certainly the economists had a field day. Several had been advisers to the president throughout his senatorial career, and they maintained their individual channels of communication to him. Galbraith had long counseled the young senator on agricultural affairs. Paul Samuelson, although originally with Stevenson as a member of the DNC advisory group, was at the zenith of his career. Kennedy sought him out, and, after a sail off Hyannis, Samuelson agreed to chair the preinaugural task force on economic policy. Kermit Gordon, then a young faculty member at Williams College, joined the advisory committee early. (He had had the audacity to ask for a fifty-dollar per diem to write his memoranda—so infuriating Bobby Kennedy that he was later to oppose Gordon's appointment to the Council of Economic Advisors.)

Other economists, as befits their status as kings of the social-science mountain, remained aloof—at least until transition time. Yale's James Tobin answered direct inquiries by White House staffer Richard Goodwin, but he was by his own account "a reasonably reluctant player" until his appointment to the council. The late Joseph Pechman of the Brookings Institution, who was to begin an unparalleled thirty-year reign as the nation's top tax adviser, was a Humphrey loyalist. He introduced another Humphrey academic supporter, Walter Heller, to Kennedy. Heller later became the new chair of the council.[57]

Originally, the economists presented neither a united nor a conventional front. Galbraith joined Truman's last council chair, Leon Keyserling, in advocating a by-then classic Keynesian policy of public works spending and easy money to the president as he entered office in recessionary times. They stood opposed to the traditional Wall Street thinking that Douglas Dillon, Kennedy's choice for secretary of the treasury, articulated—simply put, a balanced budget. Cross-pressured, the president-elect dropped a bombshell before his inaugural by making a public commitment to Wall Street doctrine. As a result, drafting the first State of the Union message became "enormously complicated." It promised a balanced budget but nonetheless contained "seven escape hatches."[58]

When the council's three advisers were in place—Heller, Gordon, and Tobin—consensus emerged on an unconventional policy. Galbraith was "eased off" to be ambassador to India, and Keyserling was politely turned aside. An initial end run by the new secretary of labor, Arthur Goldberg, to claim the price-cost turf of labor management, was cut off as well. Then the new council charged. It proposed an $11 billion tax cut, accepted the consequences of a deficit, and incurred the wrath of "one unhappy family of advisers"—to wit, the treasury and labor departments and the Federal Reserve Board. In effect, the council turned public presidential policy on its head. In the face of a business fear of inflation and a deteriorating international situation climaxed by the Soviet construction of the Berlin Wall, it persuaded Kennedy at a 1962 "summit meeting" in Hyannis to propose the tax cut as the best means for stimulating economic growth. When the president signed off, Tobin applauded his "increasing economic sophistication." The tax cut that Kennedy proposed and that Johnson later secured was an academic triumph. The economists' elite had intervened against powerful conventional wisdom in government and out. And it won.[59]

The elite's other disciplines would not secure as early a victory nor one as clear-cut. Still, even in a truncated administration, and one made politically cautious by the narrowness of its election and continued congressional sullenness, the third elite—the academic experts—blazed a trail or two. Outside economic policy, the purest example of brains joined to power was the Juvenile Delinquency and Youth Offenses Control Act of 1961. It paired the "ultimate" Kennedy politician, Robert Kennedy, with the era's most ambitious social scientists, the sociologists. It signaled the first skirmishes of the war on poverty, with consequences its authors never anticipated. Most of all, it demonstrated the difficulties that can occur when politicians, administrators, and academics talk to one another and work together.[60]

Somewhat curiously, given the broad sweep of that venture, the juvenile delinquency legislation was not a product of a transition task force. It came, instead, directly from the Kennedy family within a week of the election and in response to its continuing concern for the disability of the president's sister Rosemary. Another sister, Eunice Shriver, also had a long-standing interest in youth problems, as did an old family friend, David Hackett, who led the enterprise.

In the jargon of the public policy literature, the legislation and subsequent program stemmed from a need—"I hurt"—not from an idea—"there's this problem that needs an answer." The concern was bolstered by the continuing high level of unemployment. Lowering it was a conscious presidential priority based partly on Kennedy's personal experience campaigning among the Appalachian poor in West Virginia. It was also "in style" because it concentrated on "youth." "Juvenile delinquency" had become evident since the late 1930s and highly visible in the fifties as immigrants from the South and Puerto Rico flooded northern cities. Urban slums, street crime, and gang wars had become vexing problems for big-city mayors. They also had made *West Side Story* a Broadway hit and a subject for cocktail conversation and committee hearings in Washington.

The efficacy of political partnership became clear when Robert Kennedy courted the support of Howard Smith, the conservative Virginia chair of the House Rules Committee. Adam Clayton Powell and Edith Green became the chairs of the relevant congressional committees. They were all troubled about "the children." The difficulties of such partnerships appeared when Hackett tried to discover what remedies the academics had in mind.

The Children's Bureau in the Department of Health, Education, and Welfare and assorted foundations, not-for-profit associations, and universities had accumulated ideas about juvenile delinquency over the years, and federal demonstration projects had been authorized since the early fifties. There was, however, no consensus as to whether the problem was inside the delinquent's mind, and thus an issue for mental health, or in the community and "family setting" in which the delinquent developed. What combination of internal and external factors prompted delinquent behavior? *West Side Story* had burlesqued the dilemma with unforgetta-ble humor and poignancy in the song "Officer Krupke," as the Jets shuf-fled one of the members of the gang from judge to social worker to psychia-trist, only to reach a general conclusion that "deep down inside him, he's no good."

The Ford Foundation had supported most of the more serious research into juvenile delinquency. The talented, energetic director of its pub-lic affairs division, the late Paul Ylvisaker, was a card-carrying action-intellectual. A Harvard Ph.D. and former assistant to Philadelphia reform mayor Richard Clark, he arrived at Ford at a propitious time. In the fifties, the foundation was embarrassed by its accumulating fortune and anx-ious to invest in a major, nationwide undertaking. Ylvisaker found one in the so-called Grey Areas project—the question of what to do with that zone of deteriorating real estate which, in so many American cities, lies between downtown and the suburbs. The plight of these areas and the people who lived there, mostly minority newcomers, had been identified initially in the New York Metropolitan Region Study directed by economist Raymond Vernon in 1959.[61]

Ylvisaker took the research of Vernon and associates and, after some additional study grants to academics, funded action programs in Oak-land, California, and New York City. These included the Mobilization for Youth (MFY) in New York, which the National Institute of Mental Health also supported. It was in the launching of MFY that Ylvisaker, Hackett, and their academic intermediaries David Hunter and Dyke Bram made contact. From Ylvisaker's perspective, the scale of the problem he had identified and probed clearly required federal intervention if programs such as MFY were to go "to the roots of the problem rather than sort of dealing with palliative services."[62]

Hackett, "tired of people telling me that the only way to cure delinquency was to get inside kids' heads," responded enthusiastically to Ylvisaker's overture for MFY. A covey of experts appeared on the scene—Richard Cloward and Lloyd Ohlin from the Columbia University School of Social Work; Michael Gorman, executive director of the National Committee Against Mental Illness; and Phillip Green, director of HEW Children's Office of Juvenile Delinquency. Cloward and Ohlin took the lead position, committed to comprehensive treatment strategies involving the social and physical reclamation of entire neighborhoods and the provision of genuine opportunities for youths living in them.

This intellectual commitment to comprehensive rather than restricted treatment was never explicitly put forward in the 1961 legislation. On the contrary, the proposal used the ambiguous term "coordination" as the cover word for the interagency, interprogram attack Hackett had become committed to. The law, signed September 22, 1961, was a three-year, $30 million demonstration and training program designed to establish proto-type community based organizations in seventeen cities for more am-bitious future enterprises.

Professor Ohlin then entered the government through the recently es-tablished President's Committee on Juvenile Delinquency and Youth Crime to serve as a catalyst in the Technical Review Demonstration Proj-ects Panel. He brought with him more experts—Richard Boone of the Ford Foundation, William Lawrence of MFY, Leonard Cottrell of the Russell Sage Foundation, Sanford Kravitz from Brandeis University, and Freder-ick O'R. Hayes, a Harvard political economist then working for the budget bureau. They called themselves "Hackett's guerrillas"—a designation that suggests their sense of illegitimacy as far as standard governmental oper-ating procedure was concerned.

Frequently in consultation with Ohlin and Ylvisaker, the guerrillas expanded the field of analysis from delinquency to the problem of poverty in general. Their diagnosis focused on a critical lack of self-esteem and self-worth among the urban poor. The panel carefully delineated a "pa-thology of poverty"—"patterns of general hostility," psychologist Kenneth Clark described it, "random aggressiveness, despair, apathy, a curious fluctuation between self-deprecation and compensatory grandiosity and posturing." Ohlin and Cloward argued that the lack of self-esteem and of genuine middle-class opportunities lay at the heart of both the absence of motivation to escape poverty and the disposition to take up "illegitimate opportunities." Further, middle-class values dominated the bureaucra-cies designed to help the poor. Social workers frequently looked down upon those whom they were supposed to help and deepened their sense of hopelessness. To the experts, attitudes of both recipients and donors needed to be drastically changed.

The guerrillas' consensus on the problem did not yield consensus on remedies. The group split three ways. One prescription favored by Ylvisaker was "top down," forcing bureaucratic agencies at the local level to act by applying pressure from political power bases at the state or federal levels. The affected poor could provide information and feedback, but it was unrealistic to expect them to plan competently. A second group, led by Boone, advocated giving power to the poor through the mechanism of employing them in local programs, infiltrating the bureaucracies with them and forcing "anti-professionalism"—that is, pressuring social work-ers to abandon middle-class biases. Boone thought that in this scenario, the poor could rise through the bureaucratic ranks and influence policy from within. A third version, advanced by Cottrell and Cloward, rejected reliance on top-down planning and infiltration and argued instead that entirely new institutions built from the bottom up and shaped by the poor themselves had to be constructed. Conflict, in this view, was more effective than cooperation in achieving genuine institutional change.

These substantial differences among the guerrilla experts never surfaced in the Kennedy years. Within the executive branch, the so-called structural economists led by Robert Lampman of the Council of Economic Advisors (on leave from the University of Wisconsin) were building the case that macroeconomic "aggregatist" policies could not effectively eliminate poverty even if full employment were achieved. He argued that existing welfare programs did not bring the lowest-income families—in aggregate almost one-fifth of the population—up to the poverty line. A "no-nonsense-from-anybody" liberal, Lampman insisted that neither income tax relief nor government public works spending would effectively help the poor. He argued for income transfer and special training and assistance programs—in effect joining the guerrillas in their advocacy of general institutional change. His argument and theirs were powerfully buttressed by Dwight McDonald's long *New Yorker* piece of January 1963, which summarized the collective critiques of Galbraith's *Affluent Society,* Michael Harrington's *The Other America,* and Henry Candill's *Night Comes to the Cumberlands.*

So the pressure built within the Kennedy administration for a broader antipoverty program. It built, however, without notable public support or debate. Viewing the program as an opportunity to send "a fiscal dividend," Heller and Lampman of the CEA and William Capron of the Bureau of the Budget took the lead in June 1963 with an explicit go-ahead from the president. On November 3, Kennedy signed off on an interagency committee report emphasizing "a many pronged, coordinated attack . . . maximizing self-help, prevention, and particular attention to youth." Capron took charge of drafting a program built on individual agency responses, which were for the most part disappointing. Capron and his key associate, William Cannon, found few new ideas and even fewer proposals for coordination and collaboration among agencies and departments. They turned back to Hackett and his guerrillas.

Already in trouble with the Congress because of the dubious track records of their demonstration program, the guerrillas gladly obliged. They proposed new legislation, which, to no one's surprise, emphasized coordination and experimentation. They buried their serious conceptual and policy differences under the felicitous phrases of demonstration and planning in new and special local action agencies. Hackett's memos never discussed the kind of local agencies he and his guerrillas had in mind. As executive office staff tinkered with Hackett's language, the Community Action Program was born. "Maximum Feasible Participation" was to be

the law of the land—capable of interpretations ranging from empowerment to consultation.

This was the language that Walter Heller took to the LBJ ranch shortly
after Kennedy's assassination. Johnson transformed the program from
experimental status to a full-fledged war on poverty (the earlier phrase was
"an assault on poverty"). Planning, demonstration, and experimentation
lost out to immediate and major action programs. Still submerged in the
legislation was the guerrillas' collective emphasis on the need to "shake up
the system" and the real difference between meeting the material need of
the poor and empowering them—differences the guerrillas themselves
scarcely recognized.

The train had, however, left the station. It fell to Lyndon Johnson to
enact and then oversee a policy and program that Kennedy's experts—
economists and sociologists—had initiated. To these policies and programs, Johnson would shortly add those of the Great Society—with his
own experts and their own ideas.

3

FLOOD TIDE:
EXPERTS AND THE GREAT SOCIETY

$\mathbf{J}$ohn Kennedy, a wealthy Irish Catholic whose Harvard education made him a quasi-Boston Brahmin, used academics mostly from his home territory. Kennedy relied on them intermittently, sometimes cynically, almost always with an air of personal familiarity or friendship. Lyndon Johnson born and bred in the Texas hill country and graduate of a small Texas teachers' college, upped the academic ante exponentially, and he did so with none of Kennedy's advantages of family fortune, Ivy League education, personal self-confidence, style, and grace. Johnson's long congressional career had made him a master of national institutional politics as practiced in the Washington community. In no way did he fit easily with the stereotypic academic temperament. He was "a Washington provincial," in Harry McPherson's words, "rather than a Texas provincial."[1]

Lyndon Johnson's brilliance lay in fashioning political strategy and tactics, his intuitive grasp of personalities, and his subsequent manipulation of men and women to do what they otherwise would not have done. As his biographies, friendly and hostile, have documented, his conversational style—the now-famous "Johnson treatment"—was variously anecdotal, domineering, crudely humorous, dramatically beseeching, or frighteningly authoritarian. Careful, detached, objective, dispassionate consideration of a public problem and the logical alternatives for its resolution was not Johnson's mode.

Yet the number of task forces he established and the number of Ph.D.s (especially from Harvard and M.I.T.) he recruited for cabinet and subcabinet positions exceeded those of any other president in the republic's history. At the end of his first thirty months in office, Johnson directed Bill Moyers to produce a list of his appointees for a press release which, on Johnson's instructions, had "a good paragraph on new men from Harvard and M.I.T." Collectively, these 374 men and women held 781 degrees from colleges and universities in fifty states; 370 had advanced degrees, and 67 had earned doctorates. Throughout his six years, even as the Vietnam War first soured and then savaged administration-university relations across the country, Johnson built the most extensive network of White House academic relations in presidential history.[2]

One can speculate on the president's motives for assembling such an entourage—envy at Kennedy's Camelot, determination to better Franklin Roosevelt's record of reform, the faith of a poor boy in the power of education, the guilt of a southerner who came to realize and acknowledge the simple justice of the civil rights movement, the wisdom of a senator who recognized that the time was ripe for major domestic initiatives after Kennedy's assassination. However and in what measure these factors figured in his drive for the Great Society, the net result was a search for ideas not seen before or since in national politics. On May 22, 1964, in his famous Ann Arbor speech (crafted largely by Richard Goodwin), Johnson announced his goal—a Great Society, as distinct from a rich and powerful one—and specified "three places where we begin to build [it] . . . in our cities, in our countryside [to prevent an ugly America], and in our classrooms." As a follow-up, the president told his cabinet on July 2, 1964, well before the election, "I want to get the advice of the best brains in the country on the problems and challenges confronting America, and I want their help in devising the best approach in meeting them." He proceeded by establishing fifteen task forces, composed principally of Washington outsiders, for 1964, to be followed by twenty-seven more between 1965 to 1968. Emmette Redford and Richard McCulley broke down the forty-two groups by professional categories—academia, government, business, law. Of the 411 members of these task forces, 167 were academics. No other category came close: U.S. government officials were a poor second with 71. In the initial fifteen task forces, seven chairmen were from eastern universities, three from Harvard and two each from Princeton and M.I.T. Twenty-nine percent of the academics serving on the major task forces received their doctorates from Harvard or M.I.T., and another one-quarter came from other Ivy universities or highly competitive counterparts.[3]

The task force mechanism broke decisively the monopoly that departments and the executive office exercised over policy and program proposals, but it did not replace them. On the contrary, Johnson was careful to ensure that governmental "insiders" had their say and signaled that commitment in his July 2 cabinet meeting. "The task forces," he told the cabinet, "are *not* a new planning group in Government. Rather, their reports will provide the background for discussions among the Cabinet agencies and the White House in formulating the 1965 legislative program."[4] Given the secrecy with which the task forces operated and the scorn toward "the bureaucracy" that White House staff members such as Joseph Califano repeatedly expressed, the president's assurance was disingenuous. Still, the administration set up a dozen interagency task forces in 1965 and established ninety interagency groups from 1965 to 1968. These insider groups outnumbered the twenty-seven from outside the government by better than three to one. In considerable measure, this emphasis on insiders reflected a growing need to implement the programs that earlier task forces had created and to reduce interagency turf wars as budget stringencies set in. Nonetheless, inside groups continued to be another vehicle for generating ideas.

So was the time-honored instrument of presidential commissions. Employed throughout the twentieth century, and routinely since World War II, the presidential commission came to be used when an especially vexing policy issue became publicly visible and the White House needed to signal its concern without committing itself substantively and politically. These commissions were—and still are—of two classic types: a "Noah's Ark" whose membership is structured to include the representatives of every interest group affected by the issue, or a "tree of wise owls," a collection of particularly distinguished private citizens with a reputation for objectivity and wise judgment. Covering the spectrum of governmental affairs from adult education to voluntary services, this mechanism was used more by Johnson than by any other president. He appointed twenty-eight commissions in all, averaging more than five a year.[5]

Because they are public, temporary, and autonomous and because their conclusions are often persuasively argued in hearings and final reports as well as on national television, commissions can be troublesome to a president. Two were especially difficult for Johnson. The first was the Commission on Civil Disorder, the so-called Kerner Commission established after the 1967 urban riots, which called for a massive new city aid program and coined the phrase "two Americas—one white and one black, separate and unequal." In effect, the Kerner Report made unrelievedly clear that the president's effort to have both Vietnam guns and home-front butter was not feasible. The second was the National Commission on Urban Problems chaired by former senator Paul Douglas. With a fanfare of press releases in December 1968, it concluded among other things that "government action had destroyed far more housing units for the poor than it had built." Released publicly in the last month of the administration, the report infuriated the White House and the Department of Housing and Urban Development. Almost a foot thick, the report also provided a foundation of data, inferences, impressions, and observations from which the blistering neoconservative critiques of the Great Society would later take off.[6]

Johnson's search for ideas was not confined to Washington-based task forces and commissions. Almost immediately after Kennedy's murder, the White House dispatched Bill Moyers and Richard Goodwin to Cambridge to maintain the connection with that now-critical group of opinion makers who were, in Edelman's words, "small in number, but like editorial writers, a critical stable for governing." Thereafter, as the senior White House liaison, Moyers and then Califano visited leading universities in the South and West as well as in the East annually. In all, over the first five years, more than one hundred scholars dined with Califano, Harry McPherson, and their staffs.[7]

The results from these ad hoc exercises were varied. As the war and resistance to it escalated, it became increasingly difficult to persuade the best and/or brightest on each campus to attend the dinners. But Califano and his staff persisted, enduring passionate criticism of the war in order to fill black notebooks with "a thousand and one ideas to be staffed and costed out" and "to learn of regional differences in policy priorities." To the end of the administration, Califano used the campus visits and dinners to gather ideas for Johnson's last State of the Union message and advice on the establishment of the LBJ School of Public Policy at the University of Texas at Austin.[8]

Finally, Johnson and his key advisers continued to consult informally with individual academic stars, though not as extensively as Kennedy had. Galbraith maintained a continuing series of telephone calls and visits with the president and "enjoyed LBJ more as a person than JFK." Johnson was, in Galbraith's words, a "superb conversationalist and joke teller."[9] Until Vietnam led to a public break, Galbraith was especially active in suggesting names for task forces and commissions and in commenting on economic policy. Richard Neustadt continued his special assignments, usually worked out by friends in the Executive Office of the President, "a notch down from the White House."[10]

Eric Goldman, a Princeton history professor, replaced Arthur Schlesinger as resident academic on the recommendation of White House junior staff member Richard Nelson, who had taken his classes as an undergraduate. Goldman moved vigorously in the first months of the new administration, orchestrating semisocial Rose Garden meetings of academics, organizing small meetings on such specific issues as metropolitan affairs, and providing historical perspective on recurrent problems. By March 1964, Goldman had organized an informal brain trust responsive to the call to build a Great Society. The group included by-now familiar Cambridge scholars: Galbraith, Edwin Land of Polaroid, and me. It also included some who had not been directly involved with Kennedy: Paul Freund of the Harvard Law School, Columbia historian Richard Hofstadter, anthropologist Margaret Mead, sociologist David Riesman of

Harvard, and Paul Ylvisaker of the Ford Foundation. These experts were talking and writing in the White House weeks before the Ann Arbor speech.[11]

Initially, Goldman participated in organizing the first round of task forces as well. He lacked, however, the advantage of prior association that Schlesinger enjoyed with Kennedy, and as the inevitable personnel conflicts and struggle for presidential support broke out, Goldman lost standing. He resigned to write his bitter *Tragedy of Lyndon Johnson* and was replaced in September 1966 by political scientist John Roche of Brandeis. Roche stayed until the end, functioning mostly as an inside analyst, commentator, and speech writer. Daniel Patrick Moynihan kept reasonably close relations with McPherson and Califano, and Emmette Redford, a political scientist from Texas who literally grew up next door to the president, had personal and professional access.[12]

From a variety of perspectives and posts, then, academic experts "infiltrated" the Johnson administration, and the elite strategically positioned itself throughout the executive branch. At the White House, in the Executive Office of the President, in the great departments and line agencies, experts were applying a post–World War II stockpile of social science knowledge in a far more systematic way, with far more discernible policy results, than they had during the Kennedy years. From the beginning and throughout the administration, first Moyers and then Califano moved to put in place more or less permanent arrangements for the search and retrieval of ideas from academic sources. At the outset, however, they had to dispose of the most prominent of the policies in the Kennedy administration's pipeline—tax policy, the proposed Department of Housing and Urban Development, and the embryonic but fast-escalating war on poverty. The first two were essentially legislative undertakings, for the outline of the policies had already been hammered out. The last policy, although its major concepts were still unresolved, was partly in place, and it was still in the hands of David Hackett's guerrillas, then gathered under the aegis of Robert Kennedy's justice department. The Johnson administration and its eggheads would wrestle with its consequences, especially the Community Action Program, until the very end—and pay a heavy short-run political price.

Coping with the Legacy

If the New Frontier is interpreted now as more style than substance, a preoccupation with foreign policy almost to the exclusion of domestic policy, a haphazard, freewheeling introduction of ideas after the initial reports of preinaugural task forces were in, it nonetheless launched the most visible and most controversial program in the Great Society. True, Hackett's drafts on the strategy for the war on poverty (which William Cannon and William Capron of the Bureau of the Budget "massaged") emphasized demonstration grants to a few cities with planning and experimentation taking precedence over comprehensive action. True, too, President Johnson flipped the program emphasis completely: he demanded a full-scale operating program and insisted that it be in place by the next presidential election in November 1964. Nonetheless, the explosive concepts that lay buried in the proposed legislative language—community action and maximum feasible participation (which Moynihan would later attack in one of the beachhead books of seventies neoconservative ideology) were New Frontier in origin. They belonged to the guerrillas.[13]

The new president's policy in launching the poverty war stressed combining federal and local initiative to assure the delivery of services in a coordinated fashion. But Johnson never contemplated the poor actually participating in the process—either in Richard Boone's terms of staffing existing community agencies or Leonard Cattrell's far more radical strategy of empowerment through entirely new organizations. The president felt strongly that some tangible assistance had to be given to black America, specifically to support the Reverend Martin Luther King, Jr., and more generally to combat the general sense of alienation among minorities across the country. He also wanted *his* stamp on the program, particularly because it began in Kennedy's Justice Department and at Robert Kennedy's initiative. The emergence of professional program alternatives put forth by Johnson task forces and personal enmity (which Nicholas Lemann later chronicled) further skewed the program. But even as the administration proclaimed stewardship and fueled a political fire that would burn with increasing intensity, it steered clear of the guerrillas' ideas.[14]

The ever-prudent institutional arm of the presidency—the Bureau of the Budget—undertook to "stage" the new war, for which scheduled appropriations had multiplied fivefold to one-half billion dollars. And Johnson moved both to knock heads among federal departments resisting coordination and to blunt Robert Kennedy's political opposition by creating the Office of Economic Opportunity as a presidential agency and appointing Sargent Shriver, Kennedy's brother-in-law, as its head. In all the alarms and excursions of those early months, the question of empowering nonestablishment groups remained unexplored, undefined, even unrecognized by the key senior staff members in the Executive Office of the President.[15]

Thus the first serious venture of academic experts into social policy—conceived in an earlier administration and enacted in the inevitable confusion of a presidential transition compounded by tragedy and enmity—emerged almost completely barren of the elemental characteristic of a new hypothesis. Community action—power to the neighborhood and its people—was written into law without any experimentation, historical analysis, or planning to support it. Indeed, Boone bootlegged the phrase "maximum feasible participation" into a proposed statutory section designed to prevent segregation in the South. Neither White House staff nor executive office professionals realized what had happened.[16]

More important, after the guerrillas' legislative triumph, they infiltrated the tactically significant middle level of American bureaucracy where programs are actually carried out. They captured powerful posts in CAP as they moved into the porous federal civil service structure. Hayes, Kravitz, and Ohlin were so positioned as to be able to fund on their own discretion reform programs that challenged directly the political establishment of mayors, city councilors, and city commissioners. Conflict replaced coordination. Shriver struggled without success to place priority on youth employment programs. He saw Community Action as "a big headache," a classic case of failed communication between expert and presidential staff. Concluding her study of experts and the war on poverty in 1986, Isabel Miller wrote, "The social experts wanted to change the nature of the relationship between the poor and the institutions serving them. Yet it was precisely this relationship which kept people in power and won elections. The social experts knew their demands would threaten the establishment. Yet they believed they could alter the establishment's values and attitudes through institutional change, involvement of the poor, and conflict if necessary. What they learned was just how wrong they were."[17] A decade after the war on poverty began, Lloyd Ohlin, the expert probably most responsible for "Community Action," was asked what he learned most from the sixties. He replied, "I think we learned the enormous resistance of these institutions to change, their tremendous capacity to resiliently absorb protest, aggression against them, attempts to change their goals or directions, and the internal distributions of power and responsibility within them. Wrong analysis, wrong prescription, wrong results."[18]

Kingpins of the Great Society

If Johnson soon learned the problems experts could make in both legislation and program execution, his discoveries did not turn him against social scientists. On the contrary, they seem to have encouraged him to seek out his own academics, or, more precisely, to use under his own specified auspices and very specific terms academics who advised or were prepared to advise Kennedy. In the first wave of task forces—the Bill Moyers wave—Johnson achieved his greatest successes and the experts their greatest influence.

Born and educated in Texas, Moyers was an ordained minister, a staff aide to Johnson in the 1960 campaign, a liaison to the Kennedys, and associate director of the Peace Corps at the time of the assassination. He joined Johnson on Air Force One as it came back from Dallas on the night of November 23. He remained Johnson's key aide until his departure at the end of 1966, and he was in charge of domestic legislative policy development from November 1963 until July 1965.

Moyers's visit to Galbraith's house in Cambridge shortly after the assassination (a meeting arranged by Goodwin, a holdover from the Kennedy White House) kept open the academic channels in the period of shock and mourning. The image of Johnson as a braggadocio, a swaggering, loud, uncouth southern senator, was a popular one in the Harvard Yard, where the Kennedy style and wit had been much admired. In fact, few social scientists in Cambridge or elsewhere knew his Washington reputation and real record. During a period he remembers as his most satisfying in the White House, Moyers undertook to make sure they learned.[19]

Because he had served as campaign liaison between the Kennedy and Johnson camps in 1960, Moyers could enlist the knowledge and networks of the holdover White House staff members. This he did in the early months of 1964, when the groundwork for the Ann Arbor "Great Society" speech and the specific plans for follow-up were hammered out. Though the Kennedy preinaugural task forces were one precedent, Johnson had in fact used freewheeling ad hoc groups of experts throughout his senate career, and he would place his own stamp of confidentiality and boldness upon them. Moyers ensured that the two models would be merged.

In a June 1964 memo to White House staff members, Moyers asked four Kennedy holdovers—Goodwin, Francis Bator, Meyer Feldman, and Lee White—to join two Johnson staffers—Douglass Cater and Don Hornig—to propose topics and members. On July 6, the day after the president had adjourned the cabinet, he asked executive office senior staff—Heller and Gardner Ackley of the Council of Economic Advisors, Kermit Gordon, Charles Schultz, and Elmer Staats of the Budget Bureau—to come into the group as well.[20]

In his memo, Moyers delegated to both White House and executive office liaison members the responsibility to "line up membership . . . immediately select the list of task force members (including the chair), clear with Kermit Gordon and Charles Schultz, to assure no duplication . . . Begin at once to contact members and contact agency head on membership." That process of selection, senior staff members in the BOB recall, was an informal, casual, who-knows-whom-who-knows-what-we-need-to-know affair. Remembered professors from college days, authors of books recently read, authors of professional reviews, chance acquaintances, all were initial candidates.[21] The lists were winnowed down largely by a consensus that the most familiar names were the best. Here, the holdovers and the former academics from the executive office held a clear advantage. Eastern universities and especially the Cambridge connections dominated.

The "Big Three" of the task forces were those Johnson identified in the Ann Arbor speech. John Gardner, then president of the Carnegie Corporation, chaired the education task force. Of its twelve other members, nine qualified as academics although three were by then academic administrators. I chaired "Cities"—more formally titled Metropolitan and Urban Problems—seven of whose ten other members were academics. Charles Haar of the Harvard Law School chaired the task force on the Preservation of Natural Beauty. Eight of Haar's eleven colleagues on the committee were campus-based. The other twelve task forces covered a range of topics, four focusing on economic issues of prosperity and productivity, two on the environment and natural resources, two on improved government management, and one each on health, agriculture, and transportation. Each had a seasoned BOB staff specialist on the topic to which the task force was assigned and a White House liaison staff member. By Moyers's explicit directive, Eric Goldman was designated as ex-officio member of all task forces as well as a participant in the Rose Garden ceremonies that attended task force visits with the president. The deadline for task force reports was November 10, 1964, just after the election.[22]

There ensued a major scramble of identifying, screening, assuring security clearances, and finding funding for consultants and expenses, plus obtaining legal justification for such appointments. After this whirlwind, the exercise came off in orderly, effective, and impressive fashion. In sharp contrast to the impoverished arrangements of Kennedy task forces, the Johnson groups met in conference rooms within the Executive Office Building. Staff made their travel and lodging arrangements and provided secretarial support. Several task forces met with the president either at the beginning or end of their assignments. As one participant recalled, the original task forces were "happenings" in "a new, real atmosphere" yet replete with "blue sky planning."[23]

Although occasionally an academic would demur (Princeton's Marvin Bernstein resigned from a task force assignment in October 1964 because its schedule conflicted with the meetings of the Princeton politics department), defections were counterbalanced by letters displaying loyalty and devotion. One scholar terminally ill with cancer pledged that he would "serve until he dies on the agriculture task force."[24] In the contemporary phrase, the task forces were world-class undertakings. Moyers described the task forces as "the best of three worlds—the world of bureaucracy which would finally be responsible for implementing the ideas, . . . the world of expertise outside of government; and . . . a White House special assistant for follow-through."[25]

They were world class in their internal deliberations as well. John Gardner brought nineteen years of experience in consulting with the government to his task. "I knew a lot about how government worked," he stated, and added that he also knew "all the key players [in the field of education] from my Carnegie position, and I had worked with them. So I immediately wrote forty letters to the major actors asking that they identify key problems. I had a strong sense that I must touch all the bases to assure an effective interface between academics and policymakers. So when the task force recommendations were put together nobody could say, 'Gardner didn't consult me.' "[26] For Gardner, two secrets explained the success of his task force—the lesson he had already learned "to pay more attention to the strange tribes in the other valley than to your own troops," and the superb staff work that William Cannon of the BOB provided.

Haar's task force on the preservation of natural beauty was similarly blessed by a sophisticated and adept law professor in its chair, Laurance Rockefeller as a loyal member, and a consensus-inclined group whose recommendations would win the support of Lady Bird Johnson and accordingly the president. Besides broadening the scope of recreational and park programs to include explicitly the recognition of natural beauty, it focused on assuring amenities along highways and in national forests. The task force's work became the "beautification" programs of Mrs. Johnson and the prescient forerunner of environmental programs of the seventies and thereafter.

Consensus was harder to achieve in the urban and metropolitan task force. Its West Coast members, especially those from the University of California at Berkeley—planner Martin Meyerson, sociologist Nathan Glazer, and civil engineer Joseph Kennedy—were initially not sure there was an "urban problem," an early signal that the academic camp was divided in its analysis of city issues. But the task force did endorse the rent supplement program, support the establishment of the Department of Housing and Urban Development, and spark the first message specifically on cities that any president had sent to Congress.[27]

The education task force provided the first ten-strike for the Johnson domestic program. Although major successful laws conventionally have "many fathers," in this instance the eighteen recommendations of the eighty-three-page task force report focused on assuring access to excellent education for the children of the poor. That goal was the central thrust of the ensuing law. Frank Keppel, Harvard contemporary of Kennedy's and then commissioner of education in HEW, served as a crucial link between the task force and the Office of Education, which was in the throes of reorganization and struggling under a burden of new programs. He and Wilbur Cohen, Assistant Secretary of HEW, viewed the key portions of the legislation as being "hatched in the bureaucracy" and "refined and given respectability and legitimacy by the task force."[28]

Yet outside observers award far more credit to the task force. Norman Thomas and Harold Wolman concluded flatly in 1969 that "the major innovative programs authorized in the Elementary and Secondary Act of 1965, Title III and IV, originated with the 1964 Gardner task force." And Samuel Halperin, the key drafter of the legislation in HEW, conceded that "the final thing that broke the log jam legislatively speaking was an idea thrown into the task force."[29]

Stalled for years on the twin issues of parochial schools and states' rights, the legislation passed easily in the spring of 1965, which suggests that at a minimum the task force was the catalyst in shaping its proposals into acceptable policy. Under Gardner's skillful direction it served "to meld the aspirations of the dreamers (Zacharias, Land, and Riesman) with those of the practitioners (Commissioner Allen, Superintendent Marland)."[30] Like Kennedy's wry observation after the Bay of Pigs that "victory had a hundred fathers while defeat is an orphan," it is not surprising that the authorship of key parts of the legislation remained a matter of dispute. In any event, the task force and the office were working in tandem. Keppel was a key "broker of ideas," and the task force "thumbprint" was on every section of the new law. More dramatic evidence is the fact that Johnson tapped Gardner to be his HEW secretary at the Rose Garden ceremony celebrating the passage of the new law.[31]

By the summer of 1965, the president could view the task force operation with considerable satisfaction. His legislative triumphs of the year before had been primarily in bringing Kennedy initiatives to a successful conclusion—the tax cut and the Civil Rights Act of 1964. The Elementary and Secondary Education Act and rent supplements became law in 1965, as did environmental protection, wilderness preservation, and the creation of HUD. All in all, in the space of a year Johnson sent thirty-four first-time requests to the Congress—a post–World War II record that still stood in 1990. An unprecedented 72 percent of the House supported his social welfare legislation.[32]

These accomplishments were Johnson's and Johnson's alone. Flush with victory, he authorized Moyers to assemble the task force chairs for dinner in the White House mess on July 8, 1965. In an extraordinary evening lasting until after one the next morning, Johnson conveyed his appreciation, his determination to continue his domestic initiatives, and his conviction that guns for Vietnam and butter for the cities were possible simultaneously. Toward the end of the evening, several academics politely questioned that assumption. The first schism in the ranks of the action-intellectuals appeared, and Vietnam haunted those with a domestic agenda until the administration came to a close.[33]

The Process Rationalized

The July 8 dinner also marked the transfer of task force responsibility from Moyers to Joseph Califano, as Moyers moved to replace George Reedy as press secretary and Califano left his defense department post to take charge of preparing Johnson's domestic legislative program. The new presidential assistant was also to coordinate the legislative program with economic policy to respond to the "domestic crisis."[34]

Operating at first with only one assistant, Lawrence Levinson, Califano termed the 1964 process "hit and miss," as well as "chaotic and archaic." To him it seemed a sharp contrast to the planning-programming-budgeting system Robert McNamara was applying in the defense department. He thought little of White House assignments with "fuzzy" boundary lines such as Douglass Cater's involvement in education policy and his advocacy of a "Wednesday group on domestic affairs to balance the Tuesday group on war."[35] Ambitious, energetic, sardonic, and often abrasive, Califano would ultimately assemble a staff of four: Levinson, James Gaither, Matthew Nimetz, and Fred Bohen. All but Bohen were lawyers, and all had only limited government experience.

With this small, tightly controlled, and singularly undiplomatic group, Califano tried to "impose discipline" in the search for the best ideas from the best brains in the country through task forces, campus visits, and conversations. At the urging of the new Director of the Budget, Charles Schultz, Califano would also begin to add cost estimates to legislative proposals. Further, he would push to simplify presidential presentations by including flip charts in highly organized briefings.[36]

As Levinson recalled, "Our job was to try to harness the brain power of the country and to direct that flow of ideas into the problems of the American scene." Augmented by letters stimulated from the campus visits and solicited from the "bright people hidden away in the bureaucracy," the Califano operation put its ideas into thick black notebooks containing page upon page of proposals, one idea per page. The involvement of the president intensified; not only did Johnson authorize the broadest possible sweep for new proposals, but, Gaither observed, "he never rejected a

charter for a new task force." According to Gaither, he also became personally involved in picking experts. Johnson consciously tried to release the
eastern academic grip but succeeded only in slightly weakening it.[37]

Over time, Califano would shift the emphasis from outside task forces
to inside ones, although key ideas still clearly came from outside. In 1965,
there were four outside groups and a dozen interagency ones. With the
1964 legislative successes behind him, the president charged Califano
with three primary tasks: creating a department of transportation, securing an open housing bill, and "totally rebuilding the ghettos."[38]

In contrast to the outside groups, the interagency task forces—such as
those on education, foreign aid, labor, and food aid—often focused on
implementation and cost considerations. "Fine tuning" and "tinkering,"
they were typically conservative in orientation. Their members came from
disparate departments and agencies, and their vested interests showed.
Moreover, they were guided in 1965 by very specific "laundry lists" Califano and his staff prepared in sharp contrast to the general mandates
Moyers had encouraged. All in all, by imposing a price tag on proposals
and focusing on specific and narrow issues, Califano discouraged free-
form idea generation. Instead, he encouraged "an atmosphere of embat-
tled bureaucrats" already "drinking from a fire hydrant" to absorb and
administer the programs authorized in the preceding year.[39]

Of the four outside task forces—urban affairs, foreign aid, tax reform,
and international education—the blockbuster was urban affairs, from
which the Model Cities legislation emerged. Leonard Duhl, a National
Institute of Health psychiatrist, and Antonia Chayes, then a dean at Tufts
University, conceived the kernel of the program—to restore entire neighborhoods with a battery of physical and social support programs, an idea
that found its way into an appendix of the 1964 task force report. Its
heritage reached back to conversations and debates of the Community
Action Program guerrillas, Duhl's own advisory group (dubbed "space
cadets"), and Ylvisaker's Grey Areas Project at the Ford Foundation.

Politically, the task force found strength in its 1964 predecessor. One of
its members, Mayor Jerome Cavanaugh of Detroit, took the appendix to
Walter Reuther, president of the United Auto Workers. Reuther expanded
it in a memorandum to Johnson proposing "an urban TVA" with Detroit
as the obvious site for the new enterprise. At the very least, the Motor
City would be one of a highly select sample of six to a dozen sister cities.
The 1965 task force membership reflected this mix of ideas and politics.
Wood and Haar, veterans of the 1964 circuit, Kermit Gordon, newly de-
parted from the budget bureau to head the Brookings Institution, were by
now certified experts. Reuther, Urban League executive director Whitney
Young, Kaiser Industries CEO Edgar Kaiser, railway executive Ben Heine-

man, and Senator Abraham Ribicoff were political heavy hitters, while William Rafsky, urban renewal administrator for Philadelphia, provided a bridge perspective between "thinkers and doers."[40]

Haar and I strengthened the expert sector by adding a staff drawn from the academy. The leaders were Chester Rapkin of the University of Pennsylvania and Bernard Frieden of M.I.T., who rapidly assembled a group of young staff analysts and eighteen consultants. The staff worked under conditions of high secrecy in "a safe house," an unmarked office in the Federal Maritime Commission building. They were shielded from the biases of the political members of the task force and the professionals of the Housing and Home Finance Agency (soon to become HUD staff). Competent scholars supplied a separate stream of whatever ideas existed in the academy's stockpile.

Symbolically, the expert elite advanced another step in its relations with the politician and the administrator. Its meetings were moved from the Executive Office Building, the domain of the professional civil service elite of the Bureau of the Budget and the Council of Economic Advisors, to the White House itself. There on the third floor in Harry McPherson's conference room, the group reviewed staff papers, listed concepts, and hammered out agreements.

With a specific focus and genuine national political clout among its members, the cities task force moved at a rapid pace. Its first meeting was on October 16, and after four other weekend meetings, it sent its draft report to members on December 6. The intensive, uninterrupted Saturday and Sunday sessions were as important an innovation as the White House location and the provision of an independent staff. Harry McPherson would later write that the schedule became a prototype of a successful policy-making device; it freed the presidency from both the clamor of special interests and the cautions of the civil service.[41]

The history of the 1966 congressional battle to enact the Model Cities legislation and the trials and tribulations of its implementation have been comprehensively, if not always accurately, documented. The neoconservative interpretation is that the purity of the scholar's original concept was violated in the legislative expansion of the number of target cities and that the subsequent planning and implementation phases were further tarnished by the intrusion of "political considerations."[42]

The truth is that the task force recommendations themselves reflected considerable political deliberation. The provisions of metropolitan planning, for example, were "throw-aways" inserted with the expectation that they would be sacrificed in congressional negotiation. Nonetheless, compared to other federal grant programs, Model Cities remained a highly selective one—with barely one-third of all congressional districts benefit-

ing. It was accordingly a hard sell on Capitol Hill and insisted on the cities'
proving minimum professional standards if only for the comparative purpose of explaining to the losing congressional districts why they were
counted out. Roundly condemned as a failure of social engineering by
neoconservatives and recommended for abolition by Nixon brain trusts,
the program more than survived. It persisted under different titles and
acronyms through the inflationary, crisis-wracked Carter administration. By the 1980s, it was also a political training field for a cadre of
minority elected officials, mayors and city councilors across the country
who first learned neighborhood politics through Model Cities.

As Rufus Browning, Dale Rogers Marshall, and David Tabb concluded
in *Protest Alone Is Not Enough* (1984), Model Cities became the most important of all the federal social programs in supporting African-American
and Hispanic drives for political equality, especially in cities most resis-
tant to recognizing minority needs and rights. "Because of its strong
statutory directives, Model Cities proved more beneficial than the programs of general revenue sharing and community development that followed in the seventies . . . [it] involved stronger opportunities for local
groups to participate in the implementation process and generated significant differences in outcome." Or, as a San Francisco Model Cities participant stated, "It created organizations. It created aspirants for higher
office . . . Model Cities was worth every cent."[43]

Johnson later listed Model Cities as one of his major accomplishments.
"The proposal was an approach to the rebuilding of city neighborhoods in
a total way, bringing to bear on a blighted community all the programs
that could help in that task," he stated. "I believe this law will be regarded
as one of the major breakthroughs of the 1960s."[44]

One Bridge Too Far

The highly visible success of the 1964 Gardner and 1965 Wood task
forces—as evidenced in formal acts of the Congress followed by appropriations—emboldened Califano and his staff to push on. In 1966, his office
secured presidential authorization for eleven outside and eighteen inside
groups, some on old topics such as education, cities, and income maintenance, but others focused on an ever-widening range of new topics—
nursing homes, summer programs, wage garnishment, electric power,
information systems.

Within and outside the White House, the expert policy device now attracted attention. Mrs. Johnson's press secretary, Elizabeth Carpenter,
noted and protested the very large percentage of male members and provided å list of women for consideration. Marvin Watson came forward with

names of qualified Texans. Mike Manatos filed a list of those who would be well received in Congress. From a practical perspective, a White House legal counsel warned Califano that the funding of task forces bordered on unlawful and that statutes as old as 1909 and 1944 forbade such enterprises—unless at least two agencies were involved. Requests for copies of earlier task force reports from media and universities were frequent, and routinely denied. Philosophical objections from congressmen were also politely acknowledged but turned aside.[45]

Internal squabbles among White House staff surfaced. McPherson objected to the establishment of a second outside task force on collective bargaining to review the work of an earlier one, and substantive differences in program content continued between Califano and Douglass Cater. These squabbles were papered over, however, and the momentum for "new ideas" accelerated.

By 1967, the system of working groups had reached "a peak of systemization"—complete with a timetable for proposals and a program development book, but also with an expansion in the scale and volume of work that risked loss of oversight and, worse, loss of deliberation. The stockpile of ideas could not be replenished as quickly as it was being transformed into policy. The stresses and strains of organization within the White House were generating once again a contentious atmosphere. Preparing proposals for presidential consideration had resulted in a regular time of concentrated activity which Califano called "an indescribable part of the year."[46] Jennifer Neel depicts change in the process this way: "The size of the whole task force operation mushroomed dramatically. Task forces . . . were asked to look at specific, relatively narrow issues and to focus their attention on long-term as well as short-range recommendations." Sadly, the measures Califano instituted to capitalize on early successes and to "perfect" the technique appear to have helped reduce the effectiveness of the task forces. In short, the technique lost its impact when used as a "shotgun for policy formulation," Neel argues; it "exhausted its earlier potency . . . [and] yielded uniformly pedestrian task force performance."[47]

To the excesses in the use of the task force must be added the deterioration of the policy environment as the Vietnam War, like an insidious virus in the bloodstream, poisoned the potential for domestic reform. William Bundy, then assistant secretary of state for South Asian affairs, observed twenty years later that "the war was the president's duty which he believed he had inherited, and the Great Society was his passion. Unhappily, duty triumphed over passion."[48] In short, an idea equivalent to Gresham's currency law was underway, and the two retreaded task forces on education and cities put the problems in clear relief. A strategy of guns *and* butter could no longer be sustained. In 1965, when the Model Cities group got underway, Califano told me that there was a $12 billion surplus to be cut three ways in tax relief, defense, and the war on poverty. By 1967, when I served as HUD undersecretary, that surplus was gone, and funding for legislation already on the books was in jeopardy.

William Friday, president of the University of North Carolina, headed the last outside education task force. Cannon again assembled the group, even more academic in composition that the Gardner predecessor (ten of its thirteen members were scholars). The Friday group suffered from the president's growing preoccupation with the war. When it delivered its report, Friday recalls, "we talked five minutes about education and forty-five about Vietnam." It suffered as well from the fact that it was exploring familiar territory. Cannon observed that Gardner had the advantage of both being in on the ground floor and at the same time building the ground floor. In these circumstances, it became increasingly hard for the Friday group to follow Califano's continuing injunction to "think big" and "not let immediate political considerations get in the way."[49]

Squeezed between an agenda of items left over from the Gardner task force and the growing fiscal crisis, the second education task force nonetheless came up with new ideas: a massive "moon shot" program for poor children, metropolitan-based magnet schools, and a National Social Science Foundation. But the price tag was considerable and did not jibe with the grim budgetary realities of the day. The *New York Times* gave the task force's well-reasoned report a brief moment of publicity, after which it received a quiet burial in the White House central file.[50]

A similar fate befell the second cities task force, a mix of old and new faces largely picked by Califano. Ylvisaker, who served as chair, steered his group with singular intellectual courage to new ground—an explicit recognition that urban racism was the central component of the cities' growing agony. Clearly and precisely the task force outlined a strategy for anticipating and responding to riots which otherwise, it predicted, would be inevitable. In many ways it anticipated the findings and recommendations of the president's 1968 Commission on Civil Disorder, but its prescience was rudely unrewarded.

Ironically, Ylvisaker, then New Jersey's commissioner for community affairs, delivered the report to the White House on the day disorder broke out in Newark. He returned to that burning city to play a hero's role in quelling the immediate riot and later on to fashion creative if limited programs of state relief. Telephoning from Washington, Harry McPherson had to tell Ylvisaker that financial and political constraints prevented the White House from acting on the recommendations. Ylvisaker recalled that he was "mad as hell" and hung up on the special counsel to the president.[51]

Despite the absence of any substantial breakthroughs in legislation and executive action stimulated by the 1966 task forces, Califano pushed on. He now viewed the network of academic dinners, task forces, consultations, commissions, and conferences as mature and effective arrangements. Accordingly, he launched twenty-seven additional task forces in 1967, this time mixing outside and inside experts on several occasions and drawing particularly on former academics now in government, such as Charles Haar. But the magic had gone out of the enterprise, and, though qualitatively some of the 1967 reports were distinguished (those on suburbia, new towns, crime, and urban educational opportunities in particular), few if any significant ideas were transformed into policy. A veteran executive office senior analyst, Harold Seidman, observed of that period, "Task forceitis ran rampant . . . Papers were circulated on an 'eyes only' basis, and when agency people were included on the task forces they were reluctant to tell even their bosses about what they were doing. The task force operation bred a miasma of suspicion and distrust without producing very much that was usable . . . [it was] an obstruction to normal agency business."[52] "In the end," Neel concluded, "the originally sought 'fresh ideas' were allowed to sour and wilt during processing in the elaborate machinery designed to return and exploit those ideas. Any vitality that remained was then sucked out by the spectre of Vietnam."[53]

Coonskins on the Wall

Journalists and scholars have applied three criteria to assess the innovation and effectiveness of the Johnson task forces. The first simply correlates ideas advanced and action secured either by legislation or executive action. Here the statistics are impressive. King and Ragsdale have shown not only that Johnson topped all postwar presidents in the sheer number of requests for legislation he advanced in the first year but also that Johnson achieved the greatest number of legislative enactments. All told, Johnson secured more congressional support for his task-force-generated Great Society programs than any other modern president—72 percent.

Moreover, as an activist, Johnson took more "stand-up" positions on legislation before the Congress than any modern president, and he received in his four years the highest percentage of support from members of both parties. When one identifies the recommendations that appeared in presidential messages and then in legislative enactments (except for Medicare and Medicaid, which had for years been in the pipeline), the early task force ideas *were* the Great Society. Redford and McCulley have reported that the "major" bills of 1964 and 1965—31 and 44 respectively—were matched 29 and 56 in the next two years, though the term "major" was dropped.[54]

David Walker sums up domestic program impact on the federal system: grants-in-aid outlays doubling between 1964 and 1968, a pronounced shift in favor of urban areas, more grant programs (210) in Johnson's five years than in all of the previous years dating back to the first categorical grant in 1897, and new regulatory and managerial initiatives.[55] Whatever its original source, the process that Johnson authorized and oversaw and that Califano ultimately overextended was the principal instrument for shaping the only major domestic reform program since the New Deal.

Add to the legislative record the policy innovations introduced through executive orders, presidential memoranda, and rules and regulations, and the record is even more impressive. The major initiative was in the Planning-Programming-Budgeting System, a resource allocation innovation in the preparation and justification of the federal budget that represented "advanced" thinking in systems analysis in the most prestigious business and public management graduate schools in the country. But Johnson also actively encouraged cost reduction and personnel development programs that matched the best organizational theory of the decade. He was, as Walker has pointed out, a modern administrator as well as a legislator.

Despite his predominantly liberal outlook,

> Johnson's pragmatism and fiscal and administrative conservatism should not be ignored. In his "concert of interests" approach to legislative enactments, in his distributional approach to parceling out benefits, and especially in his dealings with individuals and groups, the pragmatist in Johnson was rarely missing. With his efforts to keep the budget under the $100 billion mark in the mid-sixties, with his worry about deficits and about the conservative criticisms they would generate, with his hostility to welfare reform, and even with his antipoverty efforts, which after all were geared to producing "tax payers, not tax eaters," a strong streak of fiscal conservatism was clearly manifested.[56]

While the scorecard of transforming academic ideas into operational programs was impressive in both legislative and executive terms, a second criterion for success was perhaps more important. Did academic experts in their new roles as consultants, dinner guests, and task force members change in any important sense the way presidents make their decisions? Close observers of presidential policy Johnson-style conclude that they did. However overextended the Califano operation became in 1967–1968, Redford and McCulley conclude, "its strength was the mobilization of intellectual resources in prompt response to a president's purpose."[57] Lester Salamon included task forces as one of four major models for policy formulation—clearly superior to the classic model of central legislative clearance Richard Neustadt described and at least occasionally as influential as the interagency "deinstitutionalized" White House working groups and the formally established domestic council which dominated the White House throughout the 1970s. Obviously, the Califano excesses in 1967 and 1968 damaged the reputation of the vehicle, but the successes of 1964 and 1965 still seemed impressive to scholars in the 1980s.[58]

If the academic experts' propositions were legislatively and executively successful to an extraordinary degree in the Johnson administration, and if scholars view the task force device as one of the best ways to organize a White House, a third standard of evaluation is inescapable. Did the ideas work? Were they any good? In response, the intellectual assault of seventies neoconservatives was savage indeed. Irving Kristol in effect argued that the social scientists who served Kennedy and Johnson were superficial thinkers, barely qualified to enter the groves of academe, "drawn like moths to the candle flame of power," scholars who "reached into their bags of half-formulated unverified hypotheses and theories and seized the opportunity to translate preposterous notions into law."[59]

In the last analysis, the neoconservative critique of the liberal experts may have boiled down to contention between outsiders and insiders. Put more directly, did the avalanche of neoconservative commentary represent consensus among impartial, uninvolved observers, or was it a heavily ideological rush to judgment, tinged with an outsider's envy of those invited to participate?

After a generation of observing and evaluating Great Society programs in operation, many—probably the majority—have established their worth. Head Start's emphasis on the importance of early childhood now enjoys bipartisan, well-nigh universal support. Concrete achievements in health care, housing, education, and manpower employment are well documented. So are the benefits of the economic growth-oriented policies, as well as the advances of medical research and preventive medicine. After twenty years, by and large, the new ventures that lay at the heart of the Great Society—programs that undertook to modify human behavior and the human condition—stand up.[60]

Even if the policy jury is still out on the quality and consequences of the ideas of the Great Society, these programs nonetheless persisted long after the Johnson administration, some until the late 1970s. They have also been rediscovered in such contemporary laws as the 1990 Housing Act. So they are of consequence and a final judgment needs to be rendered. Was this special period when White House staff, top-level civil servants from the executive office and the cabinet, and academics from prestigious universities found common cause—a political culture that John Gardner described as one "in which the groups involved understood one another"—beneficial for the country?

At the end of the sixties, and today, a considerable body of opinion viewed the coalition of the three elites as a potentially dangerous political development. On June 18, 1968, three distinguished social scientists from the University of North Carolina at Chapel Hill—Donald Matthews, James Prothro, and Thomas Cronin—addressed a memorandum to Califano designed to sound alarm about the character of the presidential advisory system that had developed:

> Presidents have always called upon outside specialists . . . to render their advice about public policy questions. But never before have so many laymen (nonpoliticians and non civil servants) been employed in this capacity . . . Some skeptics have denigrated these "thought-brigades" as an overly elitist and unrepresentative process through which to secure advice. An increasing number of permanent civil servants tend to question this tendency to look "outside," for it obviously weakens their already diminished ego and adds yet another set of superordinates to whom they must report . . . The public and federal bureaucracy need to know more about the use of experts and outside task forces. There is going to be considerably more demand to allow the public at large to play a role in the planning of the future. Reformers on university campuses and the multiplicity of groups such as consumers, black power and poor people, etc., are going to be increasingly suspicious of White House reliance on blue-ribbon panels and well-established "expert" study groups. Expert advice will increasingly be needed, as will long-range planning. But sophisticated protest groups are going to demand a role in planning this future and will have to be taken into account . . . Careful study should also be given to developing the capacity for exploring alternative futures for communities at all levels of society . . . Preserving or sustaining some semblance of democracy in an age of future planning will be a major test for the next Administration.[61]

The concern that Matthews, Prothro, and Cronin expressed with such civility in 1968 escalated throughout the 1970s and 1980s as neoconservatives were joined by the exponents of new social theory and their counterparts in law and government. An entire elaborate American version of the European philosophers Habermas and Foucault emerged asserting that the experts indeed had supplanted the bourgeoisie as a new ruling class. So Alvin Gouldner indeed described it, implying an almost all-encompassing influence through the application of critical discourse by the new intellectuals. While the neoconservatives railed against the veracity of the expert ideas Kennedy and Johnson had accepted, some social theorists were appalled by the threat they posed to democracy and the assault they leveled at the common man.[62]

As it turned out, there was no cause for alarm from either quarter because the politics of the seventies largely disposed of academic experts. Although often paying homage to the importance of academic advice, public policy from Nixon through Ford to Carter was crafted largely by legal professionals and rhetoricians. And although a cadre of distinguished scholars were actively involved in the Reagan administration, ideologues came to the fore in actual policy matters. How and why the experts were shoved aside and how the promising coalition of politicians, administrators, and experts broke apart are developments worth examining.

4

CRACKS IN THE SYSTEM

The Nixon Transition

No American president—arguably, no major contemporary American political figure—has so confounded the predictions of pundits and expectations of the public as Richard Nixon. A figure of controversy from the outset of his career, Nixon has ridden a roller coaster of victories and defeats according to his own adage that one "is not defeated until one quits." To this day he remains a man of influence and consequence, even after suffering his humiliating and shameful departure from the presidency. His capacity to perplex, confuse, and contradict the prophecies of observers and commentators is never better exemplified than in his relations with American academics.

Henry Kissinger, the most visible and influential social science expert of the generation, found his way to pinnacles of power through Nixon. The two came together from sharply adversarial positions when another academic, Richard V. Allen, acted initially as intermediary. Kissinger, a long-time adviser to Nelson Rockefeller, wrote of "a wary antagonism" between Nixon and academics. "Nixon did not really trust them any more than they accepted him," he has argued; "they could occasionally coexist, never cooperate." According to Kissinger, Nixon believed one of the "attractions" of Kissinger's appointment was that it would "demonstrate his ability to co-opt a Harvard intellectual; that I came from Rockefeller made the prospect all the more interesting."[1] Nixon's appointment of Daniel Patrick Moynihan, the other publicly prominent academic to join the senior White House staff at the beginning, also was unexpected. Moynihan's first meeting was arranged through the insistence of Nixon's New York law partner, Leonard Garment, and made more palatable by Moynihan's emerging neoconservative critique of the liberal intellectual establishment. Except through his writings, Moynihan was unknown to Nixon. So, more surprisingly given his prominence in academic and financial circles, was Arthur Burns, later a top Nixon aide.[2]

James David Barber, a distinguished student of presidential character and psychological disposition, has emphasized the special irony of Nixon's selection of Kissinger and Moynihan. Casting Nixon and Johnson as "active-negative" presidents, Barber concluded that Nixon's chief rivals were " 'Establishment' people . . . from fine and well-known families, and his confession, 'I feel ill at ease with prominence,' " clearly included the eastern Ivy League academic establishment.[3] Mel Elfin put the conundrum even more crisply. "He had the same inferiority as LBJ. *He wanted to outdo the Easterners and show them.*"[4] Accordingly, Kissinger and Moynihan, as well as Burns, Stephen Hess, and George Shultz appeared in the administration. And, though the emphasis on foreign affairs increased, so did social spending in the form of welfare entitlements and revenue sharing. Campus intellectuals might continue to disparage "Tricky Dick"; nonetheless, and ironically, as Elfin has pointed out, "intellectuals were alive and well in his administration with a lot of eggheads as assistant secretaries and holding other policy positions."[5]

More than personal insincerity, an aversion to people of prominence, and a desire to exceed their performance clouded the transition from Johnson to Nixon, however, and made the continued influence of experts unlikely. Kissinger and Moynihan were not only unexpected appointments whose relations with Nixon were untested, but a counterattack mounted by the other two intervening elites now challenged the role of the freewheeling social science experts Johnson had endorsed.

In the higher echelons of the civil service, resentment of the outside experts and their "untested" ideas, and especially the domineering air of intellectual superiority the Califano staff cultivated, had grown year by year. As Vietnam drained the nation's resources and Johnson delayed the consideration of a surtax, the Califano push for new programs became increasingly unreal, both in terms of resources and political support. To cabinet and subcabinet members charged with carrying out Great Society programs already on the books but still in the shakedown phase and grossly underfunded, new initiatives were simply "a waste of time."

Nor was the political elite content with the contributions of the academics. The continued savage attacks upon Johnson and the war from the liberal press, the campus unrest and riots, the public defection of prominent professors from Vietnam policy—all soured White House aides. Though Califano persevered in his academic dinners and McPherson tried valiantly to advance the administration's position with editors and writers, the romance between key administrators and academics strained to the breaking point.[6]

It was in this context that Nixon entered office and found waiting for him the Ben Heineman Report, the last effort of the Johnson administration to rationalize and discipline its policy process and a valiant attempt to devise an effective strategy to implement the now apparently sprawling Great Society. Soon to follow and largely confirm the Heineman diagnosis was the report of the Ash Council, Nixon's own advisory group on organization. Both reports asserted that the sheer volume of task force activity, and the consequent chore of separating wheat from chaff, had placed an impossible burden on a small White House staff. The upshot was a set of policy proposals that were insufficiently developed, lacked reliable budgetary calculations, and most of all, reflected inadequate deliberation and judgment. Trees had overwhelmed the forest, the reports concluded, and the presidential policy process had disassembled in chaos and confusion.[7]

The Campaign Ritual: Cambridge Perseveres

If Washington had become disenchanted with the academic elite, the message had not reached politicians on the campaign trail. Nixon may have been cautious, critical of Kennedy's and Johnson's "Cambridge connections," and distrustful of academics in general, but he accepted their utility to the campaign. As he had been with Moynihan, Garment was the major broker in establishing contacts with and making introductions to scholars.

Garment's principal recruit for the campaign was Martin Anderson, a young Columbia Business School professor with a doctorate from M.I.T. in industrial management and an early association with the joint M.I.T.-Harvard Center of Urban Studies, then directed by James Q. Wilson, a highly regarded and consistently conservative political scientist. Anderson had published the *Federal Bulldozer*, an uncompromising and controversial attack on the urban renewal program which had sparked considerable protest among the program's congressional supporters, mayors, and downtown business groups. Now a chance dinner with a young lawyer in the Nixon firm led to meetings with Garment and then with Nixon. The future president, "impressed," as Anderson recalls, "with the effectiveness of the Kennedy and Johnson task forces," asked the professor to run the research program for the campaign. Anderson agreed, took a sabbatical, and found himself "in the campaign headquarters, but off in a cubbyhole without a telephone—signaling a status of research and ideas fairly typical at that time."[8]

To his credit, Anderson did not stay in the cubbyhole long. On September 8, 1967, in a five-page letter to Garment, he outlined a three-point research strategy for the campaign which advocated a series of seminars on major issues, five in foreign policy and twelve in domestic affairs. By then a member of a small informal group of advisers—Garment, Patrick Buchanan, John Sears, and Raymond Price—which met weekly on policy matters for the yet-to-be-announced campaign, Anderson won approval for a full-scale research operation.[9]

By February 7, 1968, an organization chart had appeared, and two other senior experts had emerged, Richard Allen and Alan Greenspan. By April 1, the research enterprise was ready to act. Sixteen congressional aides had been canvassed for ideas and files, and a nationwide search for academic experts was underway. By May, the research division was formally established and its budget approved by Maurice Stans of the campaign finance committee. From April to August, the research operation spent about $20,000 a month, totaling $89,348 at the end of August. The staff that began in January with one member zoomed up to twenty-two as the campaign moved into high gear. A formal analysis of time allocation for twenty-two separate activities was drawn up, and division administrator Darrell Trent prepared lists of questions to be sent to outside experts. Their answers were then summarized as background reference in position papers.

Using "the first FAX machine in American politics as well as a portable telephone," Anderson became a regular on the campaign jet. Carrying a black book of the names of outside experts and a traveling library, the young academic would have the first editions of the *New York Times* and other papers Faxed to the plane in early morning so that "dawn press releases" could be distributed to the media. By August, the campaign used more than one hundred academic advisers, and Nixon had met at least once with a designated "economic advisory group."[10]

While Anderson was directing a well-organized and well-financed research division from the campaign plane, the irrepressible Richard Neustadt, who had played such a freewheeling and influential role in the transition from Eisenhower to Kennedy, reappeared. In the early fall of 1967, Neustadt suggested forming a small group of academics to think through on a nonpartisan basis the problems of the transition, regardless of who won the election. Operating under the aegis of the Harvard Institute of Politics, which he headed, Neustadt persuaded Franklin A. Lindsay, then president of the high-technology company Itek, to join Henry Kissinger, historian Ernest May, and law professor Phillip Areeda as head of this planning effort. Although not a faculty member, Lindsay had long been part of the Cambridge intellectual community and had extensive governmental experience dating back to World War II. Regarded as a "Rockefeller Republican," he nonetheless had known Nixon since the immediate postwar years when he served on the staff of a congressional committee exploring postwar aid to Europe.[11]

In January 1968, Lindsay met with Nixon in New York as one of a series of visits he made to presidential candidates of both parties. When asked if he was interested in the Harvard study, Nixon reportedly "welcomed" it. On August 15, Lindsay sent Nixon a thirty-page memorandum titled, "Preparing for the Post-Election Transition," which Areeda, as chair, signed with Lindsay and May. (Kissinger had dropped out during that period to work for Rockefeller, but, as Lindsay wrote, "he could rejoin us later.") On October 18, Lindsay wrote again, this time with the informal salutation, "Dear Dick," and transmitted a thirty-one-page memorandum, "Dealing with the Old Administration."[12]

Nixon made a point of acknowledging the work when, on December 2, 1968, he announced the appointment of Kissinger as assistant for national security. "I contacted Mr. Lindsay and found that Dr. Kissinger had done a great deal of work on that study," Nixon was quoted to state in a press release. "I met with the whole group and that triggered my thinking in that direction . . . This is the first time such a study has been made for a President-elect . . . It covers the whole transition period with recommendations as to how the transition could be carried on smoothly, and we have taken many of these recommendations."[13]

Lindsay's reward—or punishment—was to head the fifteen-member transition task force on the organization of the executive branch. Working mostly with "old hands" in both government and the Cambridge academic world, he produced a report by mid-December that Arthur Burns and Anderson, his deputy (now overseeing the entire array of transition task forces), regarded as "the first task force report he has seen that he feels the President-elect should read in its entirety."[14] As Johnson's academics prepared to depart, they could take comfort in the fact that not only had the transition been the smoothest in recent years (except for the executive search process, which Anderson considered "a disaster"), but that, thanks to Anderson and Lindsay, many of their former colleagues were arriving to take up their posts. Cambridge was surviving.

Institutionalizing the Experts

However reassuring the campaign and transition research activities may have been to academic social scientists, the truth was that the bloom was off the expert rose from the perspective of those inside the Beltway. Transition task forces could and did arrive in great number, but at best, and only in the first years of the Nixon administration, they simply coexisted with the three other policy-making channels operative since Truman's time—individual department initiatives, budget bureau reviews, and White House staffs. Outside advisers were tolerated for a while, and, indeed, they were front and center in two distinct waves. Increasingly, though,

Nixon's actions tended to substantially follow the Heineman and Ash report recommendations, which in effect heightened the influence of the two other intervening elites.

The Heineman report had argued that "resourceful administrators" in a professional Executive Office of the President should initiate and fashion policy and fix priorities. If adopted, this report would have reinvigorated the elite that the executive office had nurtured since World War II but that had been relegated to a subordinate role during the Califano years. Heineman maintained that this new executive office should "monitor the administration of Great Society programs, provide a focal point for consultation with governors and mayors and 'settle' interdepartmental issues."[15] The Ash Council took a different tack—or at least its final recommendations as modified by White House staffers John Ehrlichman and H. R. Haldeman did. The council veered away from strengthening the professional presidential staffs. Instead, it recommended the creation of a domestic council in the White House to define national domestic goals, identify policy alternatives, ensure program consistency, and function as the president's chief source of domestic policy advice. As its authors saw it, the council's role and prestige would be comparable to that of the National Security Council in foreign affairs.[16]

Fresh from the campaign, John Ehrlichman, White House assistant and second only to his fellow campaign strategist Robert Haldeman in power and influence, welcomed the Ash report. It seemed to him to promise a domestic policy power base comparable to that which Kissinger had begun to build on the international front. Ehrlichman made sure that the council would be within the White House and not subject to congressional review. He oversaw the drafting of a reorganization plan that gave the director of the Office of Management and Budget (the new title of the Bureau of the Budget) White House status as well. The power of presidential political appointees waxed accordingly, at least those within the White House. For, despite Nixon's rhetoric, the cabinet steadily lost influence, and the authority of the administrative elite waned.[17]

Presidents since Truman had found the older option—consistent reliance on the advice and recommendations of major executive departments and agencies channeled through the Executive Office of the President—too limited, and it clearly ran against the grain of Nixon's ideology and personality. Initially the president persisted in viewing his cabinet as an extension of the presidency, immune from competing pressures of the special interest and clientele groups attached to each department. Although he came late—and, in Martin Anderson's view, clumsily—to the presidential appointment process, Nixon tried to ensure that politically loyal appointees were placed strategically in the upper levels of executive

departments. He sought to have cabinet officers play essentially ministerial roles. Ehrlichman characterized the relationship between Nixon
and his secretaries: "When he says, 'Jump,' they only ask, 'how high?'"[18]

Nixon sought more than simple subservience from his secretaries and
agency heads. Long persuaded that the federal professional service was
an "ossified" and "obstructive" bureaucracy and convinced that Eisenhower had not gained effective control over a "Democrat-infested" executive branch, Nixon believed that departmental and agency proposals were
inevitably parochial and self-serving. Accordingly, he placed no reliance
on ideas that might percolate from the ranks. If the cream of the career
service in the executive office was not a dependable policy source, the
lower echelons were even less worthy. Nixon increasingly sought reliable
counsel and advice within the White House.

The president also wrote off the fourth option—continuing and fine
tuning the academically based policy task force structure Johnson had
initiated. Admittedly, as Redford and McCulley show, the Califano operation had been an open-ended affair, strong on initiative and momentum
and weak on deliberation and contemplation, playing catch-up ball to
turn academic ideas into law. But the open process of search and retrieval
might have been rationalized and improved without a major overhaul of
the White House machinery.[19]

Despite his public pronouncements, Nixon was really not disposed to
tolerate what Stephen Hess has characterized as the "hub" model of presidential organization, where several White House aides had equal access to
the chief executive. Instead, in Harold Seidman's term, he chose "a corporate type of structure with a rigid hierarchy. . . . a three-tiered structure
with assistants to the president at the top and department and agency
heads (other than those designated as counselors) at the bottom."[20] A
politicized version of the original Ash Council proposals emerged. It was
neither pure in organizational concept nor apparently hospitable to the
contributions that academic social scientists had become accustomed to
offering up. The political elite, overwhelmingly drawn from the campaign
trail, were manifestly front and center. They grew in number as they
assumed political positions "excepted" from professional civil service in
the Executive Office of the President, and they were destined to remain
there until the Watergate avalanche crashed and buried them.

Rockefeller to the Rescue

The "repoliticization" of the presidential policy process, as represented by
the emergent domestic council and the changing profiles of White House
and OMB staffs, did not occur overnight. Nor did the academic experts

disappear, either by outright exclusion from high-ranking executive-branch positions or by the elimination of outside task forces. As Elfin observed, President Nixon placed a number of Ph.D.s in high places, and he began his administration by establishing a seed catalog of, ultimately, twenty-one task forces covering almost every conceivable public policy topic. An added and special irony was that many of the appointees and task force members were, like Kissinger, protégés of Nelson Rockefeller, the chief spokesman for the liberal wing of the Republican Party and Nixon's perennial rival for the party's presidential nomination.[21]

The resort to "Rockefeller people," as well as to some Kennedy and Johnson experts, was perhaps politically curious, but it was nonetheless inescapable. The same impulse that moved Kennedy to establish the Cambridge academic advisory group now inspired Nixon, at least in the early stages. Visibly co-opting some academics for governing and appearing to engage others on the task forces made for prudent politics.[22]

Once Nixon accepted that proposition, at least for the transition period, his options were two: rely on the Democratic cadre who had already served Kennedy and Johnson, or turn to Rockefeller lists assembled over the years in the task forces he had established as governor of New York and as administrator of the Rockefeller Brothers Fund, which had periodically initiated national commissions. For the most part, he chose the latter path.

For a generation, no other Republican leader had so consciously and successfully developed a strategy for involving experts and academics in the early stages of policy-making as had Rockefeller. Most Republican politicians by instinct and disposition went the other way. Since the New Deal, most had opposed an active, involved role for government and disparaged new ideas. As the years went on, the chasm between campus and party leadership became wide and deep. Meade Alcorn had tried hard to engage the academics in the 1960 election, and the 1964 Goldwater campaign had produced a full-page advertisement, signed by more than two hundred "teachers and scholars," proclaiming that "men of ideas" supported Barry. Still, the links were not strong. Only a few academics continued to embrace laissez-faire liberalism to the degree the Old Guard espoused, and their counsel was therefore useful principally at campaign time.[23]

Rockefeller was the exception to the Republican rule and not simply because he was the national leader of the party's liberal wing. His style and strategy as a public person had always been characterized by a heavy reliance on expert advice. In a 1972 interview he commented, "Ideas come to me from all over, and it is difficult to know why one has intuitive feelings about the essence of a problem. Once I determine that there is a problem, I usually try to get a group together to study it."[24]

"Getting groups together" understates what became standard operating procedure for Rockefeller. As New York's governor from 1959 to 1970, he established eighty-one task forces, temporary commissions, and governor's conferences; thirty-one were composed of government outsiders. Moreover, Rockefeller commissioned eighty research papers for the 1958 gubernatorial campaign, and William Ronan, the former New York University dean and secretary to the governor in his first term, established forty task forces to generate new ideas and policy initiatives. Testifying on the occasion of his senate confirmation as vice president in 1973, Rockefeller acknowledged that he had, on average, thirty professors under contract and had, when necessary, advanced personal loans to them to assure their continued ability to advise him.[25]

It was on the national scene, however, that Rockefeller cast his widest net for academic social scientists of "mainstream persuasion." Twice, but a generation apart, he initiated prestigious, well-financed, quasi-research policy enterprises as part of his deliberations about seeking the Republican nomination for president.

Prospect for America was a "Special Studies Project" started in 1956, underwritten by the Rockefeller Brothers Fund, directed by Kissinger and Nancy Hanks (later director of the National Endowment for the Arts), and initially chaired by Nelson Rockefeller. The project consisted of an overall panel of thirty, six subpanels of 108 individuals, and papers commissioned from "some hundred thoughtful individuals." Rockefeller and Kissinger resigned in 1958 when Rockefeller decided to run for governor, but panel reports appeared from 1958 through 1960.[26]

Critical Choices for Americans, initiated by Rockefeller in 1973 after he left state government and before he became vice president, showed a parallel structure. The "Commission on Critical Choices for Americans" consisted of forty-two "prominent Americans" and superseded a state group studying "The Role of a Modern State in a Changing World." Again, there were six panels and "more than 100 authorities to prepare expert studies in their field of competence." Again, Rockefeller chaired the enterprise initially. As secretary of state, Kissinger was an ex-officio member of the commission.[27]

What is striking about the two undertakings is the melding of academic experts and "establishment" figures in business and government. The special blend of academics, private-sector chief executives, and partners of large law firms in the 1956 Prospect for America group prompted Eisenhower to organize his own Goals for America commission two years later. The Rockefeller initiatives also encouraged Carter in 1979 to initiate his Agenda for the Eighties. So twice, just before critical elections, Rockefeller took a powerful initiative in establishing the public agenda. Moreover, he provided the opportunity for academics to formulate, express, and *dis-*

seminate their ideas in a format that almost guaranteed media attention. In short, although he held no national office at either time, just before and after the New Frontier–Great Society years, he provided an effective, visible means by which expert ideas could receive serious attention.

Several attributes marked those scholars in the "stable of experts" Rockefeller tapped throughout his entire political career. For openers, despite the interval of eighteen years between the two commissions, a number of experts—such as Kissinger, Hanks, Edward Teller, Carroll Wilson, and Walt Rostow—served on both. Second, members were almost exclusively from the prestigious universities on the two coasts and in Chicago (Robert Dahl, Lincoln Gordon, Bayless Manning, Thomas Schelling, Lucian Pye, Wallace Sayre, and Max Milliken). Third, some scholars participating in the 1956 study would go on to serve in high Washington positions in the 1960s and 1970s (Charles Frankel, Arthur Burns, Eugene Rostow, and Harland Cleveland). Such 1973 commission members as Anderson, Daniel Boorstin, Ernest Boyer, Moynihan, George Shultz, and Elspeth Rostow had already served in national administrations or would serve again. In between both commissions, members kept enduring, prestigious, and lasting personal acquaintanceships. A substantial number would be tapped later for the Trilateral Commission that David Rockefeller formed in 1975 and for Carter's commission on the eighties. More than any single national political figure in government or out, Nelson Rockefeller identified, brought together, and maintained a hard core of academic elite.[28]

For Nixon's purposes in his first term, the support of the pool of academics Rockefeller had assembled before the 1960 campaign was critical if he was to achieve some semblance of national leadership. His victory over Hubert Humphrey had been too narrow and the war too publicly divisive to permit him to appear isolated from men and women of substance and ideas. His task, as Moynihan defined it for him, was nothing less than "to restore the authority of American institutions." Indeed, Kissinger and Moynihan were only the first of a number of experts to be drawn from the governor's "pool."

Richard Nathan, who had served Rockefeller as a sometime domestic counterpart to Kissinger and, with Bryce Harlow, had written much of the Republican platform on domestic issues in 1968, served both in the Nixon transition and later as a deputy director of OMB and deputy undersecretary in HEW, focusing on issues of revenue sharing and poverty. His experience typified what happened to many. Returning depressed by the Republican convention, and retreating to Martha's Vineyard, he received a call from Rockefeller headquarters. "Pack your bags," he was told; "you've been traded to Nixon."[29]

Others soon made the shift, with Arthur Burns leading the way. The proven Rockefeller experts knew personally most of the experts from the Kennedy-Johnson era and often asked them to stay on.[30] They also came to form a reasonably formidable cadre in the White House executive office, cabinet, and subcabinet. Highly qualified and prominent experts such as James Sundquist in Agriculture and Alice Rivlin in HEW helped out on transition teams or stayed as assistant secretaries.

The mobilization of academic talent previously identified with Rockefeller or with the Kennedy and Johnson administrations came in two waves. In 1968, transition task forces headed by Paul McCracken (designated the next chairman of the Council of Economic Advisors) and staffed by Harry Loomis were established. They reported in short order. Arthur Burns, a nationally known conservative economist who had been a member of the 1953 "overall panel" for Rockefeller and who aspired to the chairmanship of the Federal Reserve Board, with his new deputy, Martin Anderson, provided systematic oversight and followup for the McCracken operation. Indeed, the two picked the topics and membership for the task forces.

In June 1969, Nixon authorized a second series, again monitored by Burns. His executive director was Charles Clapp, a Tufts graduate who had served as legislative aide to Leverett Saltonstall of Massachusetts from 1962 to 1967.[31]

Initially, the first set of task forces was committed to undoing much of the Great Society, in particular the war on poverty and Model Cities. Initially, too, they appeared as a counterweight to the institutional hostility toward academia that the Heineman and Ash reports expressed and to Haldeman's and Ehrlichman's drive to concentrate power in the White House. They played both to that side of Nixon's personality that sought to co-opt the prestigious and to the political reality that the new administration must find and articulate a new consensus. The question remained whether the carryover in style and talent from Rockefeller and from the Kennedy-Johnson era would establish a permanently influential role for academic experts or was chiefly political window dressing, with real domestic policy being made elsewhere.[32]

Big Names and Little Deeds

With Burns at the helm, the Nixon transition team assembled an impressive array of part-time task force participants, although their aggregate characteristics differed sharply from the profiles of Kennedy and Johnson committee members. Overall, there were fewer academics and more business members in the task forces, and a considerable number of the academics were "repeaters."

Burns and Anderson initially planned twenty-three task forces, but the three on youth, agriculture, and international economic policy were never established. Of the remaining twenty, ranging from fiscal policy through housing and urban renewal to public welfare, twelve were chaired by male academics. Veterans of Rockefeller, Kennedy, and Johnson assignments were liberally sprinkled throughout: Raymond Vernon, James Sundquist, Douglas Brown, Alan Pifer, John Dunlop, Anthony Downs, Paul Ylvisaker, Steven Bailey, Frank Keppel, Richard Goodwin, Bernard Frieden, Nathan Glazer, Martin Meyerson, James Wilson, and William Cohen. "It seemed," said Frank Keppel, former commissioner of education under Johnson and returning once again to an education task force, "like old home week, or a college reunion. We had survived the transition from Democratic to Republican administrations. We felt immortal."[33]

The Burns enterprise ended on a festive note. A dinner at the Pierre Hotel in New York, on January 11, 1969, was followed by a two-day meeting in which each task force had two hours with the appropriate cabinet member. At the dinner, the president-elect and the chairs of the task forces sat at the head table. Cabinet members and White House representatives were assigned to each of the other tables. "The psychic income," observed a participant, "was considerable." (Although he maintained his Democratic "integrity," he reported, by declining to shake the president-elect's hand.)

Although Nixon's first one hundred days marked no breakthrough in legislation, indeed, were deliberately low-keyed, bipartisan, noncontroversial, the work of the transition teams seemed to satisfy him. On balance, he had rejected the advice of some of the more radical of task force advisers, such as Edward Banfield of Harvard, who wanted to dismantle the major urban programs for they ran "counter to his overarching goal of restoring the authority of American institutions." He also became increasingly attracted to Moynihan's wry suggestion that he could indeed emerge as an American Disraeli. Nonetheless, as he proceeded cautiously to frame his "new American Revolution," he sought a counterweight to "Moynihan's liberalism." On June 2, 1969, in a memorandum to the cabinet, the president observed that task forces "during the transition period produced many sound, useful ideas. I plan a new series of Task Forces to provide this Administration with ideas and recommendations for the 1970 legislative year." Accordingly, he directed that Burns, as counselor to the president and "also head of the Office of Program Development," oversee some seventeen task forces on "domestic matters," which, by the time they were in full swing, included 225 members.[34]

By now, a decade of experience lay behind marshalling and guiding these ad hoc groups; task forcing seemed on the verge of becoming a permanent visitation. As Burns's administrative officer, Charles Clapp sought to capitalize on that past experience from both the transition period and the Califano years. Procedurally, he set up a formal clearance process, including both a political and FBI check.[35] Substantively, after a conversation with his predecessor Loomis, Clapp announced that diversity was to be his principal objective in nominating members. Confidentiality was also important because otherwise "people will want to know why they are not members." Later on, this rule was abandoned because the White House came to feel leaks were inevitable. "No government officials should be members," Clapp advised, and added, "Don't let politicians name people."

As the guidelines evolved under the policy oversight of Burns and Anderson, chairs were to run their own shows; options, not recommendations, were to be sought; "Democratic members cannot be too partisan, but in welfare and some other areas you will have to include Democrats because most of the experts are of that persuasion." As a counterweight, the task force project also sought an opportunity to give "increased visibility to some Republican college presidents of talent." Following up the conversation, Clapp prepared an explicit set of rules setting a December 1, 1969, deadline for their work, focusing on the 1970 legislative program and, in a sharp break with the Johnson tradition, publicly announcing the task forces and their membership and arranging for the publication of their reports.[36]

The emphasis on nonpartisanship continued throughout the transition. In a memorandum to senior civil servant Dwight Ink, who had served in high-level positions throughout the 1960s, Clapp listed fifteen members who had "clear Democratic affiliation, including five academics who either served on Scientists for Humphrey in the 1968 campaign or had been members of the Kennedy or Johnson Administrations." Although not all task forces met the December deadline, by March 14 all had filed their final reports. At Burns's direction, Clapp forwarded the names of the chairmen to the White House social secretary with a suggestion. "You may wish to include some of them from time to time in events at the White House," he stated. "It will mean a great deal to these people and there will be further payoff for the Administration." Two hundred and eight were invited for the dinner with the president.[37]

Whether the task forces offered a commensurate policy payoff to the administration is an open question. The task forces were Burns's creation, and Burns and Anderson had picked their membership from White House staff, cabinet, and subcabinet posts, congressional staffs, and Republican National Committee nominations. The reception of their reports was muffled in an escalating fight between Burns and Moynihan over welfare reform, begun in the spring of 1969 and continuing until its institutional resolution in Ehrlichman's Domestic Policy Council. Clapp finally secured the last reports, and the Government Printing Office published them all. A new domestic program, topic by topic, was spread out for all to see and, at the suggestion of Martin Anderson, so were its authors.[38]

Anderson scored a "solo" expert triumph when he initiated in the spring of 1967 a seventeen-page memorandum on the issue of the all-volunteer armed force to replace the draft and showed it to Nixon, who, in an offhand comment to Robert Semple of the *New York Times* in November, announced his support of the proposal. On his election, Nixon established the time-honored study commission, with a staff of forty-four and a $1 million budget. Within the year the commission produced a unanimous recommendation to abolish the draft. On July 1, 1973, draft induction authority officially ended. It had taken six years, but Anderson's original proposal, sparked by a 1967 article by Milton Friedman, had become law.

Disciplining the Policy Process

The problem with the new domestic program that the two waves of task forces had produced and that Burns and Anderson had agonizingly brought to fruition was that, with the exception of Anderson's all-volunteer armed force, policy was really being made elsewhere.

Since the inauguration, the two principal academics on domestic assignment in the White House—Burns and Moynihan—had become increasingly engaged in a bitter debate over welfare reform. Substantively, the issue was whether to establish a national guaranteed income, as Moynihan argued, or emphasize job training and work requirements, assuming that the economy could function at close to full employment.[39] As both a participant and observer in the process—"I was near the White House, then, in a 'catbird seat' "—Nathan described the conflict. The task forces run by Paul McCracken were essentially nonpartisan and useful in idea-gathering, especially for the two groups Nathan chaired on poverty and revenue sharing. Later, however, he would conclude that the process of translating vague and nonspecific campaign talk (which focused mostly on the dangers of the federal bureaucracy and advocated instead a "New Federalism," highlighting revenue sharing and income-transfer programs) into policy "dragged out longer than the president wanted. This was especially true of welfare reform which at every turn became more difficult and complex than had been originally anticipated."[40]

According to Carl Brauer, Nixon "deliberately set out to create an internal debate on domestic policy" between Moynihan and Burns, but "it is unlikely that [he] anticipated the polarity of the debate."[41] It raged throughout the spring and summer of 1969 until the president arbitrarily set an August 8 deadline for his major domestic policy speech. This was substantially after the McCracken task force ideas had been worked over at White House, OMB, and department levels, but before the Burns groups had really begun.

In the end, Nixon became, in Brauer's words, "uncomfortable with acrimony," and "he did not like mediating between Moynihan and Burns." John Kessel put the matter more simply. The controversy revealed Nixon's "inability to cope psychologically with conflicting advice, and oral conflict was particularly threatening to him."[42] By the summer, under presidential directive, Ehrlichman came to referee the debate between the economist and the sociologist.

By the time the speech deadline arrived, a version of the guaranteed income plan favored by Moynihan had survived, along with provisions for revenue sharing and a restructured grants-in-aid program. The compromise involved both the intervention of George Shultz, then secretary of labor, and the mediation of Ehrlichman. In the end, both Moynihan and Burns would fade away as influential figures in the administration: Burns to chair the Federal Reserve Board, and Moynihan to return to Cambridge. The Urban Affairs Council disappeared, and, in November 1969, Ehrlichman emerged with a new title, Assistant to the President for Domestic Affairs, and chaired a new Domestic Policy Council. Nixon "considered Ehrlichman to be the ideal choice to bring to domestic policy the same intellectually wide-ranging but organizationally disciplined approach that Kissinger had brought so successfully to foreign policy."[43]

Put together in the summer of 1969, the politicized Domestic Policy Council had a staff of six assistants, now professionally legitimized by a revised Ash Council report. Kessel observed, "A Domestic Council pattern emerged in which one of Ehrlichman's staff members served as executive secretary to an in-house task force with occasional outside experts brought in. The agenda was stimulated by presidential comments on his daily newspaper clip rather than academic works on current problems and culminated in the 1971 six great goals of the inaugural address."[44]

According to Kessel, the discipline the council format imposed on the process was impressive. Usually, the president identified a problem or issue and provided some general guidance. Then a task force, chaired by a council staff member and consisting of department and executive office representatives, explored the matter with experts within or outside the government. The group settled on a preliminary decision or approach, followed up with an option paper, and, after discussion with Nixon, issued a final program and public statement. Lawyers from the justice department were almost always present. So were senior staff from OMB, and "people floated in and out" as the work went on.

The quality of these working groups seems to have varied enormously. Some chairs complained that the cabinet officers provided "a lot of turkeys . . . they obviously wouldn't give you their indispensable bright guys because they need them." Others called it "a process of trying to get the best minds we could . . . a couple of professors from major law schools."[45] One thing is certain: insiders, permanent civil servants, and political appointees, predominantly lawyers by profession, dominated the process. Academic experts did not. They had done their duty on the task forces; thereafter, they largely disappeared.

Increasingly, as the Nixon administration settled in, the council's "option paper," a notebook two to three inches thick with a summary page, back-up sections, and, most important, an "order blank" (what the president directs to be done) became the chief means by which the president arrived at a decision. Occasionally, a council staff member would spot an issue on his or her own and respond with a proposal. On even rarer occasions, a department might send a proposal directly to Nixon.[46]

Throughout the first term, the working group device remained the major instrument of domestic policy-making. It relied principally on inside departmental specialists assigned to the working group whom council staff expected to persuade their departments to accept the group's policy proposals. The technique yielded a written document as a departure point for subsequent discussions with the president, an alternative with which Nixon was vastly more comfortable than a face-to-face meeting with a policy advocate. His reaction could be noted on the margins of the option papers. Council staff became increasingly committed to "clarifying options" or providing alternatives in place of single-focused recommendations and strong advocacy. Not coincidentally, policy control remained securely in the White House.[47]

The declining use of academics and their administration supporters (Martin Anderson departed in 1971), the downgrading of the cabinet as a source of policy initiative, and the concentration of power in the White House were trends thoroughly consistent with the president's temperament and philosophy. He had campaigned against big government; his hostility toward bureaucracy, as Nathan documented, was vitriolic; his ambivalence toward intellectuals, despite the Kissinger and Moynihan appointments, remained strong. In short, an expanding domestic role for the federal government, which Johnson had advanced through his outside task forces, did not square with Nixon's philosophy. Nor could his style and manner produce a Kennedy Camelot, where academics vied for attention and involvement.

Increasingly, Nixon's attention instead fell on reorganizing the executive branch, creating "super" departments, and controlling the bureaucracy by political appointments that reached far down into the middle ranks of departments and agencies.[48] After the failure of the Family Assistance Plan and the triumph of revenue sharing, he proposed very little legislatively except structural reform related to his concept of a "New Federalism." But neither did he drastically cut back on Great Society programs. The Great Society program budgets Nixon inherited increased rapidly throughout his time in office, expanding from 34 to 51 percent of the total budget. By 1975, these appropriations exceeded by a two-to-one margin the proportion of the budget spent on defense.[49]

What did preoccupy Nixon was the mastery of the federal bureaucracy and the transfer of its programs and decision-making authority to the states. The domestic policies, ideas, and program initiatives that had so engaged his predecessors and his chief competitor, Rockefeller, did not engross him. When not focused on foreign affairs, Nixon's attention, energy, and determination in his second term were directed almost entirely to subduing the recalcitrant professional civil service. Although the budget continued to expand, the problems of cities were pronounced to have been largely solved—"the hour of crisis has passed." As Watergate came to preoccupy the White House and the nation, the domestic council's work dwindled into insignificance. In the end, neither experts or laymen, insiders or outsiders were making presidential policy for the home front.

The Ford Interregnum

To call the 895 days during which Gerald Ford was president an interregnum is not to suggest the times were uneventful. While Ford was on the White House watch, a president who had resigned to avoid impeachment was pardoned. Saigon fell, and U.S. civilians were evacuated from the embassy by helicopter. America's longest war finally ended, and 140,000 Vietnam refugees were flown to the United States. A "blue ribbon" panel headed by Vice President Rockefeller identified and reported a wide range of illegal CIA activities. Oil prices spiraled, inflation followed, and a major recession got underway. The nation celebrated its bicentennial, and the president flew to the rude bridge in Concord, Massachusetts, to mark the occasion.

This brief but event-filled period in national life was also a unique one for the new president and the country at large. Ford was the first president who had never been elected to a national office; his vice president, Nelson Rockefeller, was similarly unconfirmed by the voters. His first political task was not to continue the policies of fallen but respected predecessors, as Truman and Johnson did, but to distance himself from Nixon as quickly and as far as possible. Finally, he entered office when the prestige and support of the presidency was at its lowest ebb since systematic polling began—23 percent of the public approved of Nixon in the month of his resignation, 13 percent had confidence in the White House, and, overall, only 25 percent of Americans had confidence in the leadership of any major national institution.[50]

The task of "healing," restoring trust in the office and regaining at least the grudging compliance of the disaffected permanent bureaucracy to presidential direction, was as massive a burden as any president had assumed, at least since World War II. Yet Americans regarded the capabilities of the man thrust into the office as sharply limited, even more so than Truman's were perceived to be in 1945. With an undistinguished and largely unknown staff made up predominantly of congressional assistants and former colleagues, the leaders of the new administration scarcely qualified as a political elite of any sort. The administrative elite was clearly estranged. Although John Dunlop and George Shultz remained in the cabinet, the only truly visible expert or one-time academic who remained was Kissinger, partly because Ford, our allies, the Washington community, the media, and Kissinger himself had come to regard the man as irreplaceable.

The arrival on the scene of Nelson Rockefeller, newly retired as governor and thought to be contemplating a third try at the Republican presidential nomination, as vice president seemed to many observers an instance of inspired political casting. It was out of character for Ford and thus unexpected. Every national observer except members of the Republican right wing welcomed the choice. Ford's invitation included the explicit request that Rockefeller assume a principal role in domestic policy. He gave Rockefeller the domestic equivalent of Kissinger's portfolio in foreign affairs. "I want you on the domestic," Ford said, "and Henry on the foreign, and then we can move on these things." For the first time in American history, the vice presidency appeared likely to be an important and influential office.[51]

That transformation of the office did not, of course, occur. Three factors doomed Rockefeller's efforts to assume the command Ehrlichman had enjoyed of the Domestic Policy Council. First, the four-month delay in his confirmation as both House and Senate probed and picked over his record, especially his practice of rewarding outside experts with gifts and loans, hurt badly. While Rockefeller sparred with congressional committees, Ford's "team" of Donald Rumsfeld, Robert Hartmann, and Patrick Buchanan settled into place. One day *before* Rockefeller was finally sworn in, the White House announced a reorganization that designated these as "cabinet-rank advisees," made Rumsfeld "coordinator," and put the domestic council on a par with eight other offices. Rockefeller had no opportunity to participate in this restructuring. On the contrary, he had been deliberately excluded from the process.[52]

Second, when Rockefeller attempted to structure his role along the lines Ford originally described, he crossed swords with Rumsfeld, who was intent on transforming his coordinator role into chief of staff, as Adams had under Eisenhower and Haldeman under Nixon. Although the vice president appeared formally to prevail on the issue of his domestic council leadership and on staffing its principal positions, the senior White House staff was determined to prevent the rise of another Kissinger. They did not want a domestic "first among equals." Finally, Nixon holdovers were plentiful and departed only with the greatest reluctance, compounding the atmosphere of distrust and deceit. Hartmann, a White House staffer brought in by Ford, characterized the imperfect nature of the transition. On January 20, 1977, twenty-nine months after Nixon's resignation, he noted that there were always more "Nixon faces than new Ford ones around the table of Cabinet and senior staff."[53]

Systematically, in deputy appointments and the control of information, the president's men conspired to place Rockefeller "out of the loop." As he struggled to take the initiative in the council on energy policy, the appropriate science advisory machinery, and the review of CIA covert operations, they uniformly opposed his recommendations to the president. Consistently, they took care to advance alternative options strongly and missed few opportunities to raise the question of Rockefeller's loyalty to the president and commitment to the administration. In his aptly titled *Palace Politics*, Hartmann wrote, "The newly revitalized Domestic Council under Rockefeller never really got off the ground. It was sabotaged and strangled by his own praetorian guard . . . Behind the President's back they set out to prove to him that he had made the wrong decision, relied on the wrong adviser, and that it just wouldn't work."[54]

More than the personal hostility and bitterness that typically develops between vice presidents and presidential staff assistants confused the diffuse domestic policy-making in the White House. The single institutional focus that Ehrlichman had finally achieved began to weaken with his forced departure and then disassembled. Two new White House entities emerged in the early days of the Ford transition: the Economic Policy Board and the Energy Resources Council. Although staffed at the White House, these new bodies were composed principally of cabinet members and their designees. Partly they represented an effort to compensate for the alienation that the cabinet and its staffs came to feel in Nixon's second term. Partly they were improvisations responding to the two top issues of the administration: a deteriorating economy and the energy crisis brought on by the formation of OPEC. Whatever the inspiration, the existence of the new groups sharply reduced the scope of the domestic council's activities and eliminated any possibility that it would equal the NSC in prestige and capacity.[55]

As a result, handling issues that were already interdepartmental in character and that required orchestration throughout the executive branch became even more complicated. Now another dimension of coordination—this time within the White House itself—was required. Washington wisdom came to hold that "President Ford is served by the weakest staff in recent White House history . . . its quality falls substantially short of what he needs."[56]

In 1980, Roger Porter, who served as a White House fellow in 1974 during the Ford administration, mounted a reasoned defense of the division of labor that the three domestic offices represented. Specifically evaluating the Economic Policy Board, he noted its capacity to forge interdepartmental and interagency agreements on both macroeconomic and microeconomic issues and its success in providing timely options for tax policy, trade agreements, and the like. Adopting Hugh Heclo's formulation of the character of national policy issues—their increased scope, their growing complexity, and their interdependence—Porter identified three alternatives in organizing the White House. They were "ad hocracy," "centralized management," and "multiple advocacy." Porter opted for the last on the grounds that it gave the president genuine choices, assuming an honest broker at the staff level presented them. And he concluded that at least the EPB was usually successful in doing so.[57]

Whatever its merits, however, the Porter strategy ran directly counter to Rockefeller's philosophy of centralized operational management and in sharp contrast to a more informal style compatible with seeking or securing outside counsel. When the Office of Management and Budget, the Council of Economic Advisors, and the other fringe agencies in the Executive Office of the President were added to the three White House offices, multiple advocacy came almost to sound like a babble. Certainly their creation assumed the president's capacity to choose among multiple alternatives, a capacity Ford never quite seemed to possess.

Delayed in arriving on the scene, covertly opposed at every step in his efforts to lead domestic policy, trying to operate in a structure institutionally committed to in-house multiple advocacy, Rockefeller gave up. After a series of disagreements on staffs and programs, a clash with Rumsfeld that became a highly charged personal vendetta, and a steady drumbeat of backdoor commentary that he would be a handicap to the 1976 presidential campaign, Rockefeller withdrew from the battle in November 1975.[58]

For the expert elite, a special irony lay in the defeat of the vice president at the hands of the palace guard. More than any other national political figure, Rockefeller had established an academic network of the highest quality, used it consistently to form policy at the state and national levels, generously supported academics and experts, induced them into government, and, most important of all, skillfully and successfully harnessed their ideas and talents to public purposes. Now, finally at a position and time when he could function as a supreme broker of research and transmitter of ideas to the nation's chief policymaker, Rockefeller was unable to sustain his influence. Except for his work in reestablishing the Office of Science and Technology Policy, he was not permitted to assemble task forces and working groups drawn from universities or other outside institutions.[59] While his most notable protégé, Kissinger, continued to shape foreign policy—though with diminishing influence—Rockefeller appeared as Gulliver ensnared.

Under these circumstances—a national political figure reduced to impotence and a White House staff never thoroughly rid of the Nixon shadow, disorganized and ineffective to the end—it is not surprising that Ford failed both in policies and in ideas. On August 10, 1976, two months before the election, the RNC document "The Ford Presidency: A Portrait of the First Two Years" listed the "major Ford accomplishments." John Osborne characterized it as "pathetic." "Of the 10 claims of positive accomplishments," he wrote, "only 3—that Mr. Ford had arrested the downward trend in defense appropriations, strengthened diplomatic and economic relationships between the U.S. and industrialized partners in Europe and Japan, and begun the restoration of national confidence—could be factually attributed to anything that he and his people had done."[60]

The president's relations with Congress were reduced to a series of vetoes, more than twice as many as Johnson had issued and triple the number of Kennedy's in roughly the same amount of time. Moreover, Congress overrode twelve, which equaled the overrides of the Truman administration. Only Andrew Johnson, in the aftermath of the Civil War, accumulated more. Ford's messages to Congress appeared to commentators as "sad and disjointed mishmash—a sandwich of substance, some of it sharp and some of it muggy, placed between institutional goo."[61] He left some changes in foreign policy that his successor could follow, but, in the end, there was little to remember of what Ford said and what Ford did.

Experts in Limbo

Limited as they were, the ideas behind Ford's domestic policy emerged from a diverse and ineffective set of sources. They were, understandably, chiefly "maintenance" in character—reducing inflation and curbing a recession. Indeed, perhaps his most significant decision—to cap the 1977 federal budget at $395 billion (thereby destroying any prospect of a genuine domestic budget)—evaded any regular process at all. The decision was constructed by a junta of James Lynn, then head of OMB, Alan Greenspan of the CEA, Rumsfeld, and Richard Cheney; cabinet members, White House councils, and both inside and outside specialists were not consulted. Its results, politically, programmatically, and economically, were extremely hurtful to the nation's economy and its public programs. It was a classic example of the danger of limited group thinking paralleled only by Johnson's Tuesday group, which determined strategy for Vietnam. One of the four streams of policy initiation and validation that existed when Nixon was first elected, the ad hoc task force, had now disappeared. The remaining three—departmental, executive office, and White House—frequently overflowed their boundaries.[62]

The confusion of the Ford White House did not indicate that experts had been banished from the premises. Genuine academics—in addition to Kissinger, James Schlesinger, John Dunlop, Earl Butz, F. David Matthews, Edward Levi, and Roger Porter—were liberally sprinkled throughout the top echelons of White House and cabinet appointments. Further, during his tenure, the president established sixteen temporary commissions, committees, and boards. Most of them were technical and in-house, but at least four touched on major policy issues—refugees, productivity and the quality of working life, transportation, and employment compensation. In these, academic experts were adequately represented (Martin Anderson chaired the task force on welfare reform), though they came from quite different campuses than their predecessors had. Both in his formal and informal academic encounters, Ford tapped a different pool of experts, with quite different perceptions of the social sciences and their policy potential. Organized by White House assistant Robert Goldwin from the University of Chicago, Ford's academic experts represented a sharp break from the Kennedy-Johnson circle in character and outlook.[63]

Nathan Glazer, longtime coeditor of *The Public Interest*, exemplified the new breed. A constant and perceptive commentator on the American scene, he began as a writer and "transformed himself into a scholar." Glazer started out his expert adviser career as a Democrat. He worked for Robert Weaver, the housing and home finance administrator in the Kennedy administration, served on the 1964 Johnson task force on urban affairs, wrote major books with sociologists David Riesman and Moynihan, participated in the early stages of planning the juvenile delinquency program, and consulted at the Rand Corporation with Harry Rowan and Daniel Elsberg on a HUD research study. By his own admission initially liberal with a capital "L," he, like Moynihan, became a "rogue" Democrat.

Glazer's occasional participation in the seminar on the Great Society at Harvard in 1968 (sponsored by the Ford Foundation and directed by Moynihan and Christopher Jencks) speeded his conversion to the emerging neoconservative cult. He completed his conversion by joining the Nixon task force on urban affairs, which Edward Banfield of Harvard chaired.[64]

Goldwin, now regularly assigned to acquaint Ford with current academic thinking, invited Glazer to a White House lunch with the president. Some half-dozen such luncheon meetings were held, and Glazer attended at least three with colleagues such as Moynihan, Martin Feldstein, and Orlando Patterson. "Typically," Glazer recalls, "six to eight people attended. The talk was not organized, but far ranging, discursive, and not oriented toward policy. Ford usually listened."[65] Ford was, as Goldwin recollects, very interested in the meetings and adjusted his schedule to continue them until Reagan's victory in the 1976 North Carolina primary forced their cancellation.[66]

However, academic involvement in Ford policy-making was limited not only by the short duration of the administration and the considerable disarray in the White House. Experts were also withdrawing of their own accord. Increasingly battered by colleagues on their own campuses, they displayed almost measurable self-restraint by the mid-seventies. In economics, the certainty of the Keynesian consensus was giving way to puzzlement over the new condition of "stagflation," in which signs of both inflation and sizeable unemployment were increasingly evident. Advocates of monetary policy as an alternative to fiscal policy, such as Chicago's Milton Friedman, were once again coming into vogue. The efficacy of programmed public deficits and surpluses, manipulation of interest rates, and floating exchange rates was increasingly called into question.[67]

Sociologists, political scientists, and anthropologists who had not been involved in shaping New Frontier and Great Society politics also began to doubt the received wisdom of their disciplines and undertook to evaluate the work of their colleagues returning from Washington. The Ford Foundation–sponsored Cambridge faculty seminar on the Great Society was an initial source of criticism and review. Books by Jencks on education, Banfield on "unheavenly" cities, Moynihan on the poverty program, and Glazer on affirmative action accelerated a drumbeat of skepticism.

With the assistance of Glazer and *Public Interest* coeditor Irving Kristol, the first critiques of the Cambridge group swelled to a crescendo of unrelenting attacks on the policies forged in the sixties and the academic research that underlay them. The intellectual backlash spread to other opinion journals and popular publications. Neoconservatism took hold in the social science departments in university after university; it vied with neo-Marxism in capturing student attention and commitment. In the summer of 1976, the editors of *The American Scholar*, stimulated by a *New York Times* article by Robert Nisbet entitled "Knowledge Dethroned," put together a symposium titled "Social Science: The Public Disenchantment." Nine scholars and commentators solemnly reported that for the most part academic-based public policy did not work.[68]

Two of these neoconservative commentaries were especially critical of educational and urban reform. In education, a covey of critics assigned the major role in intellectual and monetary achievement to genes and, in a corollary effort, hypothesized racial differences based on aggregated IQ tests. The research and opinions of James Coleman, Arthur Jenson, and Richard Herrenstein, as well as of Jencks, combined to challenge sharply the efficacy of formal education and the wisdom of additional investment in schools and in teaching. These authors argued, in effect, that newer schools, better teachers, and revised curricula had little impact on educational outcomes; heredity, family background, and family behavior were more important factors. Modern Horatio Algers were born and not made; genes and blind luck, not environment or schooling, largely determined individual achievement. Hence, compensatory education programs for young and poor children would have little or no effect. Public money was being thrown after problems that were in fact intractable.[69]

Banfield and Moynihan were the eloquent if gloomy messengers of a similar critique of urban programs. Banfield's analysis of the city scene emphasized the distinction between soluble problems and intractable conditions. To him, the seamy side of urban culture—the concentration of large numbers of poor people, mostly minorities, in ghettos—was inevitable and inescapable. The behavior of these ghettoized individuals could not be modified by either carrot or stick and government intervention was therefore foolish and dangerous. In language reminiscent of the Victorian counsel of Herbert Spencer, Banfield wrote, "The lower class individual lives from moment to moment . . . Things happen *to* him, he does not *make* them happen. Impulse governs his behavior . . . Whatever he cannot consume immediately he considers valueless. His bodily needs (especially for sex) and his taste for 'action' take precedence over everything else— and certainly over any work routine. He works only as he must to stay alive." Just as bad money drives out good, Banfield concluded, so poor children cheapen good schools, unskilled, unmotivated workers reduce productivity, better housing is misused, libraries and museums are unappreciated. The principal solution Banfield proposed was semi-institutional care for the semicompetent.[70]

Banfield's second argument that would find academic favor in terms of the then-emerging critical theory protested the empiricism and "scientism" of the behavioral approach. He found that experts consistently "discovered" problems and demanded solutions where no problems had actually existed before. So it was in education, he pointed out, that in the nineteenth century almost every boy and girl "dropped out" of high school—that is, did not graduate. "Dropping out" did not become a problem until educators perceived it to be one. Accordingly, Banfield concluded, "our urban problems are like the mechanical rabbit at the race track which is set to keep just ahead of the dogs no matter how fast they run." Raising our standards and expectations guaranteed the continuation of problems. Banfield's *Unheavenly City* ran through three editions, the latest in 1990, without substantive change.[71]

Moynihan's leadership in the neoconservative movement did not rely on the essentially historical and deductive reasoning of Banfield. Both in his 1964 study of the black family and subsequently, Moynihan often presented empirical and quantitative evidence to support his positions. His statistical analyses were sharply challenged, however, and his often sweeping generalizations lacked evidential support. Nonetheless, the commitment to knowledge, not ideology, appeared clear.

In his neoconservative period, Moynihan objected to the participation of social scientists in policy-making and execution. He held that "social science is at its weakest, at its worst, when it offers theories of individual and collective behavior which raise the possibility, by controlling certain inputs, of bringing about mass behavioral change . . . The role of social science lies not in the formulation of social policy but in the measurement of its results."[72] In his public positions from the Kennedy administration through Nixon to the U.S. Senate, Moynihan would violate this injunction repeatedly, never more so than in his recommendations to Nixon for the Family Assistance Plan. Yet in his post-Nixon writings, his skepticism about the capacity of government to do anything more than mail checks and fight wars bordered on contempt. Middle-class experts might find jobs for themselves in community action programs and plan urban restoration projects, but their efforts, in the end, would not truly help the poor whom they claimed to serve.[73]

By the end of Ford's term in office, then, the action-intellectuals of the sixties were engaged in political battles not in government but in the academy. They were beset on all sides by colleagues carrying the same formal credentials. On the right, neoconservatives disparaged the capacity of government to carry out direct assistance programs, although their negative evaluations still employed the methodology of those they sought to refute. Thus they joined the "true" conservatives, part laizzez-faire liberals and part classical political philosophers, in protesting government intervention in the affairs of the private sector.

What left and right, hard and soft analysis, had in common in the mid-seventies was the disparagement of the policy innovations of the sixties. In an extraordinary rush to judgment, neoconservatives and neo-Marxists wrote off the programs of the New Frontier and the Great Society, even as the proportion of poor Americans fell by two-fifths between 1964 and 1979—from 19 percent to 12 percent of the total population. The profoundly pessimistic and laconic neoconservative commentary, which lumped together race, class, and personality structure as a single category of causation, joined the radicals' Critical Theory's new class, high-tech, low-mandarin theorist enamoured by CCD—"carefree and critical discourse."[74]

Together these sharply divergent schools and philosophies produced a judgment against the research and findings of academic social scientists that lingered through the 1980s and nearly became conventional. Beware of social engineering, the chorus sang, and of colleagues who sponsored such policies. They were guileful and irresponsible, co-opted by devious and megalomaniacal politicians. Fortunately, a recalcitrant bureaucracy and a series of calamitous events—Vietnam, the assassinations of two Kennedys and of Martin Luther King, Jr.—doomed their ill-considered, unproven schemes to failure. This was all to the good, for their plans were hopelessly utopian.

That Rockefeller, both leader and disciple of expert policy-making, was entrapped by a third-rate, sandlot White House political elite was not the only irony of the Nixon and Ford administrations. Almost covertly, these presidents increased the resources available to the programs begun in the task forces of the sixties, and by the end of the seventies both the politicians and the public had endorsed them. There would be no repeal of the health, civil rights, welfare, urban, and educational programs that went on the books between 1960 and 1968. Yet the traditionally liberal and interventionist academic community—with the exception of those directly involved in fashioning the domestic strategy—was almost unanimous in declaring these programs failures. These intellectuals succeeded in persuading print journalists, television commentators, editors, almost all of the so-called opinion-makers, that government could and should do little except develop new defense technology and conduct foreign affairs. Despite the staggering loss of resources to Vietnam, the programs more than survived to prove themselves in the 1970s and 1980s, helped especially by the success of Head Start. But the architects returned to their campuses in disrepute.

5

THE SYSTEM DISASSEMBLES

Despite the wholesale retreat—some called it rout—of the academic experts of the late sixties and early seventies, scorned by colleagues and columnists alike, the relations among the intervening elites, somewhat curiously, more than survived. By the mid-1970s, amid the first stirrings of the next presidential election and in the aftermath of Watergate, the working associations among national politicians, senior federal administrators, and scholars had settled almost into routine. The academic experts who had helped shape the domestic programs of the New Frontier, the Great Society, and the New American Revolution had long left the Beltway behind. But the proposition that substantive knowledge *should* be an integral part of campaigning and public policy-making and that much of it came from universities seemed finally established, an integral part of the political system. In campaign, transition, and governance, crops of academics continued to pop up.

A full generation had passed since Galbraith and Schlesinger led the squad of idealistic and ambitious professors to Adlai Stevenson's Libertyville, Paul Butler's Democratic National Advisory Committee began to identify policy options independent from the Democratic Congress, and Meade Alcorn tried to counter for the Republicans. Academic experts in high public places were no longer the curiosities they had been before the Kennedy-Johnson years. Genuine Ph.D.s such as George Shultz and John Dunlop forged impressive managerial records in the Nixon-Ford years. Although no policy advisers on domestic matters ever approached the public visibility of their counterparts in foreign affairs, their presence and influence in executive departments were pervasive and substantial.

Still another factor routinizing relationships was the leftover Johnson initiative of PPBS, the planning-programming-budgeting systems analysis techniques Robert McNamara introduced in the Pentagon and later mandated by executive order throughout the executive branch. Initiated by McNamara's Whiz Kids, PPBS techniques were institutionalized in policy analysis staffs in almost every department and agency. Although the Nixon administration dropped many central reporting requirements and encouraged new titles for the offices to hide PPBS's Johnson legacy, the disposition for empirical and behavioral analysis was now built into the government—in fact bureaucratized, as Arnold Meltsner has documented persuasively. With the production of social-science Ph.D.s at a record level while university faculties were being cut back sharply, it was easy to staff policy analysis units with social scientists of quality. A concern for facts—for the explicit identification of costs and benefits, for quantification of options—increasingly became standard operating procedure inside the national government.[1]

Most important of all, the academic community gave explicit encouragement to the newly emerging profession of policy analysis. Indeed, it scrambled to contribute. Universities had long responded to particular federal policy initiatives by organizing centers for research—urban and space centers proliferated in the sixties across the country. Now the academic community moved to legitimize PPBS as a professional activity by introducing new graduate programs and establishing new schools of public policy. Programs in public administration, for the most part previously a disparaged sector of political science, gave way to new policy curricula (sometimes with new degree titles) dominated by economists and substantive specialists in health, transportation, welfare, and education. A focus on quantitative techniques replaced the philosophical and institutional concerns of the older programs, and public choice analysts jostled political scientists, historians, and sociologists as the new schools took root.[2]

By the end of the seventies, more than two hundred policy schools existed. Most of them focused on providing master's degrees, and their graduates found ready employment not only in Washington but in state capitols and city halls as well. "Optimization of scarce resources" became the battle cry of the converts to policy analysis, and the long-dormant field of political economy was resurrected. "Public choice" theory endowed the private sector with new legitimacy to carry out activities heretofore publicly managed. Its quantitative methodologies, its philosophical preference for markets and public-private partnerships, and the coolly calculating dispositions of its practitioners fitted neatly into the temper of the times. With the energy crisis looming large and America losing its twenty-year competitive edge in the world, a self-appointed assembly of public policy intellectuals calling itself "the Club of Rome" mournfully proclaimed the limits of growth. California's public spending was suddenly capped by Proposition 13, and "downsizing" government seemed the order of the day. The new analysts and the new academics were ready, willing, able, and eager to provide solutions both inside and outside government.[3]

Carter and a Conventional Beginning

It is in this twin context—a by-now traditional assembly of experts for the presidential campaign and a sharply more critical and constrained approach to public policy—that Jimmy Carter's surprising appearance on the campaign trail and his subsequent behavior as president are best understood. While the media perception that this unknown Georgian governor "came out of nowhere" may have been accurate, both in philosophy and style Carter fitted the times. For all his claim to being an outsider to the national political process, Carter proceeded to assemble and display the usual academics from the usual prestigious institutions as he moved his candidacy into serious contention.

More important, the academic disposition of the new policy schools fitted well with his conservative proclivities, such as the interest in zero-based budgeting he had displayed as Georgia's governor and his education as an engineer. No "academic star" reached the inner White House circle in domestic affairs—no Schlesinger, no Gardner, no Galbraith, no Moynihan. Nonetheless the institutionalization of expert analysis and Carter's acceptance of the new "policy" discipline moved more social scientists more rapidly into place than in any other post–World War II administration.[4]

Carter began his relationship with academics cautiously, in part because academic veterans of previous policy wars were battle-weary. The Democratic academics had suffered not only from the disastrous McGovern campaign but, more painfully, from the intellectual assaults of neoconservative colleagues. Now most of them were trying to resurrect professional careers and personal lives. For their part, Republican academics still winced under the shame of Watergate.[5]

At a time when public distrust of Washington and the national government ran high and federal deficits, unheard of in the 1960s, were regular occurrences, Carter's conservative courtship of scholars was shrewdly attuned to the temper of the times. Defense needs appeared to remain prodigious, stagflation was a new and perplexing phenomenon that economists could not persuasively explain, and gas shortages abraded the public's nerves. The expansive conviction of only ten years earlier—that government could be relied on to solve heretofore intractable social problems—had disappeared.

To be sure, the first stirrings of neoliberalism—explicitly eschewing ideological design, embracing public-private partnership, and endorsing incremental, highly technical, almost whimsical approaches to public problems—were now evident in Carter's Georgia, Michael Dukakis's Massachusetts, and Jerry Brown's California. But they were scarcely visible against the old-style conservatism that proclaimed the virtue and superiority of free enterprise. On almost every policy front, neoconservatives Kristol, Banfield, Glazer, and Moynihan supported this philosophy. In their view, government was a limited instrument best suited to containing, ideologically and geopolitically, our implacable "other super-power" enemy and ensuring at home the preservation of individual and corporate rights through legal and judicial procedures.[6]

Nonetheless, however dour the political environment for mainstream Democrats and liberal Republicans and however much its technocratic conservatism fitted Carter's personal disposition, the habits of a generation prevailed at campaign time. It was now de rigueur to assemble a gaggle of academic experts. The place to start was still Cambridge, and the model to emulate remained Sorensen's 1958 advisory committee. Sorensen himself signed on early with Carter, "put him up overnight on the couch," and undertook to organize the New York delegation in his behalf.[7] But the person who actually fulfilled for Carter Sorensen's earlier role with Kennedy was Stuart Eizenstat, a young Georgian with a Harvard law degree who, like Sorensen the Nebraskan, had worked in Washington before joining Carter in the governor's office. He described himself as "a provincial who had come to know his way around."[8]

Eizenstat's cosmopolitan political experience included a summer internship in the Johnson White House in 1967, campaign staff work with Hubert Humphrey in 1968, and service as the "issue" staff person for the Democrat's 1974 national congressional campaign. Between these national assignments, Eizenstat worked with Carter in his gubernatorial campaigns.

Six months of working for the Committee to Elect Democrats under the auspices of the Democratic National Committee (co-chaired by Carter) in 1974 introduced Eizenstat to social scientists of national reputation. He compiled a "small file card box full of names like Brzezinski and Henry Owen, running from A to Z and tagged according to policy issue speciality." After the 1974 election, the young lawyer took another leave from his law firm and, with card box in hand, joined Carter full time in an operation then "remarkably thin in policy people." The Brookings Institution and the universities of Wisconsin and Pennsylvania became the first important stops to gather campaign ideas.[9]

In a manner resembling Sorensen's first excursions to Massachusetts, Eizenstat began to assemble the "idea folks." He was less successful in his recruitment inside New England, but more successful outside, than Sorensen had been. Cambridge yielded old-timers such as Harvard's Abram Chayes and Charles Haar, and, later, economists Lester Thurow and John Deutch from M.I.T. and Carolyn Bell of Wellesley. But others at Harvard and M.I.T. hung back, not "willing to devote the necessary unpaid time to a long-shot race of an ambitious peanut farmer from south Georgia."[10] Still others had their own favorite candidates—Morris Udall, Henry Jackson, Sargent Shriver—all of whom had built academic networks over the years. Not surprisingly, the New England response was tepid.

Eizenstat instead found expert advice in Nobel laureate Lawrence Klein of the University of Pennsylvania, who signed on as principal economic adviser after being impressed with a one-on-one conversation he had had with Carter in November 1975.[11] From congressional staffs and the emerging think tanks came Charles Schultz, Joseph Brouder, Arthur Okun, Joel Fleishman, Joseph Albert Starr, and Albert Sommers. All were either based in Washington or on research leave there. Eizenstat identified a smattering of others: Barry Bosworth and Al Stein of Wayne State, Richard Cooper of Yale, Donna Shalala from Columbia, and Peter Bourne, a psychiatrist with earlier Georgia associations. Old-time JFK loyalists such as Milt Girtzman and Phillip Seidman came aboard; so did Rockefeller's James L. Cannon. From this pool Eizenstat established formal campaign task forces in foreign policy, economics, and urban affairs. The most systematic, orderly, and distinguished work came from Klein's economic task force, which brought a level of sophistication and quantitative elegance to economic policy analysis unmatched since the 1960 Samuelson report for Kennedy.[12]

Eizenstat did not have to go it alone in his sweep for ideas in the campaign. Carter had his own "second track" academic links, principally through the Trilateral Commission David Rockefeller had established in 1973 to bring together business leaders, academics, and assorted "influentials" from the United States, Europe, and Japan. Invited to join in the first year, Carter found himself in a company sprinkled with nationally known academics and carefully selected labor and other interests.[13]

The Trilateral Commission was to become notorious, at least in neo-Marxist social science literature which saw it as an international conspiracy of "capitalists dividing up the world." In 1980, Richard Falk of Princeton stated that the commission was virtually "a coming out party for the ruling class," a group that exhibited the "spirit of a transnational ruling class concerned about keeping world capitalism healthy." Elaborating on this interpretation, Lawrence Shoup went on to attribute Carter's rise to power to "a small group of wealthy and powerful people—members of the corporate upper class" which "shaped the 1976 Presidential selection process, helped a relatively obscure former Governor of Georgia gain power, then molded his Administration." Shoup identified the group as "the exclusive Trilateral Commission, an organization dominated by leaders of the Eastern Establishment."[14]

One need not accept Shoup's conspiracy theory or write Carter off as a puppet of an American capitalist regime to acknowledge that the commission gave Carter an extraordinarily effective introduction to national figures in both the public and private sectors. Its American contingent— some sixty CEOs of large corporations, lawyers, public officials, and professors—represented a conscious effort on the part of Rockefeller and his close advisers to cover the continent with its membership. Carter, an internationally oriented Democratic governor from the "New South," was a natural. Seated alphabetically in the meeting next to Lloyd Cutler, a distinguished Washington lawyer who would become Carter's White House counselor in the desperate days of 1977, Carter "as a former Governor with a hat-in-the-ring spoke eloquently and impressed Cutler, Vance, and Dick Gardner," the last a Columbia economist and lawyer of international reputation.[15]

Indeed, all the academics on the Trilateral Commission and others commissioned to write papers for it were heavyweights. In 1976, they included Zbigniew Brzezinski and Gerald Curtis of Columbia; Carroll Wilson of M.I.T.; Harold Brown, president of the California Institute of Technology; Yale's Richard Cooper; the Brookings Institution's Wilfred Owen; and Harvard's Edwin Reischauer, Samuel Huntington, and Graham Allison. Many had overlapping membership on the Council on Foreign Relations. Their assignment, as White House files report, was to "write prolix reports with epochal titles."[16]

Carter's White House files are peppered with correspondence from David Rockefeller, and a special White House reception was held in the commission's honor in June 1978. Secretary of the Treasury Michael Blumenthal asked Jack Watson, then White House secretary to the cabinet, whether cabinet members should keep their memberships in Trilateral. There is no record of a response. By 1978, eighteen American Trilateral Commission members, six of whom were academics, were Carter Administration appointees.

For Shoup, Carter's Trilateral connection was sinister. "Once in office, ruling class leaders felt there was a good chance that Carter could, with liberal rhetoric and a reputation for forthrightness, mobilize the constituency needed to implement Trilateral plans for a new world order."[17] A much less dramatic interpretation suggests that, at a minimum, Carter's membership guaranteed him access to "prolix reports with epochal titles" sufficient to provide all the ideas he could absorb for campaign rhetoric and position papers. The connection almost seemed to make the Eizenstat operation irrelevant.

In another sense, the Trilateral Commission perpetuated Nelson Rockefeller's practice of assembling a "group of brains to solve a problem." His brother David's adoption of the technique, expanding it to an international scale, and mixing "doers and thinkers" was perhaps the best testimony to Nelson Rockefeller's enduring contribution to public policy. Illustrious representatives of the intervening elites were now formally brought together, and, though corporate leaders dominated and foreign affairs and international relations claimed the lion's share of the agenda, whatever academic experts had to say about domestic issues was heard carefully. Harvard's Samuel Huntington, for one, argued that a sea change in domestic politics was underway as governing authority was lost to "street people."[18] Carter had tapped into a rich reservoir of ideas, as well as a network of influence and wealth.

Short Circuit: Jordan vs. Watson

The similarity between Eizenstat and Sorensen, particularly in their search for academic experts, was not the only parallel between Carter's long-shot candidacy and Kennedy's. With due adjustment for differences in the candidates' style, character, and personality, there was a final similarity—the conflict between the "issues" managers of the campaign and those focused on more long-run matters of governance. In 1960, Sorensen's and Richard Goodwin's treatment of issues on the campaign trail had exasperated Archibald Cox, locked in his L Street boiler room. It had taken a face-to-face confrontation in Minneapolis to patch matters over between Sorensen and Cox. Now, in 1976, a more serious and potentially more damaging chasm appeared among the Carter idea people.

Eizenstat's national policy and issues staff was a part of the campaign organization headed by Hamilton Jordan, the principal architect of Carter's political strategy and one of his earliest and closest confidants. The candidate's "fuzziness" on major issues and lack of a single unifying slogan—what Carl Brauer termed Carter's "lack of clarity about his goals"—was partly mitigated by the effective staff Eizenstat had assembled. Occasionally, Trilateral "stars" made uninvited and unexpected proposals. In foreign affairs, second-track experts Brzezinski, Owen, and Gardner were likely to spin speech drafts and suggestions off freely. So were task forces on nuclear and defense policy, which included such stalwarts as Paul Doty, Kenneth Arrow, Carl Kaysen, and George Rathgens. On domestic matters, Ted Sorensen, with authority derived from the Kennedy years, typically worked independently. Hamilton Jordan resented the intervention of these scholars, for his entire campaign strategy was based on banishing Washington insiders and cultivating outsiders. "Jimmy Who?" was programmed to burst on the national political scene to "give the American people a government as good as they are."[19]

At least through the primaries, Jordan and Eizenstat prevailed against the experts of the Trilateral commission. As Lawrence Klein recalls, Eizenstat "ran the intellectuals in the campaign, although as the campaign progressed, it became more establishment oriented, less radical in ideas, and the influence by academics declined dramatically."[20] Barry Bosworth confirmed Klein's perception that Eizenstat orchestrated the "issues" work throughout the campaign and that the role of academics "was progressively diminished during the campaign and became even less thereafter . . . a much different role than in the sixties when academics were looked up to as objective, wise, pure in their ivory towers."[21]

The star wars with Trilateral members and Carter's personal penchant for informal meetings with task forces aside, Eizenstat and Jordan had a more serious challenge to confront, one that surpassed Cox's dispute with Sorensen. Another young Georgian, Jack Watson, had persuaded the candidate to establish a policy planning team in anticipation of winning the election and preparing for an orderly, Atlanta-based transition to power. By summer of 1976, Watson had assembled a staff. As Brauer reports, "most of whom were in their thirties, and had some Washington experience. All worked long hours for subsistence wages in an atmosphere of idealism, expectation, and ambition."[22]

The Watson operation concerned Eizenstat (though he considered the team "crackerjack"), and it infuriated Jordan, especially because it diverted $150,000 from scarce campaign funds. In August, the *New York Times* reported that young foreign policy experts had been divided between the two staffs, as well as that Carter continued to seek his own council from members of the Trilateral Commission and the Council on Foreign Relations.[23] Jordan regarded both as "fifth columns," new kids on the block, and he was especially concerned that Watson had responsibility to search for key appointments.[24]

But as the campaign wore on and Carter seemed to stumble, an increasingly pressured Jordan became preoccupied with falling opinion polls and day-to-day crises. Watson, on the other hand, flourished as a media favorite and soon after the election was greeted in Washington as the whiz-kid to watch.[25] After the election, however, Jordan counterattacked. At a postelection retreat on Sea Island, Georgia, in early November, Jordan took over the key personnel function in what Eizenstat remembers as "a short and bitter fight. Watson was left with a staff of about half a dozen. Mondale took over national security."[26] Brauer reported, "At the very moment that Watson's star appeared brightest, it was eclipsed by Jordan . . . . He barely managed to stay in the picture."[27]

Actually, the press got the picture upside down. Over and beyond the struggle for experts and their ideas, the Jordan-Watson affair is a classic illustration of the limitations of media coverage, its tendency to misinterpret and oversimplify its picture of politics. In the November 11, 1976, *New York Times*, under the headline "Watson, Head of Planning Staff in Campaign, Gets Key Post in 'Duel' with Hamilton Jordan," James Wooten reported on the Sea Island meeting:

> Post-election competition between two of Carter's chief aides has apparently left Jack Watson, Mr. Carter's liaison with the Ford Administration, in charge of a major share of all transitional responsibilities . . . Mr. Watson's rival [Jordan] in what one insider called a "bloodless duel" will head the assembly of a White House staff.
>
> While Mr. Jordan is not seen as a waning figure on the Carter staff, his restriction to specifically defined duties is viewed by some here and in Washington as evidence of Mr. Watson's rising star . . . Mr. Watson, a Harvard-educated Texan seemed to have the clear advantage [in directing the transition]. On a meager budget from campaign funds, he and 15 other men and women meticulously combed thousands of sources for information and ideas that would be useful to Mr. Carter only in the event that he won.

However, Wooten and other media observers had failed to note the critical element of power signified in these personnel assignments and the fact that transition planning, in Brauer's words, "was largely a paper exercise until Cabinet members and agency heads themselves were chosen. Not surprisingly, some Cabinet members and agency heads filed [the transition team's] products in their wastebaskets and started over again with their own people."[28] So it was Watson's star that in fact was sinking and with it the grand notions of planning, efficiency, coordination, and rationality that the new politics of neoliberal technocracy and the new schools of public policy embraced. The old-fashioned politics of personal power held sway: Carter continued the tradition of making his top campaign assistants his top White House assistants.

Because Jordan won in the first struggle in the Carter White House, Eizenstat also won. A week after the Sea Island shoot-out, *U.S. News and World Report* named him one of twelve advisers sure to "move to the inner circle" and consistently thereafter placed his name above Watson's.[29] In January, their relative positions were confirmed: Eizenstat was named assistant to the president for domestic affairs and policy, in effect inheriting the post Ehrlichman had fashioned for himself in the Nixon administration. Watson was relegated to a post perceived to be mostly ministerial—cabinet secretary and assistant for intergovernmental relations.[30]

If Jordan's victory over Watson was clear-cut, he lost more generally in his battle with the eastern establishment's old guard. In particular, he lost to Trilateral. Repeatedly he had emphasized the candidate's commitment to fresh faces—Washington outsiders, "a new generation of leaders." During the campaign, Jordan had stated that appointments of such establishment figures as Brzezinski and Vance would provoke his resignation. But Brzezinski and Vance both joined the administration, along with fellow Trilateral Commission members Harold Brown, Mike Blumenthal, Warren Christopher, Richard Cooper, Eliot Richardson, and Lucy Benson, all of whom assumed cabinet and subcabinet posts. Over all, Shoup counted twenty Trilateral Commission members, fifty-four Council on Foreign Relations members, and five trustees or senior fellows from Brookings and the Committee for Economic Development.[31] Carter nominated Sorensen to direct the CIA (although, under fire, he withdrew the nomination). Since Klein was not an active candidate for the CEA, Charles Schultz became its chair.[32]

All in all, Hedrick Smith concluded in the *New York Times*, the Carter cabinet was "neatly balanced" and "carefully selected to reflect the political face of America in the 1970s, . . . [but] in the most sensitive policy areas, Mr. Carter leaned almost exclusively on veterans of the Johnson and Kennedy administrations and on his own intimate friends from Georgia."[33] A formula emerged from the transition—young Georgians in command in the White House; Washington old-timers and insiders in command elsewhere within the executive branch. As time went on, more and more observers concluded that reversing these assignments might have served Carter better.

The Domestic Policy Staff: The Triumph of Lawyering

Watson's struggle to remain chief policy planner and Jordan's attempt to banish the establishment failed in the transition. Academic experts in domestic affairs lost out as well. Eizenstat himself was in no peril. As a colleague of Jordan, not of Watson, and an effective campaign adviser reporting directly to Carter, he was secure in the Georgian White House. Directing the newly established domestic policy staff, he was now the central figure in translating campaign promises into policy initiatives. Further, his earlier associations with Carter in 1970 and 1974 gave him an identity independent of Jordan. There were constraints, to be sure: an unclear presidential mandate and vague guidelines governing his relations to the cabinet and the Office of Management and Budget. The new assistant for domestic policy was, however, free to choose his immediate staff and his mode of operation.[34]

Not surprisingly, Burt Carp, who had been with Eizenstat during the campaign and a Mondale congressional staffer before that, became Eizenstat's deputy. The rest of his staff were chiefly, like him, lawyers. The group resembled the small, informal, and freewheeling staff Califano had gathered for Johnson. The Nixon and Ford administrations added another dimension, which Eizenstat also accepted: his new staff were insiders. Unlike Califano's lawyers, compulsively canvassing the campuses for "new ideas," the members of the new domestic policy staff were more like Ehrlichman. Although Eizenstat would deny any break with academics or outside experts in general (he kept in touch with Klein and other veterans), no major academic figure served as an architect of public policy in the Carter administration. No raft of task forces and commissions paralleled those of Johnson or Nixon. From Eizenstat's perspective, the new schools of public policy and the new curricula of public choice superseded the old campus networks. Indeed, "issue networks" in Washington had now appeared, new coalitions to run in tandem with internal groups and their iron triangles. "Carter's domestic council," Eizenstat has argued, "represented not a break with the JFK and LBJ tradition, but an evolution in the most effective means of harnessing ideas. A new generation of public policy types such as young Ben Heineman appeared."[35]

Erwin Hargrove, working with Carter's oral histories (compiled at the University of Virginia's Miller Center), adds to the Eizenstat sketch of his operation:

> On behalf of the President the DPS would test policy ideas against what the political traffic would bear. He therefore recruited staff members with Washington experience, whether on Congressional committee staffs or in public interest law firms . . . For the most part, however, they were not technical experts in what is often called policy analysis, which has cost-benefit analysis as its core methodology. In Eizenstat's view, expertise at policy analysis in this technical sense should reside in the departments and agencies where program proposals would be developed.[36]

Hargrove goes on to draw a sharp distinction between how Carter staffed the Council of Economic Advisers and the National Security Council. "The three CEA members and fifteen or so professional staff members are economists, the majority drawn from university faculties," he wrote in 1988. "NSC staff members are usually a combination of academic experts and experienced government professionals but, in both cases, a premium is placed on substantive expertise."[37]

Charles Jones, another distinguished scholar who has analyzed the Carter years, rounds out the profile of the domestic policy staff:

> For President Carter, the DPS performed vital functions in preparing the legislative program . . . When he became director of the DPS, Eizenstat knew

the President very well both in terms of substantive policy preferences and political style . . . DPS members emphasized that their influence was a consequence primarily of becoming familiar with what the President wanted rather than of giving him direct advice on an issue . . . It was important that the DPS be seen as a relatively neutral manager of information and options, again within the context of the President's clear preferences.[38]

DPS's initial emphasis, then, was constricted. It stressed analysis rather than advice and gave attention to the process of bringing issues to the Oval Office rather than arguing substance. Staff estimated what the political traffic would bear; they did not engage in political lobbying directly, as Califano had done.

However modest his beginnings, Eizenstat found his influence unexpectedly expanded by Carter's first major blunder—the Bert Lance affair. Having invited Lance to join the administration as director of OMB, the White House was traumatized throughout the summer of 1977 by the consequences of Lance's apparent mishandling of his personal financial affairs. Not only was Lance to suffer as an individual when he was finally forced to resign, but the institutional damage to OMB, a key agency through which the professional senior federal service elite typically weighed in most effectively on policy, would be even greater. Its reputation for professionalism had already been hurt by the fact that Nixon politicized its top staff, but it remained an executive agency with longevity, a strong sense of institutional history, and high professional competence. Before Carter could bring himself to accept the resignation of his closest Georgian associate, OMB's influence and prestige had been seriously impaired. As Jones puts it, "In order to make the OMB work for him, the President must be able to take control of the agency through his appointments . . . The loss of Lance was a serious blow to the President. Lance's successor, James McIntyre, could not expect to override advice on domestic policy [as Lance could]. Rather he was a contestant in the struggle to gain access to the President . . . [A] great deal of chaos and confusion [ensued]."[39]

With OMB crippled and McIntyre forced to concentrate on repairing the internal disarray, DPS stepped up to bat. Eizenstat's staff had far more flexibility than the OMB in choosing its priorities, and Eizenstat's personal standing with the president was greater than McIntyre's. Furthermore, the White House viewed many of the OMB senior staff as "holdover Republicans" and accordingly was suspicious of their policy recommendations.[40] To enhance Eizenstat's position even more, as Hargrove reports, Jordan foreswore any competence or interest in policy, "a hole that Eizenstat eventually discovered he had to fill." He became the heretofore missing link between political calculations and policy analysis as "he kept in touch with interest groups, sounded out Congressional opinion as policy was being developed, and compensated for Carter's limited interest."[41]

While his predecessors Califano and Ehrlichman had deliberately taken policy into the political White House and out of the institutional Executive Office of the President, Eizenstat was now forced to accept a policy role. Key administration professionals, along with academics, were out of the loop. In a curious way, the process of policy-making seemed to return to Harry Truman days. The prime movers became the departments and agencies and their cluster of interest groups and issue networks. There was a process for achieving presidential sanction, but there was no agenda of priorities and little disposition to "knock heads" and impose discipline among the warring cabinet barons.[42]

What emerged in the first year of the Carter administration was something of a "seed catalog" of presidential proposals. Separately, Hargrove and Jones examine four major Carter policies entailing legislation—the economic growth policy, an energy program, welfare reform, and the establishment of the Department of Education. They also analyze four other key domestic policy initiatives extending through 1980—wage and price guidelines, minimum wage, hospital cost containment, and civil service reform. With the exception of the civil service reform, the major attributes of these policies and the process by which they were shaped appear strikingly similar.

They were, first of all, "insider" products, heavily dependent on the analyses of permanent policy staffs within the concerned departments and agencies, with all the built-in institutional biases of the providers. Sometimes, Carter gave the assignment to one or two principals. He directed James Schlesinger to work on the first energy package and secretaries Califano and Marshall to investigate welfare reform. Sometimes, he divided assignments between executive office and departmental staffs, as he did with the economic growth policy. But Carter farmed few, if any, out to independent expert review. Where task forces were used, they were predominantly composed of government experts and analysts. "The role of academics not only diminished over time during the campaign, but it became even less during transition and administration, . . ." Barry Bosworth observes. "Many academics couldn't translate principles into concrete terms. Compared to the sixties, academics were no longer looked up to as sitting in an ivory tower. Departments and agencies began simply to hire their own economists and other experts. . . . [The] civil service was much more highly trained than in the sixties and academics failed to understand their role at this point."[43]

A second characteristic of Carter policy-making, especially in the cases of energy and welfare, was that proposals usually lacked a cohesive theme or even slogan. In place of an overarching approach or thesis capable of being captured in a single word or phrase—Four Freedoms, New Frontier, Great Society, Head Start, Upward Bound, Model Cities—a laundry list of specific subsidies and regulations appeared. As James Fallows was to write in his devastating *Atlantic* article of 1979, "The Passionless Presidency,"

> In each of these areas [taxes, welfare, energy, reorganization of government], Carter's passionate campaign commitments turned out to be commitments to generalities, not to specific programs or policies . . . Carter had not given us an *idea* to follow . . . No one could carry out the Carter program because Carter has resisted providing the overall guidelines that might explain what his program is. I came to think that Carter believes fifty things but no one thing . . . When goals conflict, spelling out these choices makes the difference between a position and a philosophy, but it is an act foreign to Carter's mind.[44]

Third, as each executive department and agency with a possible interest had its inning in policy-making, specific proposals not only grew more numerous, but they became contradictory and inconsistent. In the case of the energy package, Hargrove reports, "The President wished Congress to consider 113 interlocking proposals." The first economic proposals never reconciled the call for a tax rebate with public works expenditures until serious congressional damage had occurred. The welfare proposals carried water on both shoulders: income maintenance and jobs. James Fallows again:

> Carter is a smart man but not an intellectual, in the sense of liking the play of ideas, of pushing concepts to their limits to examine their implications . . . He thinks in lists, not arguments; as long as his items are there, their order does not matter, nor does the hierarchy among them. Whenever he gave us an outline for a speech, it would consist of six or seven subjects ('inflation, need to fight (?)') rather than a theme or tone.[45]

Finally, at least in the first years when Carter remained committed to "cabinet" government and wary of congressional intent, the political consequences of a major policy were rarely anticipated. Toward the end of the administration, Eizenstat would come to recognize the fatal flaws in the original policy-making design. "You simply couldn't run a major study on a major issue out of Cabinet departments . . . the welfare policy . . . is an excellent example of what happens when the White House doesn't coordinate policy . . . Carter ended up getting a decision memorandum on welfare which was some 60 single-spaced typewritten pages, utterly incomprehensible, in which Labor and HEW could not agree even on the language to be used in various sections."[46]

Burned by adverse congressional reaction to the almost endless array of complex, inconsistent, and frequently incomprehensible policies generated within the executive branch, the White House finally withdrew from the "vintage Carter" approach a rational response "to a national problem requiring a comprehensive solution so there was no need to compromise or consult."[47] Yet neither the professionalization of the DPS approach nor ultimately the president's delegation to Eizenstat of genuine power to coordinate policy-making heralded the return of the outside scholar. DPS continued to rely on departments and agencies to supply "the numbers," the hard data, and the original concepts. Lloyd Cutler summed up the situation this way: "Carter had more academics—certified, card-carrying Ph.D.s—than any previous administration, but they were rarely, if ever, influential in the White House." Eizenstat concurred: "I did not often think of advisers with the category of academics in mind."[48]

When genuine crisis broke, the idea people were not present. The most dramatic example was at the Camp David "summit" of July 5 through 15, 1979, after Carter had returned from Japan to find nationwide gasoline shortages, consumer revolts, and important energy price controls scheduled to expire. What began as a retreat to prepare a major speech on a new energy policy turned into ten days of "wide ranging and philosophical" review and evaluation of the administration's overall performance since the inauguration.[49]

Not surprisingly, the list of summit attendees July day after July day became a conventional Noah's Ark of prominent Americans—except for academics. Eight governors came first, then six "wise men"—Clark Clifford, Lane Kirkland, and Sol Linowitz among them. On July 8, a mixed bag of leftover governors, oil executives, and university presidents (Jerome Wiesner of M.I.T. and John Sawhill of New York University being the most prominent) arrived—the so-called energy group. July 9 was Congress's day, with eleven senators and eleven representatives in attendance. July 10 made clear that of all scholarly advisers, only economists were still valued—or, more precisely, only economists who had achieved public or political notoriety such as Klein, Okun, Whitman, Heller, Sommers, and, of course, Galbraith. A religious delegation (skewed heavily to the Baptists) followed, with one Berkeley sociologist thrown in. On July 11 twenty-two visited Camp David—six governors, four state legislators, nine mayors, another economist (Columbia's Eli Ginsberg), and labor and business representatives. Carter flew to Carnegie, Pennsylvania, and Martinsburg, West Virginia, on July 12 to meet with "common folk" families and returned on July 13 to lunch with seventeen journalists, counting Walter Cronkite, who arrived late.[50]

On July 15, Carter delivered his best-remembered national address, now known as the "malaise" speech, although the word never appeared in the prepared text. Over the strenuous objections of Eizenstat and Mondale, the Camp David ruminations had come down on the side of philosophy and not policy, with the issue of energy tacked on at the end. "This specific program will begin to solve this bigger problem," is how participants remembered the address. Overwhelmingly, the "crisis of confidence" theme prevailed. Although the initial public reaction was favorable, as the message sank in Americans came to understand that the president elected to office pledging to rebuild a government "worthy of the American people" had concluded that the people weren't good enough. It was not a politically viable philosophy.[51]

Before his speech, Carter spent the afternoon with his communications adviser, Gerald Rafshoon, and his pollster, Patrick Caddell. Presumably the last word on the condition of America—its economic and social health, its culture, its wants and needs, and its politics—came from individuals whose skills derived from hand-me-down psychology and sociology simply and often shallowly applied. To be sure, these rhetorical skills are now central components of political campaigns. But they were not social science.[52] Nor, as things turned out for the president, were they satisfactory substitutes for policies that responded to reality. Compared to the rhetoric and public philosophies of JFK and LBJ, the malaise speech was superficial and unsatisfying. Inside experts, as well as outside experts, had lost out decisively and with Iran and the hostages waiting in the wings, the Carter administration stumbled inconclusively to its end.

Bootlegging New Policy: Two Last Flings

To record the substantial decline of the academics as an important intervening elite in national domestic policy during the Carter era is not to suggest that disaster befell the republic. A series of unhappy events combined to bedevil what Jones has termed the "trusteeship presidency" of Jimmy Carter. Hargrove reminds us that many of Carter's difficulties were "manifestations of problems of governance in a 'no-win presidency' characterized by weak parties, fragmented coalitions, voracious interest groups, and unrealistic public expectations . . . He faced extremely difficult contradictions in domestic policy among competing forces in the Democratic camp and his choices in economic policy were seriously constrained by the realities of economic life."[53]

There were no magic elixirs on any university campus to resolve the perplexities of most of the major policies Carter chose to tackle. Indeed, by the mid-1970s, academic experts were wallowing in their own perplexities. Keynesian economics was coming under increasing attack as stagflation persisted. The scathing neoconservative criticism of the public policy of the sixties continued unabated. New philosophical voices were also abroad in the land. They cautioned against the scientific and technological establishment, reasoned a priori that a "new class" of intellectuals and intelligentsia was emerging with a strong cultural and moral basis for transforming the "system," and depreciated experimentation and observation as valid routes to "true" knowledge. These intramural battles left policy-oriented scholars little time to add to the stock of policy ideas developed since the sixties.[54]

Meanwhile, Eizenstat was right in supposing that the new schools of public policy and the emerging policy analysis staffs within the executive branch and Congress had capabilities scarcely visible in earlier administrations and could, if properly tapped, produce new and effective policies. Once stubborn resisters of change and impediments to new policies, the senior civil service elite now had policy-generating capacity of its own. Two cases, one relatively early in the Carter administration and one at the end, showed that the insiders could propose and secure reform as well as the task forces of the sixties. They showed too that the talents and knowledge of outsiders were still tapped, if surreptitiously.

The first was legislation for civil service reform. Technically, the proposal was not an "insider" policy, for the insider who sparked the effort was an "in-and-outer," a prototypical action-intellectual serving for the first time as a full-time presidential appointee. Alan Campbell, newly appointed chair of the Civil Service Commission and later director of personnel management, had been lured to Washington just after he had become dean of the LBJ School at the University of Texas. Earlier, he had been dean of the Maxwell School of Public Administration at Syracuse University and had worked with Nelson Rockefeller as deputy controller of New York state. Campbell's closest political allegiance had been to Robert Kennedy, and he maintained his mainstream Democratic loyalty.[55]

Campbell had met Carter in the 1976 campaign and had, at Eizenstat's request, prepared a memo on federal interns. ("The memo got screwed up, and there was no speech," Campbell recalled; "only a press release.") Campbell was an old hand on Great Society task forces and active with both public interest groups and the Advisory Commission on Intergovernmental Relations in Washington. These organizations recommended him to the White House. After interviews with Jordan, Lance, and Robert Strauss, Campbell met with Carter, who agreed with his proposal for major civil service reform and accepted a seven-page memorandum that Campbell prepared as the basis for legislation. This was, as Jones observed, not a policy brought forward by overwhelming popular demand. Scholars talked about it, good government advocates at every level talked about it, but no political ground swell existed in its behalf. "Here was," in Jones's words, "another 'right thing to do' with no perceivable electoral benefits for Congress or the President."[56]

In a manner unlike most Carter policy practice, Campbell gave almost single-minded attention to the task. With an executive office perspective and an assignment affecting the entire executive branch, he made sure that an able deputy managed the internal affairs of the Civil Service Commission. Campbell himself took the responsibility for developing and advocating the reform agenda. He began in April with a large task force of civil servants. For six months, 120 people reported on departmental and agency problems and issues from every part of the public service.

From these deliberations, Campbell drafted legislation that maintained intact the key concepts of his initial memo—flexibility, decentralization, and the creation of a senior executive service. In October 1977, Carter voiced a public commitment to the reform in a press conference. Senators Abraham Ribicoff and Charles Percy—Democratic and Republican committee leaders on civil service—were persuaded by their staffs to send out a comprehensive questionnaire to "leading lights" in public administration. With supportive feedback from the questionnaire, the endorsement of the National Academy of Public Administration (the peer group for theoreticians and practitioners of public organization), a small group of corporate vice presidents as personnel, and satisfactory negotiations with the key federal service unions, Campbell was ready to move.

By 1978, the administration committed itself to a presidential message on civil service reform. Released on March 2, its legislation followed the next day. Campbell, according to his own account, had assembled "a range of support a mile wide but an inch deep."[57] Accordingly, having shaped the legislation largely on his own, he gave full attention to the interagency task force the White House congressional liaison staff had formed. Campbell encouraged "a full court press," and on October 13 his program became a law incorporating the most fundamental change in government organization in a century. As Campbell wryly observed, "No intellectual of high stature was involved anywhere down the line unless you count me." Yet he had two bases for his authority and clout—not only a presidential appointment with Senate confirmation but twenty years of distinguished scholarship in the precise field of his responsibilities as well. Coordination and a consistent central theme came easily in these circumstances.

The second "bootlegged" policy was the Youth Employment program, popular with Congress but, having been proposed at the end of Carter's term, not enacted before time ran out. The principal actor was Peter Edelman, by his own account "a quasi-academic . . . a closet intellectual."[58] A distinguished graduate of Harvard Law School who taught law at Georgetown and is now associate dean, Edelman is a scarce commodity in national politics—a reliable, enormously attractive, reassuring, and skillful bridge person between politicians and experts. Ever since his early years as principal staff assistant to Robert Kennedy, Edelman demonstrated a rare capacity for translating complex but effective proposals for solving important domestic problems into politically viable, popularly understandable language. He had served as "idea chief" for Arthur Goldberg in his New York senatorial race and played the same role in the presidential campaigns of Walter Mondale and Edward Kennedy. His record and reputation were especially strong in urban affairs, education, and disadvantaged youth; he had begun to investigate the last topic while working with Robert Kennedy. After directing New York State's Youth Services Program, Edelman had returned to Washington to practice law in a firm from his home state of Minnesota early in Carter's administration. Through his client search, he secured a modest contract in 1979 with the newly established Vice President's Task Force on Youth Employment.

At the time, the Carter administration, though enfeebled, was more seasoned, ready for a last legislative go-round. The idea of the task force had actually come from William Spring, a senior-level analyst in the DPS and himself a refugee from the Great Society. Edelman joined Spring as a consultant and in turn brought in another "idea type," Tom Glenn. What emerged was a policy process that mixed outside and inside participation. Although an interagency task force was established, it never met. Spring had witnessed the consequences of passive departmental foot-dragging in DPS, and the interagency task force thus served only as an informational medium. In that way, the task force avoided the debilitating "lowest common denominator" effects of the Carter interagency groups that had gone before.[59]

Two factors account for the effectiveness of the youth employment task force. First, its quasi-independent staff wrote all major proposals. Department and agency representatives functioned as liaisons to their own organizations, testing out propositions and reporting back but never initiating them. Accordingly, no seed catalog of inconsistent, equally weighted proposals appeared. Second, all key actors signed on in advance. What transpired, in Edelman's words, was "a five-ring circus . . . We invited academic papers, we sought out major discussions with principal interest groups such as mayors and governors, we held public hearings and organized conferences to stimulate public interest. We continuously engaged the staffs of key committees on the Hill, and we briefed the media. We received policy memos from the departments and agencies, but we never used them. We steered clear of the two bêtes noires of youth employment—

vocational education and community-based organizations—though we pieced them off with a minimum budget."[60]

In September, Edelman wrote the major policy memorandum describing the process by which mostly poor, mostly urban adolescents could make an effective transition from school to work. Its form was an amendment to an existing and popular law, the Elementary and Secondary Education Act of 1965. Its central provisions were logical and linked: remedial education in basic skills, support for public agencies building effective bridges to the world of work, and partnership with community-based private industrial councils to match trainees to jobs. In its coherent and clear theme, the plan reassembled the best of Great Society programs. A "glossy" report released with fanfare brought almost unanimous acclaim.

"All interests were aboard," Edelman remembers, "all we ran out of was time. A year earlier, the youth employment amendments would have sailed through . . . Now Iran, the election, a Congress not responsive to a president (the way it had been in LBJ's last few months when the 'blockbuster' 1968 Housing Act was enacted) all conspired to block consideration. Carter had finally gotten it right, but too late."[61]

Civil service reform and the youth employment program were not the only examples of effective policy-making under Carter. As Jones shows, the president's overall batting average in roll-call votes was better than the Nixon-Ford era, and not too far behind Johnson's spectacular record.[62] In foreign affairs, there were genuine successes—the Camp David negotiations with Israel and Egypt, the Panama Canal treaties—and, in the end, a reasonably workable energy package was enacted. But the perceived overload on Congress, especially in the early years, and the inability to move prime measures such as welfare reform, hospital cost containment, and tax reform created a reputation for failure. With it came the conclusion that a trusteeship presidency—aloof from the rough-and-tumble of congressional politics, responding to the new "consolidation" issues of the day, uncomfortable with political bargaining, trade-offs and piece-offs—could not be sustained in contemporary Washington. "Carter was," in Jones words, "a circumstantial president."[63]

Yet even in the inhospitable 1970s, civil service reform and the youth employment program indicate that policy built on social science knowledge, with a consistent internal logic and thrust, could survive. Neither was global in concept, neither was ideological. One was based on political scientists' sustained observation and evaluation of the executive branch since Franklin Roosevelt's time. Historical understanding, as well as contemporary organizational theory, went into Campbell's first memorandum and carried through to the final legislation. The youth employment program represented Edelman's best synthesis of a generation of ideas about youth behavior, poverty, learning processes, community group action, and employment practices. While certainly not highly visible, both continued the approach of the action-intellectuals Theodore White had identified in the early sixties. They eschew general theories of society born of dialogue and dialectic, they look for reliable observations and experiments, and they proceed with a respect for facts. In Edelman's words, they "tackle problems that you can get your hands around."[64] Though criticized, subdued, and in part supplanted by insiders with equivalent credentials, academic experts remained in the wings of public policy—and occasionally on stage.

The Policy President: All by Himself

There is still the final factor in assaying the respective roles of intervening elites in policy-making during the Carter years—the president himself. What the literature and staff recollections of his administration reveal is more than a policy agenda put together by insiders who labored under extraordinary difficulties. Stipulate a professional Executive Office of the President enfeebled by Lance's departure, academics back on their campuses in disarray and under attack, a political outsider in a sullen if not mutinous Washington, a Congress still reacting querulously to the Nixon imperial presidency. Stipulate too, a hostile economic and social environment in which both peace and prosperity seem in peril, an intransigent Soviet Union, an arrogant OPEC, sharply climbing inflation, and barely measurable productivity gains. These forces combined to make forging presidential policy a hard job. Still, the record is not complete if it does not recognize Carter's determination to be his own chief policymaker, to do it "all by himself."

Erwin Hargrove makes this presidential determination the central theme of his research. In his exploration of Carter's "policy leadership," he finds a president suspicious of interest groups and therefore of a public interest fashioned through a compromise of the separate claims. Rather, Carter's focus was on "public goods" and "the public good." Accordingly, the right policy arose from a combination of "study and good will." "A planner and a moralist . . . Carter preferred a comprehensive proposal . . . that deals with all facets of a problem." So Carter "fashioned executive decision-making processes to emphasize homework and free discussion, putting himself at the center of this process, since he was to make decisions. He was not comfortable with intermediaries who might stand between him and the process of exploration and discussion but preferred to work directly with small groups of advisers."[65] "Collegiality" (working with a small group) and "homework" (delving into all details himself) were the twin principles Hargrove found in analyzing Carter's "policy leadership," as he undeniably placed new issues on the public agenda.

But these principles carry consequences that, unless anticipated and managed, ensure policy disasters. The quality of colleagues and their advice, and hence the quality of the homework, and the capacity of the student to assess and recognize the problem and the limitations of one's research are bedrock essentials. In the Carter administration neither quality nor capacity met the requirements.

The most severe critique falls on Carter's colleagues, the Georgians in the White House. Lloyd Cutler's observation that more academics were farmed out throughout the executive branch as presidential appointees than in any other administration appears to be correct. But John Gardner is also correct to note that these administrators found it hard to function as "idea people" as the pressures of office descended upon them. With his strongest Georgian, Lance, out of action early and with the executive office accordingly sidelined, the burden of policy-making fell on the necessarily political White House. More important, while Eizenstat clearly matched Sorensen, Goodwin, Moyers, Califano, and Ehrlichman in intelligence and judgment, he initially lacked access to the president, and he foreswore access to the academic experts his predecessors had assembled. As Fallows commented in 1979: "Stuart Eizenstat . . . was pleasant and less high strung and vain than Brzezinski; everyone liked Stu. But as Eizenstat himself admitted, he was a skilled version of an unimaginative breed. He would give you a lucid diagnosis of the four options placed before him, but would be the last man to suggest that some unlisted fifth option might be the necessary answer."[66] Lawyerlike, composed, and consistent, Eizenstat was the best the White House offered in policy-making, except, perhaps, for Watson. But like Watson, Eizenstat was put down in the end at Camp David. The quality of Carter's advice was thus neither fully imagined nor realized.

As for Carter himself, his limitations as a student became generally acknowledged. "Carter's skills were well matched to the tackling of specific problems in which his capacity for mastery of details . . . could make an important difference . . ." Hargrove writes, yet "his strategic leadership had a disjointed character . . . His capacity for leadership caused him to treat decisions in isolation from each other."[67] Jones's analysis of Carter's capabilities is similar. "When he judged an issue to be his, he considered it his duty to master the details. He wanted to understand the issue as well as any member of Congress did . . . Carter thought Congress should support the President because he spent time on an issue, demonstrated public support, and personally avoided the strictly political in his definition."[68]

Accepting so much urgent homework is a heavy burden, even after Carter authorized speed-reading sessions in the White House. Fallows too viewed Carter as not up to the task. "Carter's cast of mind: his view of problems as technical not historical, his lack of curiosity about how the story turned out before" limited his ability to respond effectively to issues, Fallows argued:

> Carter came into office determined to set a national plan for his time but soon showed in practice that he was still the detail man used to running his own warehouse, the perfectionist accustomed to thinking that to do a job right you must do it yourself . . . After six months had passed Carter learned that this was ridiculous . . . but his preference was still to try to do it all—to complain that he was receiving too many memos and that they were too long, but to act nonetheless on everything that reached his desk . . . He said "unless there's a holocaust, I'll take care of everything the same day it comes in."[69]

Fallows explained why he had originally signed on for Carter in the campaign and why, toward the end of the administration, he felt compelled to kiss and tell.

> I thought he had learned from hard experience about the perils of organization life . . . that . . . he would stay one step ahead of staff jealousies, information blockages, monopolization of his time. When I heard him recommend, early in the campaign, repealing the mortgage tax deduction, I assumed that Carter must have thought deeply about the tax system . . . When I read his famous Law Day speech of 1974 . . . I thought he must understand the excesses of a legal system which siphons off so much of the nation's talent . . . When Carter spoke about a strong defense but promised to cut five billion or more from the defense budget, I took it not as campaign hyperbole but as proof that he recognized the danger of setting military budgets by ideology or platitude . . . Perhaps this list is a testament to nothing more than my naivete . . . but by the time Bert Lance resigned as budget director in September, 1977, most of the original hopes had departed as well. These weren't the tips of icebergs we were seeing (indicating vast, hidden extensions below); they were pieces of ice."[70]

Whether they were pieces of ice or icebergs, and whatever the quality of Carter's mind, his administration could not make an effective transition from broad and moral goals to policies that were politically acceptable and programmatically workable. The thirst for ideas in policy development that Johnson cultivated, for example, did not depend on Johnson's grasp of detail. "Go do something for poor mothers in slums," might well have been the extent of LBJ's initial involvement. Indeed, no president successful in domestic affairs has done much homework except as a translator from problem to solution, from cost-benefit analysis to the demands of the political arena—or has demonstrated a taste for much more than, as

James Burns has put it, "blarney, boodle, and bludgeon." Carter, until the end, disclaimed such a critical assignment.

Relying chiefly on politically seasoned veterans, "non-idea" people, for his major initiatives in energy and welfare reform, filtering their proposals belatedly through the Georgians, and then closeting himself away to make the final judgments, Carter imposed an isolation that, with few exceptions, guaranteed the failure of policy. He discovered too late that in this complex world driven by science and technology, one cannot rely on modern rhetoric—or upon ideology. One must work problem by problem, policy by policy, with those who have spent their careers coming to know "what can be done" or what "people will accept" rather than "what ought to be done." Ultimately the self-confidence and stubbornness that won Carter the presidency were the qualities that limited and depreciated his time in office.

6

TAKEOVER:
THE REAGAN RECESS

The Quick Consensus

Within two years after Ronald Reagan left the presidency, more than ninety books—including his own autobiography—had appeared about the man and his administration. Written from various perspectives, ranging from superficial memoirs of insiders to serious scholarly analyses, these accounts come to at least one common conclusion. Reagan was a man of beliefs, not ideas, "a stubborn dreamer, a radical reformer," Barrett Seaman wrote, with "vivid and clearly defined views of the world," quite capable of ignoring and then plowing through "the loose gravel of facts and consequences that life kicks up along the way."[1]

The fortieth president's mangling of facts, his penchant for leadership by allegory and anecdote, his absence of intellectual curiosity, and his failure to articulate a national purpose were detectable early in his first term. As David Stockman directed the first drastic round of budget reductions in 1981, he confessed, "None of us really understand what's going on with these numbers."[2] Writing in 1984, John Palmer and Isabel Sawhill found at work a simplistic philosophy: "that economic growth will flow from the inherent entrepreneurial spirit of enterprise of the American people; that social problems can be largely solved by church, family, and neighborhood; that freedom is the greatest national asset and that its protection requires, above all, military strength."[3]

In 1987, in his sixth book on an American president, Gary Wills portrays Reagan as uncritically embracing the myths of the market and the frontier, the "perfect carrier" of the American legend of a genuinely New World, individualistic and optimistic, forever young. "Never a boy genius," Wills writes of the actor turned politician, but surely at home "in the place

139

where legends of boy geniuses were fabricated . . . He is an icon . . . a durable daylight 'bundle of meanings' "—that is, a myth.[4]

By 1990, Larry Berman had termed Reagan's presidency "a legacy of paradoxes" in which ideology confronts pragmatism, "a choreographed Presidency . . . a performer with beliefs."[5] Stephen Weatherford and Lorraine McDonnell push the point more explicitly viewing the Reagan era as "an ideological presidency . . . a cluster of ideas . . . the lodestone against which options can be compared in particular situations," and in Reagan's case, "two central beliefs—individualism and populism."[6]

So, the consensus runs, secure in his convictions, maintaining a short and simple public agenda, unencumbered by complex analyses of complex issues, Reagan was content to reside passively in the Oval Office. Except when he cared intensely about a given issue, he seldom reached out for the views of others and maintained a "hands-off" management style. Whenever his key fiscal commitment was concerned, according to Stockman, Reagan was as far above the detail work of supply-side economics as a ceremonial monarch is above politics. In short, "Dr. Feelgood," "the Gipper," "the Great Communicator" excelled in projecting an image and provoking a reaction, but his style never invited intellectual response or measured debate. Single-minded and stable in his conviction about how the world worked, Reagan persisted in pursuing public policies that most biographers and commentators viewed to have been far removed from reality.

Second Thoughts on the Consensus

Given this practically unanimous judgment about the ideological source of Reagan's ideas—essentially an overriding commitment to capitalism, American style—its triumph over pragmatism and empirical knowledge is impressive. It is also deceptive, for it suggests that the three kinds of talk that carry presidential messages from campaign to government proceed in isolation. In fact, however, such linguistic purity had rarely been found in any of the administrations that had gone before, and the ideas that shaped Ronald Reagan's talk were less pure than commentators perceived. The interaction of rhetoric, ideology, and knowledge in the 1980s was, in fact, particularly complex.

Distinguished, credentialed, Nobel Prize–winning social scientists signed on with Ronald Reagan from the beginning of his 1976 presidential campaign and flocked to his banner in greater numbers by 1980. Martin Anderson, who earlier had served as Nixon's director of research and White House aide, reappeared to organize and direct Reagan's search for and use of academic experts in both the 1976 and the 1980 campaigns. Holding an M.I.T. doctorate in industrial management, Anderson had served on Rockefeller's Critical Choices for Americans Commission and was then employed as an economist at the Hoover Institution on war, revolution, and peace in Stanford, California. Now he built on both his campaign and White House experience with Nixon and his network of fellow Rockefeller panel members to structure Reagan's advisory groups. In this, his second time around, Anderson's sweep of universities and consulting firms was impressive. There were carryovers from the Nixon era—most prominently Richard Allen, Alan Greenspan, and George Shultz—but there were new faces in both campaigns.[7]

The 1976 effort, by Anderson's account, was a catch-as-catch-can affair. Anderson himself only signed on after a dinner at Toberio's in Washington, D.C., on October 16, 1975, with John Sears, Lyn Nofziger, and Jeffrey Bell. Ten days later, he joined the campaign team meeting at the Beverly Wilshire Hotel in Los Angeles. With only selective briefings and uncertain about the availability of some experts, Anderson came to conclude that "Reagan's 1976 Presidential campaign had only a skeleton staff of researchers and speech writers. . . . Basically, the governor did not have the kind of policy and speech writing support that is minimally necessary to run an effective Presidential campaign. . . . Perhaps our greatest deficiency in 1976 was the lack of an in-depth policy development and speech writing team that could provide support material to the Governor."[8]

Anderson set out to ensure that the same mistakes were not made in the 1980 campaign. In the summer of 1978, he gave Reagan's top campaign staff a checklist of the functions of the National Campaign Research Headquarters, including "in depth policy papers on all major cases, criticisms of Democrats' policies, a truth squad, and the establishment of 20 to 25 campaign task forces, composed of 15 to 20 members each."[9] For the key policy/speech-writing team, Anderson identified four who met another set of explicit criteria—longtime support of Reagan, basic philosophical agreement with the candidate, prior presidential campaign experience, substantial government experience, excellent writing skills, a wide range of media contacts, youth, and being "nice people to work with."[10]

On August 17, Anderson sent Reagan a six-page memorandum on the uses and structuring of task forces that made Sorensen's and Califano's formats for Kennedy and Johnson look primitive by comparison. The memo identified the principal value of task forces to "wrestle with policy issues which have become so complex that few, if any, individuals have the knowledge and the skill to deal with them alone." These task forces were thus to provide an intellectual "'critical mass' to cope with problems of this magnitude." The memo went on to point out that by becoming acquainted with "literally hundreds of the country's top experts," a valuable pool of talent would emerge, and the national media would become aware that Reagan had his own share of the "best and the brightest," a "wealth of talent" to counterbalance "the resources of an incumbent president."[11]

The memorandum then detailed the composition, logistics, and timing of a typical task force and reviewed the experience of both campaign and presidential task forces since the Johnson administration. In arguing for publicizing task force membership but keeping the reports themselves confidential, Anderson sought a midway position between the Johnson and Nixon experiences. Reagan concurred, and on April 20, 1980, well ahead of Anderson's original timetable, he announced the names of sixty-eight foreign policy and defense advisers.[12] A month later Anderson had compiled a working list of 155 potential domestic and economic policy advisers, of whom 106 ultimately signed on.

The collective profile of these advisers was quite different from those of earlier campaigns, either for Democratic or Republican presidential candidates. There were substantially fewer women (seven) and minorities (six). Regional differences were even more striking. The Cambridge concentration was decisively broken—only three of the one hundred and six task force members came from Massachusetts, only five more from the rest of New England. Old Washington hands—seventeen former cabinet and subcabinet officials and Beltway think-tank senior members—were strongly represented. The task forces included sixteen New Yorkers, including business and financial advisers as well as academics. Eastern advisers still accounted for 44 percent of the total, but California now claimed 36 percent and the South and Midwest together claimed the remaining 20 percent of task force membership.

Twenty-six academic institutions were represented in the task forces, but now the core of brainpower was Palo Alto. Nine of Anderson's colleagues from the Hoover Institution and six Stanford faculty were included. Three more task force members were from the University of California, Los Angeles, and the University of California-Santa Barbara, Claremont College, and California State University-Hayward contributed one each. In sharp contrast, Harvard was represented by only three domestic advisers; there the Cambridge network stopped. Yale and Dartmouth faculties offered two advisers each, but then New England disappeared. The universities of Rochester and Chicago provided three each, Carnegie-Mellon and Virginia Polytechnic Institute two each, and a wide scatter of midwestern, mid-Atlantic, and southern institutions, a mix of distinguished institutions such as Michigan, Columbia, Texas, Rutgers, and Emory were also represented. So were scholars from surprising sources such as Temple, SUNY-Buffalo, and East Carolina University.[13]

Throughout the summer, Anderson and his deputy, Darrell Trent, followed the guidelines of the 1978 memo faithfully as they structured the economic and domestic task forces and recruited members. On October 23, 1980, too late in the campaign for the media to notice, the Reagan-Bush Committee announced the formation of twenty-three domestic and economic policy task forces with 329 advisers to join the foreign policy and defense advisers whose ranks had now swelled to 132 individuals organized into twenty-five "working groups." The additions to the domestic roster did not significantly expand the academic component. Indeed, most of the newcomers came from business and government with a particularly strong contingent from congressional staffs. Nonetheless, the task forces would provide grist for the policy mill, by now an inevitable process in presidential transitions. Their reports would serve as counterweight to what the Reagan team regarded as an intransigent bureaucracy, still committed, however surreptitiously, to the liberal agenda.

Acknowledging that the press release inspired in campaign headquarters "an air of bemused tolerance about all these intellectuals running around in a political campaign," Anderson saw three benefits of assembling them. First, they were "on call" when specific questions arose in the course of the campaign, "able to provide small nuggets of information that stopped small policy problems from growing into major political embarrassments."[14] Second, they constituted "a primary pool for talent" for high-level appointments. Third, simply by publicly supporting the candidate, they "gave a powerful boost to credibility." To Anderson, that the campaign staff—and most of the media—did not view the task forces as central to campaign strategy did not diminish their benefits to the candidate.[15]

However bad the timing of the announcement and the lack of public acknowledgment, the assembled experts collectively displayed two attributes that suggest they were more than window dressing. In economics, the social science that would matter most in Reagan's domestic policy-making, Anderson had assembled genuine heavyweights. Noble Prize—winner Milton Friedman had been one of the "charter members of Reagan's economic team since December 1975," when the challenge to Ford began in earnest. So had C. Lowell Harris of Columbia, Richard Muth and Ezra Solomon of Stanford, and Arthur Laffer of the University of California at Los Angeles, whose advocacy of supply-side economics would soon capture media attention. In 1978, Anderson recruited George Shultz, already well known for his cabinet service in the Nixon administration and a highly respected academic who had received his doctorate from M.I.T. and had served as dean of business administration at the University of Chicago.[16]

In 1980, Shultz agreed to chair the Economic Policy Coordinating Committee, overseeing the six economic task forces. The committee consisted of the task force chairs plus six others who were prominent in economic policy, either in government or in the private sector. Like Shultz, the economists on the committee were all recognized and established figures. Arthur Burns had been actively engaged in national policy since Eisenhower's time; Paul McCracken had chaired Nixon's CEA; Alan Greenspan had been a major player for the Republicans since the 1968 election (although he did not formally earn his doctorate from NYU until 1979); Murray Weidenbaum chaired a first-rate economics department at Washington University in St. Louis; and, of course, Milton Friedman had been the foremost spokesman for the libertarian school of Chicago economics for more than a decade. In professional stature and academic influence, these men clearly seemed on a par with their Kennedy/Johnson/Carter counterparts, Samuelson and Harris of Cambridge, and Democratic CEA chairs Walter Heller of Minnesota, Arthur Okun of Yale, and Charles Schultz of Brookings and the University of Maryland.

A second factor enhanced the influence of the coordinating committee: they came together at a time when their discipline appeared in considerable disarray. The Keynesian consensus, forged for the most part after World War II, legitimized government intervention in the economy, however much the specific timing of tax cuts versus increasing public spending was disputed. Toward the end of the 1970s, however, a disenchantment which the Keynesian approach set in within the profession. An influential article by Harvard's Martin Feldstein made the case against demand-oriented policies.[17] Feldstein argued for a greater emphasis on factors that would increase the growth in potential output—such as increased savings and investment, regulatory reform, and reduced taxation of capital income.

Throughout the 1970s, inflation and unemployment had risen together, contrary to the conventional Keynesian doctrine that their simultaneous increase was theoretically implausible. As Anderson was to outline in his campaign Policy Memorandum No. 1, inflation, according to the textbook, came about in a "too hot" economy close to full employment. Unemployment meant a decrease in consumption expenditures and eventually falling prices. But the United States under Carter was experiencing stagflation—spiraling inflation, sluggish productivity rates, and substantial unemployment, all unresponsive to the various policies Carter struggled to put in place.[18]

At the Federal Reserve Board, chairman Paul Volcker prepared to invoke interest rate and money supply policies that appeared to be modeled closely on Friedman's counsel. On campuses across the country, economists vigorously debated the prime causes of stagflation and, more fundamentally, the nature of the post-Keynesian world. Computer forecasts of national economies and new economic models pioneered by Otto Eckstein at Harvard and Lawrence Klein at Pennsylvania tumbled one after another, but economists reached no real agreement as to what government should do next. No longer pledging wholehearted allegiance to demand-oriented Keynesian theory, "mainstream" economics sought increased output and growth through supply incentives. With such turbulence in economic theory, the time was ripe for the counsel of "wise owls," especially if they were successful, self-confident, and worldly.

Historically, of course, economists had always favored the marketplace as the most effective allocator of scarce resources. Moreover, modern presidents from Roosevelt through Carter, including John Kennedy, remained skeptical of the Keynesian revolution. They required repeated persuasion to authorize government intervention, and, though Keynesian advice ultimately prevailed throughout the sixties, no politician was totally satisfied with the outcome. Nixon's early lurches toward a new international economic policy and wage and price controls, as well as Carter's ineffective initiatives, served to underscore the suspicion that an era Keynesian theory could not explain had arrived.

Thus, both national disposition and prevailing circumstances combined to return the coordinating committee to more conventional economic wisdom. Anderson's Memorandum No. 1 had already sketched out the principal components: the policy was to seek as wide a sphere for private-sector decision-making as possible; key sectors of the economy—most prominently, transportation and banking—were to be deregulated; taxes were to be reduced; and enforcement of antitrust laws was to be restrained. Twenty years of government tinkering with market forces had demonstrated the heavy counterproductive hand of the public sector. It was time to restore the marketplace and the production function to their proper roles. Although Say's Law did not reassert itself, Leon Walras and Alfred Marshall and their refined and updated followers were fashionable again. Now, not just the ideologues and rhetoricians trumpeted the virtues of capitalism; intelligent, creative, academically credentialed economists familiar with the Washington scene were also in camp. For the first time since academic experts had appeared on the scene, the intervening elites appeared to carry equal weight.

The fact that the right experts appeared at the right time, in Anderson's view, sharply shifted the terms of their assignment. Instead of devising and advocating policy, persuading presidents of the "salability" of their views, and fencing off the competing arguments of other elites, the policy goals of the three elites harmonized. And no one had to persuade Reagan of the virtues of the marketplace. The person most responsible for creating the economic program that came to be known as "Reaganomics" was in fact Reagan himself. Anderson wrote, "For over twenty years he observed the American economy, read and studied the writings of some of the best economists in the world . . . and he spoke and wrote on the economy, going through the rigorous mental discipline of explaining his thoughts to others."[19]

The issue now was faithful implementation, making sure that the clear vision of the Reagan revolution was not compromised. After the election, in his new position as White House domestic adviser, Anderson arranged for the campaign committee to continue with Shultz as chair but with a new name, the President's Economic Policy Advisory Board, and one new member, Herbert Stein, who had chaired Nixon's CEA after McCracken. Concerned that the execution of economic policy might be compromised by the Treasury Department, OMB, or the Council of Economic Advisors, Anderson conceived the new board "as a secret intellectual weapon, one that could be called upon if Reagan's economic program started to veer off track." On February 10, 1981, the board was formally established. It met six times in the first year with the president, and, despite an effort by Donald Regan to "ambush" it in 1985, it continued throughout the Reagan years. It was, in Anderson's view, an effective "policy choke point"— ensuring that the president heard "directly from private economists who were independently analyzing and judging his policies," but from "inside the Reagan tent."[20]

In effect, at least for the economists, outside domestic policy experts had never had it so good. Over and beyond their institutional outpost of CEA, staffed to do bureaucratic battle with Treasury and the Federal Reserve Board, they constituted another layer of advice superimposed by executive order. They equipped the White House with a capability at least equivalent to what existed anywhere else in the government. In no previous administration had an academic discipline seemed to rise so high: economists were on top as well as on tap.

The question comes, then, how fared these Reagan experts—especially the Coordinating Committee turned Board, the six economic task forces, and the rest of the pack? Certainly, the circumstances were favorable. They had a limited agenda committed to a massive downsizing of government after twenty years of expansion and experimentation, with few if any domestic initiatives. Furthermore, a conscious, articulate strategy developed during the campaign was in place by "the most elaborate transition machinery in history . . . a blizzard of task forces, committees, and teams" who advised Reagan and "a relatively small number of aides and advisers" making the key decisions about personnel, policy, and organization. For the first time, subcabinet appointments were tightly screened for their fidelity to the president's policy. Finally, a "cabinet council" system, with White House staff directly at the table for seven subcommittees of the cabinet, was formally established. These conditions seemed to enhance the probability that the views of the economic brain trust would prevail, as they had in the days of JFK.[21]

Yet for all the thrust toward simplicity in agenda and accountability in implementation, the final result at least in economic policy seemed more ideological than analytical. The new skepticism about demand-oriented Keynesian economics, the revived debate on monetary versus fiscal policy, the advocacy of measures to enhance aggregate supply fell prey to gross oversimplification, distortion, take-overs by political and media figures. In the end, none of the three major domestic reforms the Reagan administration undertook—shrinking the public sector, devolving government to the lower echelons of the federal system, and restoring the marketplace as a major device in urban development—came out as planned. Other elites, other political actors, and other branches of government intervened to produce results that serious policy analysts viewed as a far cry from the vision of economic experts.

Experts at Work: Supply-Side Made Simple

If the boundaries between serious social science and ideology are never clear cut, if ideological goals and values surreptitiously cohabit with empirical analysis, nonetheless the *degree* to which the borders are protected is always important. Harold Lasswell drew the distinction almost thirty years ago when he wrote, "The science of politics states conditions; the philosophy of politics justifies preferences."[22] He went on to state the conditions of contemporary political systems. When dogma overwhelms proof, subverts facts, and the dialectic triumphs over observation, then ideology drives policy. Throughout the 1980s, supply-side economics stood poised at the border.

The theory was born within the domain of mainstream economics or at least linked to the monetary and neoclassical critique of the excessive management of aggregate demand, which had characterized policy since Kennedy. Supply-siders concurred with the majority of conservative economists that Keynesian policy had become increasingly ineffective in the 1970s. They also agreed that recovery required new incentives to entrepreneurship, increased savings and investment rewards for hard work, and that the key to economic recovery was substantial tax cuts. Tax cuts, the argument ran, would raise the return on capital and labor, encourage innovation and productivity, and yield an impressive increase in aggregate supply.

Supply-siders broke with most other economists and moved toward the ideological boundary lines in their additional assertion that a major tax cut could actually *increase* total revenue. The key conceptual notion was the so-called Laffer Curve introduced by Arthur Laffer, a University of Chicago scholar transplanted to California. A member of the advisory board, Laffer had established separate access to Reagan early in the 1980 campaign through Jack Kemp, the principal congressional advocate of the supply-side school. The Laffer Curve purported to demonstrate that when the tax rate exceeded a certain percent (usually identified as 50 percent) the disincentive to work and invest would grow so strong that tax revenues would actually decline. Ergo, if the tax rate were reduced, the best of all possible worlds appeared: an administration could cut taxes, increase productivity, and raise revenue. Who would ask for anything more? It was painless prosperity.*

It is at this juncture that economist Laffer found political company and support from noneconomists strategically placed to popularize and advance the cause. The most politically visible and influential was Kemp, cosponsor of 1977 legislation to cut the mean tax rate by 30 percent. Early in 1980, Kemp arranged for Laffer to meet with Reagan for "a pow wow out in California" and concluded that Reagan had been converted. Joining Kemp and Laffer at that meeting was journalist Jude Wanniski, who had been a supply-side disciple since the early 1970s. Backed by the Richardson Foundation, Wanniski publicly made the supply-side case in *The Way The World Works*, published in 1978.[23] In 1980, in a *Village*

---

*With supply-side economics, I here consider a much-disputed economic theorem about tax incidence and its effect on the level of economic activity. Contemporary textbooks such as those by Samuelson and Lindblom treat the subject respectfully but skeptically, especially with regard to the impact on working and saving. A good analysis is Thomas R. Swartz, Frank J. Bonello, and Andrew F. Kozak, *The Supply-Side: Debating Economic Issues* (Guilford, Conn.: Dushkin, 1983). Anderson devotes a chapter in *Revolution* to "The Legend of the Supply-Sider," 140–63, emphasizing especially the fallacy of expecting aggregate tax revenues to rise. In a letter to me, August 31, 1991, he elaborates on his analysis in *Revolution* and the erroneous rush to judgment on the part of many academic economists: "I know powerful myths are hard to shake, but I have been searching now for over four years and still cannot find any evidence of 'supply-side' economists asserting that if tax rates are cut government revenue will immediately increase over and above what it would have been if those tax rates had not been cut . . . Moreover, the important point is that neither Reagan nor any of his key economic advisers ever acted according to the alleged charge. The 1980 campaign document that officially spelled out the details of Reagan's economic plan predicted only a 17 percent 'flowback' from the proposed tax cut—i.e., as tax rates were lowered the revenue loss would not be dollar for dollar; because of economic growth the tax revenue loss would be only 83 cents, not the full dollar. I'm pretty sure of this because I wrote the document."

Voice interview that Anderson believes introduced "the great myth of the supply-siders," Wanniski, Laffer, and Kemp were described as fighting a "battle for Reagan's mind" against Shultz, Burns, and Friedman. The three supply-siders were depicted as "wild men" arrayed against the establishment.[24]

The political fallout from the *Village Voice* interview had the immediate effect of "dropping" Wanniski from the campaign adviser circle. It also generated a barrage of professional criticism largely from Cambridge economists led by Samuelson and Robert Solow and so vigorously advanced that Anderson openly questioned its fairness and accuracy. Concluding that they were "just plain wrong," Anderson felt that Laffer, Kemp, and Wanniski had unjustly linked the Reagan administration with the perception that a painless solution—growth in public revenue without taxation—was at hand.[25]

Stockman believed that the president accepted the doctrine of "revenue feedback." "The whole California gang," he wrote, "had taken [the Laffer Curve] literally (and primitively)."[26] For his part, however, Anderson felt the administration was never genuinely on board. He asserted on the contrary that to assure Kemp's support at the 1980 convention and in the campaign, Reagan endorsed Kemp's tax proposal "as part of a political deal."[27] With an ironic twist of Gresham's Law, "pure" economics was set aside to allow a politicized version of policy to become accepted as "Reaganomics" (George Bush's 1980 campaign tag line "voodoo economics" also long endured). As Stephen Weatherford and Lorraine McDonnell concluded in 1990, supply-siders were "less economic experts than popularizers and disseminators of a theory."[28] Stockman's judgment was blunter: "All the palaver about growth and gold solving the deficit problem was just that . . . The supply-siders keep pretending that the fiscal truth is escapable, an illusion that makes them more dangerous than ever . . . They are now trying to rescue their free lunch economics with easy money and inflation."[29]

When one sifts through the several versions of the Reagan record, the weight of the evidence seems to fall with Anderson's view. The immediate focus of Reagan's principal economic advisers was to bring inflation under control, even if Paul Volcker at the Federal Reserve Board had already become the point man in that exercise. For the long run, their objectives and the president's were minimalist government, deregulation, and a larger sphere for the workings of the marketplace. Indeed, privatization of formerly public programs and vouchers for housing and education were favorite items on the domestic agenda. Tax cuts were therefore a prerequisite to downsizing the federal government, but a balanced budget was also a necessity.

Reagan's senior neoclassical advisers became especially concerned as the deficit grew. Martin Feldstein in particular would break openly with the president and be discharged from his post as chair of the CEA. The monetarists also expressed concern, though their focus remained on the money supply and interest rates. David Stockman's dissent intensified as the "magic asterisk" in his budgets promising "future savings to be identified" proved to be an empty citation. Unable to persuade the president to cut defense spending or enhance revenues or to talk Congress into further domestic reductions, Stockman's position as OMB director became untenable. Convinced that "the fundamental reality of 1984 was not the advent of a new day, but a lapse into fiscal indiscipline on a scale never before experienced in peacetime," he left Washington in August 1985.[30]

As the supply-side tax cuts failed to provide an equivalent revenue feedback, the president was not as despairing about the deficit as either Feldstein or Stockman. In Weatherford's and McDonnell's judgment, "This area was not central to Reagan's economic ideology. For Ronald Reagan, reducing the budget deficit provided yet another rationale for shrinking the size of the Federal government, but he never regarded it as an economic policy goal in and of itself."[31] In short, while the 1981 tax and budget cuts and the 1986 tax reform were critical to Reagan's economics and were accordingly pieces of legislation on which he took the initiative, the deficit was not. To Reagan, deficit reduction was instrumental to the "minimalization" of the public sector, but it was not a matter for strategic concern like inflation, productivity, or private investment patterns.

The final Reagan resolution of the deficit issue, at least in theoretical terms, was more political than economic. To be sure, economist James Buchanan has gained Nobel fame for discovering and reporting to his colleagues that by paying due attention to their constituencies and therefore their own reelection, most congressmen simultaneously favor tax cuts and budget increases in their favorite programs. Yet this is essentially a truism derived from and demonstrated by political science, and Anderson had come to the same conclusion as early as Policy Memorandum No. 1. After disposing of the long-established "myth" of trade-off between inflation and employment and recommending tax and spending cuts and deregulation, the 1979 memorandum concluded with an "Economic Bill of Rights."[32] Anderson proposed that these five rights be incorporated in a single constitutional amendment imposing a ceiling on federal expenditures, mandating a balanced budget, giving line-item veto power to the president, forbidding wage and price controls, and requiring a two-thirds vote of Congress on all major spending bills. These proposals became constants in the Reagan creed, and as late as the spring of 1987 Anderson—by then back at the Hoover Institution—was called on to expand the 1984 version of his original memorandum.[33]

In the end, then, supply-side economics was politicized not only in practice (to which Stockman fell prey) but also in theory. If tax cuts cannot
produce painless equilibrium, and if the pluralism of interest groups and
congressional lobbies remains too spendthrift to collaborate in budget
limits, then constitutional discipline must be imposed. That is not a
theoretical economic concept. Certainly, it was not the doctrine Reagan's mainstream economists, however conservative, embraced. With the
White House political realists, they came to the reluctant conclusion that
more taxes were in order. It was left to the succeeding administration of
George Bush to accept this judgment, dispose of "voodoo economics,"
and, with Congress in the car seat, renege on his own first campaign
pledge of "no new taxes." To Reagan's principal economic experts, this
consequence had been foreseen, and the president forewarned.

Experts at Work: The New New Federalism

If supply-side economics distorted sensible advice and so unbalanced the
national budget, there was another way out of the dilemma of too-big and
too-costly government in Washington. That option was a structural, political one—a massive devolution of government to the states and localities.
Programs nationally initiated and in large measure nationally financed
could be sent back downstairs in the American federal system.

Even more than Reagan's initial economic policy, his "new Federalism"
reflected the consensus judgment of scholars and practitioners. In the
words of the prestigious Advisory Commission on Intergovernmental Relations (ACIR), the permanent, nonpartisan monitor established by Congress in 1959, "The tripartite system involving shared and separate powers among the federal, state, and local levels of government is in trouble."
On the first page of its 1980 summary report, the commission cited the
conclusion of Daniel Elazar, the preeminent political scientist in the
study of federalism, that "the American people and their representatives
are very much lost in the woods, or at least, seriously bewildered."[34]

"The current network of intergovernmental relations has become dan-
gerously overloaded, . . ." the ACIR report observed, "as a consequence of a
rapid expansion in the overall scope, range of specific concerns, and
coercive character of the federal role in the federal system."[35] The "overload" had been created by both the sharp increase in the amount of federal
grants-in-aid and the proliferation of grant programs between 1960 and
1980. Federal grants to state and local governments rose from $7 billion to
$88 billion in those twenty years—from 2.0 percent to 3.4 percent of the
Gross National Product and, more significantly, from a 15 percent share of
total state-local expenditures to 23 percent. The number of programs

jumped even more dramatically, from 132 to about 530 (the exact count seemed in doubt in 1980). The amount of federal revenue flowing directly to local governments had increased from 8 percent to 25 percent. The fifty states had received 97 percent of federal funds in 1960. By 1980, more than sixty thousand "subnational" governments were receiving federal money. Federal regulations to audit and monitor the disbursements grew accordingly, from less than ten to more than one hundred each year; by 1980, 1,259 rules governed federal grants-in-aid. Another index of regulation is the *Federal Register*, which soared from twenty thousand pages a year in 1960 to sixty thousand in 1980. Finally, "off-budget" credit assistance—loans and loan guarantees to state and local governments amounted to $221 billion in 1979.[36]

What moved these fiscal statistics from the pages of scholarly journals and government reports to the pages of daily newspapers and onto television and radio news shows were accounts of redundancy and apparent largesse in these programs. It was not the big-ticket items—transportation, social security, or even welfare and employment programs—that caught the public eye. Instead, it was the "silly" little programs—eleven federal agencies funding local fire departments in fifty-two separate programs, $2.3 billion in support of local libraries, and finally, reportedly at the initiative of New York City, federal aid for pothole repair. Cumulatively these stories pushed a political hot button and made a dry and dull academic speciality a front-page topic or a catchy sound bite.

Lyndon Johnson's "creative federalism" had embraced the concepts of cooperation, of partnership and mutual interdependence, of shared national and state purpose, and of fiscal equity. Richard Nixon's support of general revenue sharing as an improved model of "New Federalism" was based on the same ideas. But these principles seemed almost absurd by the time Reagan took office. Four hundred and twenty categorical grant programs accounted for only 10 percent of the total federal aid package, but each came with separate needs, regulations, and management. ACIR's conclusion that government had "gone awry" and that "decongestion" of the federal grant system was "long overdue" seemed amply demonstrated.[37] Given these perhaps inevitable by-products of program expansion and neoconservative disparagement of the Great Society, few informed observers could quarrel with President Reagan when he announced in his first inaugural address that he intended "to cut the size and influence of the federal establishment and to demand recognition of the distinction between the powers granted to the federal government [and] those reserved to the states or to the people." Even those who were committed to the domestic reform programs of the 1960s were troubled by the cumbersome and frequently malfunctioning systems that delivered their services.

Reagan's announcement of yet another new "New Federalism" as the centerpiece of his 1982 inaugural address was thus well within mainstream administrative theory and political counsel. There was less consensus, however, on his effort to restrict the size of the public sector and to shift the public expenditure burden to subnational partners. Yet at a minimum, both strategies seemed to some degree plausible ways to cope with the deficit the supply-siders had handed him. If he had inherited both an intergovernmental system that, in the words of Urban Institute senior associate George Peterson, "in many respects was frustratingly out of control" and a presidency turned imperial under Nixon and ineffective under Ford and Carter, devolution of public authority seemed an eminently reasonable idea.[38]

Reagan's new version of New Federalism came in three specific parts. The first, an explicit plan for sorting out government responsibilities and functions, was a "purist" vision of intergovernmental relations harking back to pre-New Deal notions of "dual federalism" during a time when the tubs of state and nation stood on their own sovereign bottoms. Here Reagan proposed that the states assume responsibility for the basic income support programs (Aid to Families with Dependent Children [AFDC] and food stamps), while the federal government took over Medicaid entirely. Additionally, sixty-one smaller grant programs would be transferred to the states together with a comparable amount of tax revenue. This "swapping" exercise went considerably beyond ACIR recommendations and envisioned a clear-cut reduction in Washington's domestic policy role.[39]

The two other components of the new New Federalism were reducing and restricting public spending consistently at every level and simplifying program implementation. The latter was to be achieved chiefly by packaging the almost five hundred categorical grant programs in "block" grants covering broad policy areas and giving the states the chief responsibility for managing operations. Local governments' access to Washington was to be limited sharply.

In both reducing spending and consolidating programs, the Reagan administration achieved substantial success. In the first two years, the total number of federal grants dropped by 27 percent and project grant obligations by 31 percent.[40] Grants to state and local governments between 1978 and 1983 fell by 20 percent, from $49 billion to $39 billion in constant dollars. As a percent of the domestic federal budget, grants returned to the 1960 level. Fifty-four previously categorical grants were consolidated into nine block grants, with an overall $6.6 billion cut in projected expenditure—an average cut of 25 percent.[41]

An early reckoning of the impact of budget reductions and simplified management showed that the Reagan strategy of restricting public expenditures at every level was working. Studying the budgetary impact on fourteen states and forty local governments in 1983, Richard Nathan and Fred Doolittle found that few federal funding cuts were replaced by state and local funds; nonfederal funds replaced federal dollars most frequently in well-off places or generally liberal state and local governments. The most pronounced effects, the early study showed, "have been on people, especially the working poor."[42] A year later, however, states and localities anted up their own money much more vigorously. Eleven states had fully replaced federal cuts in social services, twelve in drug abuse, and nine in health services. The change from categorical to block grants, which theoretically should have reduced the incentives for state spending and changed priorities according to state circumstances, was having the reverse effect. States were beginning to substitute their own dollars for federal ones, and their priorities seemed roughly the same.[43]

By 1985, a pattern emerged in which entitlements for the middle class were well preserved, essentially on a national scale. On the other hand, urban minority populations continued to carry the major burden of the cuts in federal grant programs. They were adversely affected both as program clients and public-sector employees. To the degree that minorities represented a growing political force, first in urban and then in state politics, they triggered a continuing countervailing response to the Reagan effort to reduce domestic spending. The pattern Peterson detected in 1984 accelerated throughout the decade, supported by the surpluses that state and local governments received as unexpected windfalls from their consumer-oriented tax systems, while the federal deficit grew. Although states frequently reduced taxes in this era of prosperity, they also continued to replace federal funds in substantial measure. The time of genuine reckoning throughout the federal system did not arrive until 1990. Then, facing a recession turning into a depression, states in region after region faced fiscal deficits and political crises. Telltale signs were evident as early as 1986. State and local debt had doubled since 1980, from $334 to $705 billion, and expenditures almost doubled in those six years, from $342 to $604 billion.[44]

In budget and management terms, then, the new New Federalism at least applied a brake on expansive tendencies. Yet its third objective—the devolution of government, the permanent "swap" of functions—never materialized. This goal was, of course, the most radical part of the overall strategy, seeming to most political scientists as the Laffer Curve seemed to economists—a concept at the boundary line between fact and ideology. It was an idea that could be resolved not by debate or discourse among political theorists but in the crucible of pluralistic politics. Here, as Peterson observed, "The New Federalism debate . . . tested for the first time how large a constituency there was for devolution among directly affected interest groups, among the states and localities that would inherit new responsibilities, and among taxpayers. The results of this test were decisive. They revealed virtually no constituency for a devolution of basic Federal authority, but strong support for devolution of implementation responsibilities."[45]

Ideology was thus put down as governors, mayors, and affected constituencies examined program after program and decided not only that they did not want to assume the burdens of federal authority but also that these programs involved national interest. In their view, setting eligibility standards and income maintenance payments state by state would trigger a competitive economic race akin to domestic mercantilism, and the states would come to resemble a herd of carnivores around the last waterhole. Neither did governors, mayors, or interest groups clamor for a devolution of regulatory powers. To the surprise of the administration, business did not seek—indeed, it opposed—the delegation of regulatory authority for product liability, hazardous waste, and environmental protection. The private sector viewed with distaste the possibility of fifty sets of standards replacing a single national policy.[46]

Thus, though the "purist" formulation of an unambiguous swap of functions and separation of responsibilities did not prevail, or, indeed, move beyond the White House talk stage, the fiscal and management goals were substantially realized. For critical programs, costs were shifted to the states and localities who ultimately replaced severe federal cuts with their own funds. The expenditures of local governments were reduced sharply, and the states became the prime recipients of federal funds. Block grants did reduce the number of categorical aid programs and simplified management and oversight procedures. If Reagan had not succeeded in restoring dual federalism, he had at least, in Peterson's words, "succeeded beyond reasonable expectation in resisting new commitments to intergovernmental assistance. A political consensus . . . appears to have been reached that lower levels of government are better off and the Federal system healthier when they possess greater self-sufficiency, both in fiscal resources and policy design."[47]

Although the current recession-driven near-bankruptcy of the states may conceivably call for a return to national programs, the federal deficit escalated by supply-side economics is sure to be a heavy and continuing obstacle to doing so.

Nevertheless, even confirmed liberals such as Paul Ylvisaker, architect of the first Great Society experiments and a Cambridge academic par excellence, was not offended by the new New Federalism. Considering its impact in 1985, he wrote: "The American Federal system is ingeniously contrived: an undulating process of moving programmatically with the times, a digestive mechanism that absorbs partisan ideologies and reduces them to assimilative practicalities. And fortunately, one that is malleable."[48]

Experts at Work: The Triumph of Urban Enterprise

Reagan could rely on respected and responsible academics for counsel and support in shaping much of his economic and intergovernmental policy, and reality in many instances tempered his ideological impulses. But he found no consensus in urban policy. To the contrary, he inherited from Carter's swan song—his Commission for a National Agenda for the Eighties—a rousing endorsement of his instinctive predilection for the marketplace. In the absence of clear expert advice, Reagan's ideology in the urban field could reign unchecked.

Carter's urban policy was made up largely of a laundry list of programs and initiatives left over from the Great Society and repackaged by Nixon. To these were added some early versions of block grants and cross-cutting entitlement regulations. Brought up short by the energy crisis and inflation, appropriations for urban purposes were frozen, and whatever momentum had built during the sixties waned by the mid-1970s. With federal activity at a standstill, Carter's final policy pronouncement followed the example of Dwight Eisenhower in recommending to an indifferent successor policies and strategies he himself had not found possible to carry out. Overall, Carter's Commission for a National Agenda for the Eighties was downbeat on America and especially on government's capacity to cope with the demographic, energy, and environmental crises it foresaw. Specifically, its panel on urban and metropolitan issues challenged the very idea that there were distinctive urban problems, let alone appropriate solutions, and wrote off large cities as matters of concern. At a time when Snow Belt vs. Sun Belt disparities in economic and population growth captured public attention, Carter's commission believed almost perforce that labor mobility would maintain a strong national economy. Displaced auto workers from the Rust Belt should "go with the flow: and settle in Texas to make computer chips." The commission's report declared in flat-out terms, "There are no 'national urban problems,' only an endless variety of local ones. Consequently, a centrally administered national urban policy that legitimizes activities inconsistent with the revitalization of the larger national economy may be ill advised."[49]

Carter's disinclination to develop an urban policy was more the rule than the exception among modern American presidents. Except for the brief years of the Great Society, the nation's attention to its cities had always been bootlegged, smuggled aboard the public agenda under the guise of another overarching national crusade. Housing assistance to the poor and home mortgages for the middle class were New Deal measures designed principally to stimulate economic recovery. Post–World War II housing subsidies that sparked the migration to suburbia were essentially disguised as a veterans' bonus. The urban renewal program of the fifties was a measure of the panic and political power of downtown retail merchants as they watched their customers abandon them for shopping centers near their suburban homes.

In the historical sweep of city-building in the United States, the establishment of HUD in 1965, the Housing and Urban Development Acts of 1966 and 1968, and the mandated annual presidential report on national urban policy were blips on the screen, brief efforts to assert the nation's uncertain interest in its cities. Although the Great Society programs continued until the end of the seventies, federal commitment formally ceased in 1972 when Nixon declared the crisis of the cities to have ended. In its place loomed the crisis of the environment, far more appealing to middle-class political activists than the conditions of the ghetto and the problems posed by the newest wave of urban immigrants. In effect, Reagan could start with a fresh slate.

Aiding and abetting the intellectual renaissance of the marketplace was continuing neoconservative pessimism about the Great Society's efforts. Continuing throughout the seventies, the disciples of Irving Kristol increasingly disdained urban policies and programs. Edward Banfield regarded the situation of the urban poor as hopeless; Daniel Patrick Moynihan pronounced the war on poverty an absurd, quixotic adventure. Nathan Glazer queried the efficacy of affirmative action in hastening the realization of the American melting pot. The essays, articles, expositions, and occasional research studies of neoconservatives dominated the policy debates.[50]

A policy vacuum arose as all past efforts were written off as naive, excessive exercises in social engineering and as the marketplace was once again identified as the preferred instrument for urban development. So the old urban programs were fair game, and a principal target for Stockman's budget exercise. Between 1980 and 1987, the White House cut HUD's operating budget by 57 percent, from $36 billion to $18 billion, and reduced the authorization for assisted housing from $27 billion to $7.5 billion. The administration also sliced the number of new rental housing units from 129,000 to 19,000, dropped public housing authorizations (technically, reservations for financing) 93 percent (from 205,000 to 14,000 units), and advocated a voucher program in which 62 percent of the applicants reported no housing was available.[51]

Meanwhile, throughout the 1980s, the marketplace turned enthusiastically to the task of building two new urban forms—the entrepreneurial city and the urban village. In brief summary,

> The entrepreneurial cities . . . depict the 'hot' urban places where national developers concluded in the 1980s their complex, equity-conditioned, front-loading financial arrangements for commercial ventures which architects enclosed in shining glass towers: Boston's Fanueil Hall, Chicago's Water Tower Place, Baltimore's Inner Harbor, Atlanta's Underground.
>   The urban villages . . . were outer cities: the Princeton Strip in New Jersey, Tyson's Corner outside Washington, Walnut Creek east of San Francisco, Post Oak Galleria next to Houston. They were new office, industrial, retail, housing, entertainment focal points—almost a low density cityscape.
>   Private sector conceived, private sector built, private sector domiciled, entrepreneurial cities [and] urban villages are the new urban places. The buzz words of public policy of the 1980s were public-private partnership."[52]

The Reagan administration did offer a fig leaf to existing urban areas more as a concession to place-oriented public officials and interest groups than to experts—"enterprise zone" legislation. As it had with supply-side economics, the administration endorsed the program at the behest of Jack Kemp, point man for the program throughout the decade. Kemp tried nine times unsuccessfully to secure legislative authorization for enterprise zones. In 1987, he finally achieved a victory of sorts—statutory authority, but without appropriations.[53]

Essentially, enterprise zones were specific poor urban neighborhoods in which public officials and developers were to attempt to generate business activity, either retail or manufacturing. The basic assumptions are that government regulations and/or taxes inhibited urban growth. Originally proposed by the British professor Peter Hall and adopted in 1981 by the new Thatcher government, refined by Stuart Butler of the Heritage Foundation, Enterprise zones are aimed primarily at reducing the costs small businesses incur in older city neighborhoods. The program offers public loans, waivers of local zoning or building code requirements, suspension of tax and wage reporting requirements, outright exemption from certain taxes, grants for new jobs for local residents, and technical marketing assistance to employers. At the core of the concept is the incubator notion of stimulating business innovation and experimentation. The zones are to function as start-up places where space is cheap, labor easily available, and inventions can be transformed into products and successfully marketed.

Congress hesitated and, in the end, provided no substantial legislation on enterprise zones during the 1980s, but thirty-seven states nonetheless found the concept politically attractive. Such zones promised help to small business, which is always politically appealing, and they "did something" in the gray areas where both structures and residents were abandoned. As most of the state programs provided neither subsidies nor significant tax exemptions, they did not cost much; neither after five to ten years had they done much to turn neighborhoods around. Glowing state estimates of job creation and job retention were hard to sustain upon careful examination. Optimistic HUD and Commerce reports were counterbalanced by more sober evaluations from the General Accounting Office.[54] Unless coordinated with physical renewal programs and educational and social reforms, few state programs could demonstrate substantial increases in small business activity. Perhaps the most tangible accomplishment in the national discussion was the establishment of the American Association of Enterprise Zones in Washington, a development that exemplified the great American tradition that every idea has its lobby.

Three university studies confirmed the General Accounting Office's skepticism about state enterprise zones. They found such a paucity of data and such a web of contradictory cause-effect associations as to make any assertion of their success unwarranted. In 1989, even the director of the American Association of Enterprise Zones admitted that "unfortunately there really has not been much more than anecdotal academic research in this field." He went on to suggest that the major value of the program was symbolic, "a positive message to the business community . . . the sign of the city and state that they want these avenues improved . . . a carrot to prompt more activity . . . a Hail Mary pass."[55]

In the parade of witnesses through the Senate and House Committees on Small Business in 1989, congressmen, state and local officials, and trade association representatives appeared by the dozen. But no academic figure was called to testify, and no respectable urban initiative emerged in the Reagan years.

The Revolution on Hold

Looking at the Reagan record in at least three major areas of domestic policy makes clear that the 1980s were not really years of ideological abandon. Ideological talk there was, in abundance, and the president's view of the proper role of government and the liberating power of free enterprise was undeniably simplistic. But in the *execution* of Reagan's goals, as opposed to his articulation of them, a conservative version of the best and the brightest was at hand to turn policies into law and to make significant programmatic changes in the executive branch. The Economic Coordinating Committee-turned-Advisory Board was a group made up mostly of internationally distinguished economists. It was no gang of wild-eyed reactionaries, nor were most of them officeholders with formal responsibilities in economic affairs. The call for a New Federalism, the substantial devolution of responsibilities to the states, and disciplining the federal budget were exercises supported at least in their broadest outlines by a close-to-unanimous roster of expert opinion.

In urban affairs, where no opinion prevailed, or, more precisely, where sharply contradictory policy positions canceled each other out, nothing was done. The Reagan administration simply accepted the counsel of the decade's prevailing academic sentiment that a coherent national urban policy was unfeasible. Time will tell whether the federal government must develop policy for places as well as people, but the academics, not the Reagan administration, must take responsibility for the inaction in this field.

In economic development and tax policy, where ideology in its rawest sense prevailed, either nothing of policy substance occurred in the Reagan years or disaster loomed on the horizon. Reducing the role of government, especially at the federal level, and enhancing the role of the private sector departed from mainstream academic advice in two ways. The first was supply-side economics; here the consequence, to the distress of many of the president's economic advisers, was the deficit. Even here in a post-Keynesian world, there were reputable rationales for transforming the United States from a creditor to a debtor nation. Nonetheless, ideological stubbornness clearly played the major role in the advocacy of supply-side measures, and the Bush administration struggled with that legacy.

It struggled as well with the consequences of the reckless rush to deregulation and the blind commitment to private decision-making which did so much to bring on the savings and loans and HUD scandals. Turning loose inexperienced but greedy private entrepreneurs in the complex world of housing finance has proved disastrous, in the precise meaning of the word. In the stranglehold of ideology, the reality of the marketplace was twisted out of all recognition. In the effort to restructure federalism, however, ideology did not prevail, and the workings of the system in a managerial sense improved.

In short, the pattern of advice and counsel from the social sciences not only persisted in the Reagan administration; it was expanded and, in its implementation, perfected. Liberally disposed experts may have been replaced by conservatively disposed ones, but the reliance on data, the disciplined use of inference, the articulated distinction between fact and value persisted in the shaping of policy. The government's sphere of influence was thereby reduced, budgets were cut, and block grants were made to the states. One can argue about how desirable and feasible these policies were, but they were not just rhetorical or ideological talk. They were mainstream social science.

As historians struggle with the Reagan legacy, one principal caution seems in order. Whatever the verdict on specific policies, foreign or domestic, it is unlikely that the Reagan era will appear revolutionary in any precise sense.[56] The public sector is already expanding once more. All governments are struggling with the ideological hangovers of deficit and deregulation—and all are raising revenue once more. The countercyclical clock of Arthur Schlesinger, Jr.'s, fifteen-year interval of conservative and then liberal dominance is ticking. And the experts are still there.

7

THE NEW ORDER

The University Disassembles

Although they were conservative, Reagan's experts in the social sciences shared more than equivalent academic pedigree and professional status with their liberal predecessors. Friedman, Shultz, Feldstein, Weidenbaum, and company were of the same generation that advised Kennedy and Johnson. Arthur Burns and Kenneth Galbraith, Friedman and Samuelson, Buchanan and Solow paired comfortably in age and renown. They rose through faculty ranks and wrote their more influential books in the "golden age" of the American university—the post–World War II period of expansion triggered by the GI Bill, perpetuated by the shock of Sputnik, and sustained through most of the 1960s. Almost all politically active social scientists were part of that new "multiversity." Clark Kerr, president of the University of California system, proudly and repeatedly proclaimed that they stood ready to take on any policy problem, domestic or foreign.

By the time Reagan was assembling his task forces in the late 1970s, however, the academic good times were clearly gone. Wracked first by the Vietnam controversy, then pinched and squeezed by inflation and the oil crisis, the campuses of the great universities became unhappy places. Moreover, the distractions of student riots, warring faculties, and budget-tightening exercises so preoccupied university administrations that they overlooked more long-range, fundamental, and onerous societal and economic forces that later threatened their institutions' well-being.

The first of these forces was simply a change in demography, the smaller college-age cohort of the population. Baby boomers had passed through the pipeline; the baby-boom "echo" was fifteen years away. A second new condition lay in the public consequences of an older population: the post–65-year-old cohort, the most rapidly growing group of dependents, were now accorded new priority. The third was inflation, resulting inescapably from the way in which the Vietnam War had been financed and from the emergence of genuine foreign competition in major sectors of the U.S. economy.

Like administrators, social science faculties at the great research universities failed to acknowledge their changed circumstances. Apparently oblivious to the demographic and economic sea-changes that sharply reduced undergraduate demand, increasingly constrained revenue, and severely limited the number of new academic jobs, many academic departments continued their graduate programs. A sizeable surplus of Ph.D.s appeared, and young men and women who had spent eight years or more becoming credentialed found few prospects in the colleges and universities. According to the folklore of the time, they found themselves driving taxis and "selling soap." John Kessel of Ohio State University recalls the experience of his political science department this way:

> As the supply of academic jobs diminished . . . the number of good students going to graduate schools also shrank. By the late 70s we were admitting many more MA students just to stay in business. At first we thought it was something we were doing (or not doing). Then we discovered that Berkeley had only *one* entering graduate student in American politics and that things were bad all over. Unfortunately, the brightest students were the first to pick up cues and so the students we were getting weren't all that good.[1]

By the mid 1970s, as the economy began its downswing, the effect of these new forces had been further intensified by the recognition of resource scarcity—or, in Dennis Meadow's graceful phrase, "the limits to growth." When international economic problems proved unresponsive to wage or price freezes and a floating dollar, a full-blown recession followed. With fewer and less qualified students and sharp budget restraints, it is not surprising that the euphoric associations of "being a professor" disappeared. It was replaced by a sour, sullen, defensive posture, as more and more academics perceived themselves to be unappreciated and unwanted.

Two scars were especially visible. One was the internal loss of community brought about by the Vietnam War; the second was the neoconservative attack on the universities' principal public contributions of the sixties, the New Frontier and the Great Society. Both marred the face of an academy which for more than two generations had proceeded in the special American tradition of pragmatic positivism that John Dewey and William James had stamped upon the emerging social sciences at the turn of the century.

The aftermath of Vietnam, the student protests, and the campus riots that culminated in the murders at Kent State triggered nothing less than the destruction of a scholarly community already made fragile by its rapid growth a decade earlier. The disruption of university life that began in the sixties spilled over into the seventies. The disintegration was wrenching, and it spread like wildfire—Berkeley first, then Columbia, then Harvard and M.I.T., then to other elite research campuses.

Administrators who had spent their time raising funds or overseeing the classic chores of admissions, class scheduling, and fee collection were thrust into crisis management. Deans developed tactics to handle unruly assemblies; presidents agonized over when to call in local police or the National Guard. In the late sixties and throughout the seventies, once-routine meetings of faculty senates or governing assemblies became arenas of violent debate. Hours of argument, flights of rhetoric, outbursts of violence set colleague against colleague. Vehement conflict shattered lifetime friendships. Students anointed instant heroes and villains. Campuses purporting to be citadels of reason were transformed into ideological battlegrounds until, finally, a presidential commission chaired by William Scranton acknowledged the unrest to be a "national problem." In January 1969, I returned to M.I.T., having served three years as undersecretary and secretary of HUD. In the first week, the students classified me as a "war criminal." In the second week, given my experience in the 1967 urban riots, I counseled then-President Howard Johnson on the consistently unruly conduct of faculty meetings. Later in the spring, students would storm the Hermann Building, where the Center for International Affairs was located, to engage in loud debate and occasionally throw a punch or two at faculty members and graduate students. It was a rude awakening, contrasting sharply with the orderly, essentially nonpolitical institution I had left in 1966.

The academic experts who were to serve Reagan were as much members of these warring and contentious communities as those returning from Johnson's and Nixon's administrations. Reagan's advisers, however, were more often estranged and angry spectators than participants. They did not suffer the personal and sometimes physical attacks that the "action intellectuals" of the New Frontier and the Great Society endured, the designation as "war criminals," physical assaults during protests and sit-ins. Nonetheless, their dismay at what was going on in their universities, the disorder, disrespect, intolerance, and violence was clear.[2]

Most important, for conservative and liberal scholar alike, this continued disarray and turmoil consumed enormous amounts of time. The academic enterprise seemed no longer geared primarily to serving faculty research interests. Instead, it placed what appeared to be inordinate demands upon them to help preserve the institutions. Alienation was a common faculty reaction, and it was widespread at the end of the seventies.

The 1970s had seen another untoward development directed especially

at the social sciences. Chiefly within the confines of mainstream behavioralism, intramural debate broke out on the efficacy of the programs
of the sixties. In sociology, James Coleman, the principal investigator in
the first large-scale and generally positive evaluation of the educational
effects of classroom desegregation, now reversed his position. In a series
of reports, Coleman concluded first that white flight was undercutting
integration efforts and second that private schools, especially parochial
ones, were academically superior to public schools. To Coleman, the 1964
and 1965 Elementary and Secondary School Acts, earlier regarded as
watersheds in legitimizing a new federal role in education, were in fact
inconsequential or even harmful.[3]

Coleman's sobering, if sometimes contradictory, conclusions about
education were paralleled by the judgments of two distinguished urban
planners, Bernard Frieden and Marshall Kaplan, about Model Cities.
Assessing the program in 1975, they concluded that design flaws and
implementation ineptness combined with America's cumbersome federal
structure to make "the gap between promise and performance . . . con-
spicuously large" in Model Cities. Planners would have to go "back to the
drawing board" if they wished to "really help American cities."[4] Both
Frieden and Kaplan had actively participated in the design and execution
of Model Cities, and their judgment was accordingly given special weight.
It reinforced the neoconservative laments of Harvard's Edward Banfield in
Unheavenly Cities and Daniel Patrick Moynihan's major indictment of
the Community Action Program in *Maximum Feasible Misunderstanding*, which had surfaced in the Ford years.[5]

Taking note of this new propensity for critical and public evaluation,
James Allen Smith concluded that the academic base for policy-oriented
research had been eroded as much by internal disputes as by the external
forces of ideology or rhetoric. Disillusionment with the social sciences, in
his view, derived not so much from the excessive expectations of the
sixties as from the "lingering perception that social scientists cannot
agree on what had been accomplished and what had failed to work."
Because of the new focus on critical evaluation, academic social science
"had become a source not of ideas but of institutionalized skepticism—
and potentially a more conservative political force."[6] Yet a contradictory
movement has arisen in the social sciences, as my colleague Hal Wolman
of Wayne State University has noted in reviewing this manuscript, of
"academic monism," a retreat to disciplinary minutiae and publication in
professional journals and an exclusion of policy interests, chiefly in the
interest of academic career advancement. Put more bluntly, the academy
had shot itself in the foot.

By the eighties, the instability of the university and the growing penchant of social scientists to disparage one another's policy initiatives had corroded the link between reliable knowledge and responsible policy. Academic experts so disposed no longer found the campus a hospitable community of scholars. For a full generation, faculty stars had engaged in "campus hopping" with grant programs and graduate students in tow. Now, they were impelled to find environments more welcoming than other universities. The think tank, a free-standing intellectual enterprise without students and committee meetings, seemed more appealing. So did government service, as its pay scales grew more generous.[7]

New and Hostile Horizons

More than psychic disillusionment, economic hard times, and intellectual infighting made the university unattractive. Social scientists who maintained a respect for facts were not only being pulled toward other professional locations; they were also being pushed toward them by two new ideologies. The conservative classicism of the Western tradition reasserted itself, and a radical new class-based humanism emerged. Both sides attacked policy-oriented scholars for their "moral relativism," for passing themselves off as "value-free."

Lance deHaven-Smith, author of a prizewinning study on the Great Society, has offered perhaps the most dispassionate indictment of the methodological limits of the public policy field. Having struggled since his graduate days to bridge the gap between "behavioralists and theorists," deHaven-Smith concluded that behavioralists had dominated the policy field in both the Kennedy-Johnson and Reagan years that their approaches were too narrow, their programs too specifically focused, and the assessment of their impact too simplistic. "The standard approach to policy analysis rests implicitly on a military model which has been inappropriately applied to the evaluation of social programs," he asserted, and his contention was that "the study of policy issues required a focus not on programs but 'policy frameworks' which in turn required political theory, 'a broadened domain of inquiry.'" Policy analysis properly conceived, deHaven-Smith argued, set aside "questionable empiricist presuppositions" and examined the entire political process from electorate to political leadership, to see where the "weight of the evidence" of comprehensive, broad-scaled, contemporary but conflicting theoretical "templates" might fall.[8]

DeHaven-Smith's analysis, based on the theories of Charles Lindblom and Jurgen Habermas, failed to determine whether or not the Great Society had been a good thing. "It all depends on how you look at it," DeHaven-Smith wrote, but he argued nonetheless that its behavioral approach was wrong. "The source of our confusion," he declared, "is a methodology of policy research that produces evidence devoid of clear theoretical implications." Hence, the restoration of "comprehensive social and political theory" seeking to reform entire cultural systems was now urgently required. The social sciences had been led astray since World War II by false analogies to the natural sciences. Now they should return to the tradition of great thinkers. They should abandon the behavioralism of the last generation as an unfortunate digression, a misguided detour.[9]

DeHaven-Smith's counsel was prelude to the more concerted assault that followed. The first wave was the angry critique of classical conservative ideology, enunciated and typified by Allan Bloom. The second wave was an unvarnished repudiation of modern science from new schools of literary criticism. In the guise of critiquing established modes of inquiry, linguistics and deconstructionism discounted facts, warned against the reliance on data, and called for the return to "first principles." As James Smith has observed, "The conservative revolt was really a frontal assault on the pragmatic philosophical assumptions that have been at the core of American politics—and, not coincidentally, of social science expertise— since the turn of the century . . . [it was] a common belief in the primacy of ideas and their historical reality. [To conservatives] ideas precede the talk about policy, shaping responses to the realm of facts, even reshaping the facts themselves."[10]

Conservatism notwithstanding, what really transformed the universities was not the espousal of Western civilization, a replay of the century-old conflict between utilitarians and idealists. Rather it was/is the largely linguistics-based assertion by the "New Class" and the "legal critics" that manifest words do, in fact, mask latent "social knowledge," and that knowledge *is* power. Elites rule because they command words, and words—rhetoric—condition and direct behavior. Or, as Jurgen Habermas holds, communication, discourse, the force of the better argument— the "fundamental norms of rational speech that we must always presuppose if we discourse at all"—is the foundation of substantive, legitimate social and political order. In this context, the "practical reason" of the common man—not the "technical reason" of the instrumental expert, dominated by the ruling class—should guide the economy and specify the technology.[11]

This linguistic interpretation of power as expressed through discourse appeared on campus in radical, not conservative, garb. The debate over the liberal arts curriculum, which broke open in the late eighties at Stanford, concerned how its reform could become an instrument of social transformation. It is the replacement, as John Searle points out, of the conservative "canon" of Allan Bloom and E. D. Hirsch, Jr., with the works of Derrida, Gramsci, and Foucault so that "something that is multicultural and non-hierarchical finds its way onto the syllabus."[12]

Ironically, although its proponents identify themselves with the cultural left, the new canon attacks the "liberal" empirical behavioral social science even more directly than it does the conservative idealism of such traditionalists as Richard Weaver, Russell Kirk, and Leo Strauss. It is not only the "hegemonic discourse" and the historical oppressiveness of Western civilization that its advocates protest. They also reject the positivist ideal of objectivity and disinterest. At rock bottom, these new radicals assert the dual claim that political power influences any scholarly inquiry, and that—especially in the humanities—scholars are obliged to be "explicitly and beneficially political instead of being disguised vehicles of oppression."[13]

This assertion is, of course, a basic challenge to both the natural and the social sciences. Still, as John Searle put it in a 1990 article on the debate, though "we can all learn about the nature of politics, culture, and history from Shakespeare . . . the study of poetry, plays, and novels is hardly the ideal basis for understanding modern structures of power or the mechanisms of revolutionary change." Searle surmises that the recent migration of radical politics from the social sciences to the humanities "comes about by the bankruptcy of Marxism, Leninism, and its subsequent formulation in Maoism and Castroism as empirical theories of economics and politics." Hence, its "most congenial home . . . is in departments of literary criticism."[14] It is appropriate here to recall Daniel Lerner's critical distinction between logical disputation and scientific knowledge. "For the needs of debate," Lerner wrote, "dialectic is a superb instrument. It cancels certainty by casting doubt; while feuding with the mind, it delivers a verbal blow to the solar plexus that leaves the opponent gasping and speechless. It scores, in short, debaters points . . . On this point, dialectic decisively departs company from science."[15]

Whatever the merits of the new humanism, the sheer hubbub generated by the new radical left, the din of the debate over curriculum reform, the noise overwhelming the standard signals of scholarship are now major depressants in academic life. They also present sizeable barriers to effective scholarly participation in the political system "as is." If the ultimate aim of the "new discourse" is to "empower" people, then nothing less than the thoroughgoing reconstruction of political and economic systems is acceptable. Yet this "critical theory" does little to encourage real links with real political actors within the system. As an intervening elite, policy-oriented social scientists can inform and educate politicians, administrators, and the public; they can incrementally enhance the capabilities and skills of all three. As revolutionaries, academics have little prospect for sympathetic response from any quarter—save students and alienated persons existing outside the system.

Major segments of the academy are thus, and again, increasingly antagonistic to the disciplines that give its work credibility in other sectors of the society. American campuses seem increasingly hostile to the social sciences, chastised for their perceived clumsy imitation of the natural sciences, their struggle to understand complex phenomena, and their effort to identify solutions for problems that cheapen the human condition. Colleagues are not only indifferent to one's work, they are opposed to it. The dialectic based on "secret" knowledge is everything; observation and experimentation are worse than trivial. They are immoral. Academic Luddites appear poised to demolish the laboratories and libraries. Policy-oriented scientists seem best advised to look elsewhere to ply their trade.

The Rise of the Think Tanks

One long-standing myth in American academic folklore is that teaching and research go hand in hand. Good scholarship, so the truism runs, enlivens instruction. Like sponges, eager young minds absorb the research-enhanced wisdom of the professors, who in turn are inspired to return to their inquiries with fresh perspectives drawn from classroom discourse.

In point of fact, good teaching at most universities and colleges is a sheer accident, but not because "good teachers are born not made," as many poor teachers assert. It is rather because graduate students heading for the academy are told again and again that research is their overwhelming obligation, their professional calling. Teaching is a necessary burden, a duty to be discharged; one either cannot truly prepare for it, and, even if one could, one should not give time to it. So teaching remains largely amateur and ineffective. Young professors are not taught to teach and older ones are not held accountable.

Given this deeply ingrained folk wisdom, it is not surprising that when the academic life turned sour in the elite universities, the attraction of alternative institutions grew substantially among policy-oriented scholars. The pull was increased exponentially when the salaries and other material rewards such places offered rivaled or surpassed what the academy delivered. For the generation of social scientists coming of professional age in the 1980s, think tanks offered an ever more appealing option as Ph.D.s glutted the academic market and affirmative action changed the faculty hiring process.*

*Robert D. Reischauer, director of the Congressional Budget Office, then senior vice president of the Urban Institute, wrote the author on May 16, 1985, about the

Almost simultaneously, the perspective of the national policymakers was shifting: the university increasingly seemed an unreliable source of counsel and advice. When a beleaguered White House staff member looked north to Cambridge or west to the Bay Area, even the new schools of public policy seemed apt to contribute uncertain, unuseful, or untimely responses. As Sorensen had discovered with Harvard's Mark Howe in 1959, professors continued to be beset by a long list of campus distractions: classes, blue books, long-term research, commitments to publishers. Costs in time and travel and the difficulties of scheduling work on presidential messages and legislation around classes and examinations also inhibited them. Over the years, as the search for viable policy ideas became more systematic and widespread, seeking scholarly advice often entailed slippages in time and relevance that became more costly. Too often, policy solutions to vexing problems suddenly high on the political agenda arrived too late from the campus experts, were of uneven quality, were not clearly focused, promised to be difficult to implement, or even seemed "tossed off." Increasingly, what the policy staffs needed and wanted were Washington-based experts, on call and ready to respond.[16]

The push off campus and the pull to the Capitol combined to make the Seventies the decade of the "think tanks." As Ken Fox describes it, "The think tanks have become places to make it as an academic without entering the bureaucracy or going back to the campus. One thinks always of Joe Pechman, Alice Rivlin, Henry Aaron, Tony Downs."[17]

What think tanks *are* precisely, their number, and their major functions are still topics of debate. James Smith traces the origin to World War II jargon, when it signified a closed, secure room connected with the establishment of the Rand Corporation." It is a curious phrase," he writes, "suggesting both the rarified isolation of those who think about policy, as well as their prominent public display, like some rare species of fish or reptile confined behind the glass of an aquarium or zoo." They are "quintessentially American planning and advisory institutions . . . private, non-

---

evolution of think tanks and the declining use of outside experts. "As time has gone by the White House 'Task Force,' consisting of outside and inside experts has withered as a device to formulate policy options . . . The expertise within government grew tremendously [in the 1970s] . . . Intellectual and academic input was gathered, sifted, and simplified in [departmental and agency] policy shops and fed to the White House. In part this was necessary because of the increasing sophistication of the methodology used by the academic/outside experts which became so complex that non-experts had a difficult time digesting it." Reischauer goes on to point out that in 1980 task forces were a useful device for drawing on "a stable of conservative thinkers" because the Republicans did not have faith in the "inside" experts, but essentially the freestanding think tanks, mostly in Washington, became central in fashioning policy ideas.

profit research groups that operate on the margins of this nation's formal political processes." Smith estimates that more than one thousand private, not-for-profit think tanks operate in the nation, about one hundred of which are in or around Washington.[18]

Kent Weaver sets think tanks down as a growth service industry sparked by intellectual entrepreneurs. Although no accepted definition nor accurate count of them exists, Weaver cites Peter Kelley's definition as valid. In Kelley's words, think tanks are "an arrangement by which millions of dollars are removed from the accounts of willing corporations, the government, and the eccentric wealthy and given to researchers who spend much of their time competing to get their names in print." Less cynically, he pushes on to classify think tanks in three categories: "universities without students," contract research organizations, and "advocacy" tanks. All are sources of policy ideas, evaluators of policy proposals and public programs, media commentators, and not infrequently, suppliers of personnel to the higher echelons of government.[19]

Whatever their real power and influence, the international perception sees think tanks as "in." Gorbachev read the Hoover Institution's *The United States in the 1980s*.[20] In Japan, Mizuno Takanori called think tanks a "threat" and titled his analysis of them *The Fourth Power: The Shadowed Leaders Who Drive Bush*. Takanori not only identified them as homes of the new "intervening elites" but also as the principal sources for "Japan-bashing."[21] Though the interests of corporations and foundations for think tanks ebbs and flows, there seems little doubt that they are permanent Washington fixtures.

Smith identifies thirty policy-research organizations as "a sampler" of the one thousand plus he estimates to be currently in existence. According to Smith, the Brookings Institution is the grandfather of think tanks and was established in 1916 when statistics became essential to economics and the impulse for structural reform and efficiency drove political scientists. It was soon followed by the Hoover Institution (1919). The Committee for Economic Development and the Rand Corporation were World War II creations. The former was devoted to liberalizing business positions on economic policy, or, as one staffer put it, reconciling corporate thinking to Keynes. Rand, the first contract research organization, was originally concerned with defense policy and strategy.[22]

Ranking think tanks by the size of their 1987 operating revenues, Weaver identified eleven whose annual income exceeded $2 million. Rand and Brookings led the list with $77 million and $15 million respectively. The Heritage Foundation and the Hoover Institution, both conservative advocacy organizations, were close behind Brookings; the Urban Institute then followed.[23]

Rand and the Urban Institute are the two that the federal government originally established. Rand came into existence as the brainchild of Air Force General Hap Arnold as the first signs of the Cold War appeared and the role of the Air Force in the air defense structure was uncertain. Rand was originally given hardware and science questions related to aircraft, missiles, and satellites. National security issues have dominated Rand's research, although in the late 1960s HUD supported its entry into domestic issues—a beachhead that has broadened over the years. Concentrating on public policy issues and program performance, its work is "in the public domain"; Rand accepts no commercial contracts.

The Urban Institute originated in the deliberations of the first Johnson urban task force and was specifically the inspiration of one member, Martin Meyerson. The analogy to Rand was explicit, and the driving concept was to formulate domestic strategy by a means parallel to that guiding national security. The proposal lay dormant until near the end of the Johnson administration, when the torrent of neoconservative academic criticism descended on the Great Society programs. The White House and domestic secretaries realized that some responsibly objective evaluation of Great Society efforts must occur or they would be savaged by ideological critics with prestigious credentials. The Urban Institute was designed to provide an autonomous capacity for timely and forthright evaluation within a context of sympathetic concern for urban issues.[24]

The Urban Institute continues to carry out its evaluative function, but it has broadened its scope considerably. Over the years it has undertaken more comprehensive and ambitious research assignments in health and social service, family life, immigration, and the labor force that take it considerably beyond its initial mandate. The institute's stated goal now is "to help shape thinking about societal problems and efforts to solve them" as well as "to improve government decisions and performance."[25]

To the think tanks originating before 1970 and deemed more or less establishment (or counterestablishment) in their staying power have been added a rash of new centers in the last twenty years. In 1989, the *Congressional Quarterly* listed twenty and, in the temper of the times, classified eleven as conservative in orientation, two as libertarian, four as liberal, and three as "centrist." Moreover, their stance has shifted visibly to outright "advocacy" postures and away from contract research and the presumably more objective model of "universities without students."[26]

As a historian, Smith seems to view this trend with mixed emotions. On the one hand, he remains skeptical of the American social sciences, rooted as they are in Dewey's and James's pragmatism and empiricism. "They have too hastily and uncritically embraced metaphors from the natural sciences . . . held out excessive hopes that social scientists could be society's doctors . . . [as well as] the impossible promise of escaping from politics." On the other hand he is equally suspicious of the think tanks' "modern metaphors of marketing and intellectual combat" arising "out of disappointments with scientific claims of social research. These images suggest that the enterprise of experts largely involves creating and peddling innovative policy measures to citizen consumers or battling for ideas in a hostile arena in which the winner takes all." Too often, Smith believes, the experts "drawn into the Washington community have limited themselves to serving a narrow stratum of political leaders and cognoscenti of policies" and have neglected the public at large. In the end, he seems to despair at both academic and think-tank experts, yet fears the time when "the wizard with his basket untethered floats rudderless, higher and farther from the Emerald City, leaving the Scarecrow—or someone less capable—to rule in his stead."[27]

Far less skittish in taking the measure of think tanks, Weaver cites their ruthless search for financing and the development of attractive "product lines" designed to reach "target" markets. Their institutional vulnerability is apparent in their sources of revenue. Of the top ten think tanks, three get 85 percent of their income from government contracts; for four, private grants cover 82 percent. In the case of the most vigorous advocates—the Heritage Foundation and the Center for Strategic and International Studies—private and corporate gifts dominate. None of the ten have endowments that cover even a third of their costs.[28]

In Weaver's analysis, think tanks emerge as income-driven organizations, seeking to complete research, write and publish their findings, assure their relevance to the contemporary political agenda, and place the reports in influential hands. They then establish new deadlines toward which the staff struggles to assure that the enterprise stays afloat. In Ken Fox's words: "What would happen at the Urban Institute was that people would sit in strategy sessions and try to think up gimmicks that would capture someone's attention . . . Within certain disciplinary and ideological bounds (it had to sound like economics and be liberal) the premium was on how tricky and innovative a proposal could be . . . the way research and knowledge were to be used . . . appealed to me and still [does]. What I did not like was the personal objectives of the Institute staff . . . intent primarily on their own career trajectories."[29]

In Weaver's words,

> Think tank managers must be certain that the financing, image, staffing, and product line decisions that they make are consistent with one another . . . When there were just a few think tanks on the scene, with strong reputations for objectivity in research, their views carried a high degree of authority. Now there are many voices clamoring to be heard. Moreover, these organizations vary widely in their standards and claim to objectivity. In this

new environment, it is difficult for either the public or policymakers to know the difference between sound reliable research and propagandizing. And it is easier for policymakers to find some think tank study to support their current views, no matter what they may be.[30]

In short, in think tanks as in universities, the battle between the ideologues and the social scientists continues—and in both, the current fashion favors ideology. Whether grounded in religion, western tradition, or contemporary multiculturalism, both are committed to grand ideas, first principles, discourses, and subjectivity. In the think tanks, however, the perspective is short-run, the time is now, and the task is to persuade the policymaker to act whatever the reality, the issue, or the circumstance. With few exceptions, they are institutions designed to make plausible "the word" which, for the most part, is derived from an encompassing world view—an ideology—that rarely admits exceptions or inconvenient facts.

The Future of Policy Experts

What happens when ideology and rhetoric win in political talk, especially presidential political talk? What happens when the social sciences are devalued and the Academy retreats into abstract discourse and a seemingly sophisticated recourse to the normative wisdom of ancient times?

One way to answer these questions is to review what actually endured in domestic policy from the New Frontier and the Great Society. What kind of policies, what sort of political debate took the place of these heavily criticized and disparaged schemes? Clearly, government undertook to "downsize" itself, although the impact of cuts in dollars and personnel in domestic programs was offset by an expanding defense sector. The Nixon and Carter administrations witnessed a standoff in welfare policy that was finally resolved by ideological assertions of the value of "work" and of the continued relevance of the Protestant ethic. The Reagan years grudgingly sustained the patchwork of separate assistance programs from AFDC through food stamps to Medicare. Overall, however, the major programs of social security, health care, education, welfare, and environmental protection endured. In housing, to be sure, vouchers signaled a move toward "privatization." A similar approach was evident in education. Everywhere complaints arose about rising costs. Nonetheless, for all their apparent shortfalls and the impulse to "privatize," the nation seemed to have signed off on these programmatic creations of the sixties. In their essence, they satisfied public and professional evaluators alike.

In the late seventies and with a vengeance in the eighties, a resurgence of fervor for capitalism emerged, along with an intense moral and religious debate over abortion and a revival of racism that bids fair to undercut the laboriously achieved advances since the civil rights acts of the mid-1960s. The basic ideological contentions that government as established and practiced in the United States is "the problem," that only death (and not taxes) is inevitable, and that deficits in public finance can be cheerfully ignored permitted the economy to deteriorate. It also permitted the consensus of professional economists, conservative and liberal alike, about the danger of the deficit to be ignored. The debate over abortion, unleashed by a conservative but increasingly activist Supreme Court, ill-disposed to both natural and social science, carries even more unvarnished ideology. It issued uncompromising pronouncements about the beginning of "life" without reference to the biological sciences. Predictably, moral debates about "death" and euthanasia followed. Moral arguments also surrounded the "injustices" that affirmative action laws and programs designed to redress past injustices toward African-American and other minorities visited on white Americans.

When social science is set aside, advocacy in place of evidence comes to command political debate. Deductive *interpretations* of conditions and events, "obtained," in Daniel Lerner's words, "by some secret process" take precedence over politics extracted by detailed observation and experiment. Sweeping moral criticisms of existing institutions and systems— replete with moral fervor—take the place of rigorous evaluations of actual performance. As moral absolutes become prominent, compromise becomes an increasingly unacceptable option for political participants. So violence becomes increasingly a quasi-legitimate alternative, in protests before abortion clinics, in city street behavior, even in the conduct of everyday life: in the dissolution of family relations, the availability and use of firearms enhance the likelihood of unpremeditated accidental assault.

What the past generation has witnessed, as social science as an aid to policymaking has been systematically disparaged, has been an escalation of rhetoric in presidential campaigns and an ever-increasing reliance on the assertion of anecdotal, undocumented propositions about "the way the world works." Most curiously, from the university cultural left comes the social critic distrust of the paradigms of science. Resolute in the validity of their own interpretations, scholars on the left are convinced not only that things are not as they appear, but that things can only be known subjectively. Knowledge, in other words, cannot be "known."

With increasing religious fervor, the right calls for "pure" individualism, even if the first outcome of an unfettered market is a failed banking system. All things are possible if the psyche and the soul of each citizen is in conformity with right principles. Have the ghetto children "just say no" to drugs. Have the ghetto adolescents "just say no" to sex, or learn safe sex.

Find family values again and all will be well. For a decade at least, ideology has shaped not only the rhetoric of the campaign but also, increasingly, both the presidential and the national agenda.

Does it follow, then, that the republic is doomed unless social scientists in the American pragmatic tradition are placed in key policy positions? At the dawn of the twenty-first century, should they be enthroned again as the new philosopher-kings to continue the social engineering of the nation? How should social scientists respond to the negative caricature ideologues of all persuasions have drawn of them—value-free, pretentious examiners of the human condition, ignorantly parroting the metaphors of the natural sciences, arrogantly proclaiming their capacity to demonstrate a reality independent of subjective perception?

A first step is to disabuse commentators—academic and lay alike—of the false dichotomies that have been inferred from the ambiguities of the undertaking. For openers, it is important to acknowledge that ideologies—Philip Pomper's "developed doctrines containing evils to be combatted and goods to be pursued in a secular world"—do shape action, and they are always intertwined with the languages of knowledge and rhetoric. The approaches of professional social sciences are not either/or affairs. They can be inductive or deductive. They can embrace both empirical observation and speculative thinking. They can eschew value judgments or reflect value preferences. If they are not abstract theory, they need not be plodding classification. Philosophical assertion of "subjective interaction" to the contrary, the social sciences, like the natural sciences, are cosmopolitan in their methodologies. They size up and try to understand puzzles, in the southern vernacular, "every which way they can."

In short, the social sciences are no more a perfectly rational, passionless, positivist set of disciplined inquiries than the natural sciences are. None is in a steady state. A ceaseless flow of facts tumbles down on the researcher, from laboratory experiments, archaeological digs, censuses, public opinion surveys, case studies, and psychological tests. This is an ever-expanding stock of knowledge to be understood and transmitted to policymakers, and anticipating the consequences of any policy is always difficult at best.

Given the prevailing skepticism about the social sciences and their generally marginal role in contemporary public policy-making, especially in the presidential cockpit, seasoned social scientists venture into the waters of political advising with considerable caution. They must be serious about their entry—frivolous propositions lightly advocated have no place in policy-making in any government. New ideas are to be welcomed and new paradigms embraced, but not if they are advanced untested and irresponsibly. The political arena is not a playpen, a sandbox, or a social laboratory for interesting ideas. The presidential arena, especially, is not suitable as a social laboratory. The obligation remains that any policy must be rooted in solid data, not in the latest unverified fad that captivates academic attention at the moment. Third, and perhaps most important, the expert advisers need to accept at least some of the responsibility for the consequences of the policy they have persuaded politicians and administrators to adopt and carry out. They cannot leave their colleagues in the policy arena, the other intervening elites, hanging out to dry.

Appreciating social sciences properly, then, means acknowledging that all too often academic propositions for public policy, including those made to a president, have been ill considered. Veterans looking back on the New Frontier and the Great Society often cringe when they review the list of unexamined, untested ideas that became task force recommendations. "New math" and "new physics" appeared in education, and, after a few years, they slunk away. "New communities" did the same. Deinstitutionalization in mental health was solid as a concept, but the consequences of its implementation on community life were not anticipated. The list includes many programs from the seventies and the eighties, from the war on drugs to the Job Training Partnership Act.

But judgments between these competing ideas, of rhetoric and ideology, versus social science knowledge, are, in the end, comparative. "Silly" social science does not portray reality nor identify correctly the attributes of a problem and the options for its resolution. "Sensible" social science, however, has a capacity to anticipate problems and their future political consequences *before* they are apparent to political actors; at their best, the New Frontier and Great Society programs anticipated both the problems and possible solutions that had yet to emerge. They did so in a systematic way—linking one component to another—and in the three great areas of health, education, and urban life provided start-up models *independent* of political demand. No interest group, no calculating "establishment" demanded these reforms. To the contrary, they were either barely aware or ignorant of the problems.

So, at least for most of one decade, the politics of innovation stood alongside the politics of distribution and redistribution, the classic concerns of ideology and rhetoric. First-generation programs, perhaps as primitive as model Ts and biplanes when they first appeared, were designed to help people in ghettos before black power was a reality. They were there to respond to the needs of the mentally ill, young children, and the dispossessed who could not or did not vote. The capacity to foresee needs and wants, to simulate conflicts, and to design their resolutions was enhanced by sympathetic politicians and bureaucracies. Those domestic innovations endured well beyond the decade, in hostile political circumstances and under unceasing ideological attack.

The question becomes what today's comparative schools of "ideas" have to offer in domestic public policy. Models of capitalism, American style, are not persuasive in view of the faltering economy and the international competition that lies ahead. Models of revolution, neighborhood autonomy, republics in miniature, or little sovereign communities hold even less promise. They deny or ignore reality. So, one turns again to the pragmatism and incrementalism of the painful progress of science, natural and social, well aware of the uncertainties, false starts, and risks of failure. But the alternatives seem worse: politicians who rule by anecdote, analogy, or metaphor, who misread history, who look back to past solutions no longer appropriate; and government officials who still proceed by the numbers, repeating their experiences and searching for things as they used to be.

It is better that presidents be possessed of what knowledge we have, however incomplete, than to act on beliefs and convictions that simply cannot come to pass.

NOTES

Introduction

1. H. Mark Roelofs, *The Language of Modern Politics* (Homewood, Ill.: The Dorsey Press, 1967), 19, 28, 33.

2. Philip Pomper, *The Russian Revolutionary Intelligentsia* (Arlington Heights, Ill.: Harlan Davidson, 1993), 23 [seen in page proofs].

3. Gary King and Lyn Ragsdale, *The Elusive Executive: Discovering Statistical Patterns in the Presidency* (Washington, D.C.: Congressional Quarterly, 1988), 6.

1. Helping Presidents Talk

1. David Truman so titles chapter 10 of his *Politics and Government in the United States* (New York: Harcourt Brace, 1965). A comprehensive identification of the literature on the modern presidency fills a five-foot shelf or more. One can begin with Dennis A. Barton, James B. Rhoads, and Raymond W. Smock, eds. and comps., *A Guide to Manuscripts in the Presidential Libraries* (College Park, Md.: Research Materials Corporations, 1985), and the various works of the Center for the Study of the Presidency, most prominently its *Presidential Studies Quarterly*. The archival records of the respective presidential libraries include those held in Alexandria, Virginia, as in the case of President Nixon. The U.S. Government National Archives, "Records of Temporary Committees," Washington, D.C.: Commissions and Boards Record Group 220, August 14, 1985 (typescript), and William E. Reachtenburg, ed., *American Presidents Research Collections* (Bethesda, Md.: University Publications of America, 1991 annual edition), are also valuable. Especially useful in helping to identify academic experts who have served on public advisory bodies is Steven D. Zink, *Guide to the Presidential Advisory Commissions, 1973–1984* (New York: Chadwyck-Healey, 1987) and Thomas R. Wolanin, *Presidential Advisory Commission: Truman to Nixon* (Madison: University of Wisconsin Press, 1975). The most comprehensive recent general bibliography of which I am aware is Herbert B. Asher, *Presidential Elections: American Politics*, 5th ed. (Pacific Grove, Calif.: Brooks/Cole Publishing Co., 1992). For the office's attributes identified here, I have relied mostly on the "classics" in political science and history, most notably works by James MacGregor Burns, Cary R. Covington, Thomas E. Cronin, Erwin C. Hargrove, Hugh Heclo, John H. Kessel, Louis Koenig, Lester G.

Seligman, Richard Neustadt, Clinton Rossiter, Arthur M. Schlesinger, Jr., James Sundquist, David Truman, and Aaron Wildavsky. Later on, when the specific topic indicates, I identify particular books and articles supporting the analysis, including my own works. Here it is the "mainstream" authorities with which I begin.

2. James David Barber cataloged differences in the chief executives' character in his ground-breaking political psychological study *Presidential Character: Predicting Performance in the White House* (Englewood Cliffs, N.J.: Prentice-Hall, 1972). His specific characterization of Eisenhower is challenged by Fred Greenstein, *The Hidden-Hand Presidency* (New York: Basic Books, 1982). Greenstein more recently edited *Leadership in the Modern Presidency* (Cambridge: Harvard University Press, 1988). See also Dean Keith Simonton, *Why Presidents Succeed: A Political Psychology of Leadership* (New Haven: Yale University Press, 1987). I continue to find Barber's analysis highly useful as an organizing perspective.

3. Richard Neustadt's most recent book, *Presidential Power and the Modern Presidents: The Politics of Leadership from Roosevelt to Reagan* (New York: Free Press, 1991), taken as a logical progression from his earlier *Presidential Power* (New York: John Wiley and Sons, 1960), is the authoritative statement of the presidential capacity to govern. On influencing the public directly, see James P. Pfiffner, *The Strategic Presidency: Hitting the Ground Running* (Chicago and Pacific Groves, Calif.: Brooks/Cole Publishing Co., 1988). Also instructive is Samuel Kernell, *Going Public: New Strategies of Presidential Leadership* (Washington, D.C.: Congressional Quarterly, 1986).

4. Arguably the preeminent American theorist treating political pluralism is Yale's Robert A. Dahl. From his *Who Governs: Democracy and Power in an American City* (New Haven: Yale University Press, 1961) to his most recent *After the Revolution? Authority in a Good Society* (New Haven: Yale University Press, 1990), Dahl has provided an authoritative analysis and reasoned defense of pluralism, American style. James Q. Wilson has introduced other "kinds" of politics—majoritarian, client, entrepreneurial—and other "theories"—Marxist, elitist, bureaucratic—which he suggests limit the scope of pluralism as an explanatory concept. See his textbook, *American Government: Institutions and Policies*, 5th ed. Chap. 23 (Lexington, Mass.: Heath, 1992). I find the formulation of intervening elites superimposed upon a pluralistic system the most effective framework in characterizing present-day national politics.

5. See, for example, Laurence H. Shoup, *The Carter Presidency and Beyond: Power and Politics in the 1980s* (Palo Alto, Calif.: Ramparts Press, 1980) and its foreword by Richard A. Falk.

6. At the outset of the period here examined, William C. Mitchell wrote an article destined to become a classic, "The Ambivalent Social Status of the American Politician," *Western Political Quarterly* 12, (September 1959). He begins, "The literature of American political science indicates an almost total lack of interest in the social status of the elective public official. Sociologists interested in social stratification and status have, unfortunately, also ignored the politician." In November 1965, giving the annual John Gaus lectures at the University of Alabama, I reviewed the state of the literature again and found it still limited, although some dissertations on political recruitment and socialization were underway. One of them, by David Schwartz at M.I.T., "Toward a Theory of Political Recruitment," appeared in summary form, again in *Western Political Quarterly*, 20, (September 1969), I use it as a point of departure.

7. A principal authority on modern campaign financing is Herbert E. Alexander, who since 1960 has regularly reported on the financing of presidential elections and the major changes since Kennedy. See his *Financing Politics: Money, Elections and Political Reform*, 3d ed. (Washington, D.C.: Congressional Quarterly, 1984). Also notable are the works of Alexander Heard, Frank Sorauf, David Adamany, and George E. Agree. Elizabeth Drew's "Politics and Money" is a shrewd journalistic account (*New Yorker*, May 17, 1976, 126–56). A recent comprehensive analysis is Herbert B. Asher, *Presidential Elections, American Politics*, 5th ed. (Pacific Grove, Calif.: Brooks/Cole, 1992).

8. Although Barber and Greenstein are arguably the most prominent contemporary students of presidential personality, the study of political psychology is a substantial field linking political science, history, psychology, and psychiatry. Both are indebted to the towering analyses of Erik Erikson and Harold Lasswell and to more limited inquiries into adolescent political behavior, well represented by M. Kent Jennings and Richard G. Niemi. An especially intriguing recent analysis is Simonton, *Why Presidents Succeed*. Using four criteria for presidential success, Simonton gives generally high marks in his appraisal of the capacities of the majority of American presidents. He also provides an impressive interdisciplinary bibliography. From a wide array of sources, I have chosen to emphasize Lloyd S. Etheridge's depiction of "hardball" politics in *A World of Men: The Private Sources of Foreign Policy* (Cambridge: M.I.T. Press, 1978). I do so not only because Etheridge's formulation is succinct and rigorous in its formal expression, but also because it most closely corresponds to my forty years as a participant-observer of political actors, including sheriffs in Florida, mayors in Boston, governors in half a dozen states, representatives, senators, and the four presidents for whom I have worked. However widely these men and women have varied in other aspects of their personalities, Etheridge has captured their common attributes as I have observed them.

9. For a recent comprehensive review of American voting behavior and corresponding campaign strategies, specifically focusing on the presidency, see John H. Kessel, *Presidential Campaign Politics*, 4th ed. (Pacific Grove, Calif.: Brooks-Cole, 1992).

10. Ibid., 133–39. Kessel's identification of the triple test for new ideas was explicitly standard operating procedure in the three presidential task forces on which I served between 1960 and 1965.

11. Ibid., 150; see also Asher, *Presidential Elections*, 117–20.

12. John W. Kingdon, *Agenda, Alternatives and Public Policy* (Boston: Little, Brown and Co., 1984), 1.

13. The National Commission on the Public Service, *Leadership for America: Rebuilding the Public Service* (Washington, D.C., 1989), 20. The commission's report, together with those of its five task forces, provides the most comprehensive recent profile of the administrative elite and its current status. See especially the report of the Task Force on the Relations between Political Appointees and Career Executives, beginning on 239.

14. James W. Fesler and Donald F. Kettl, *The Politics of the Administrative Process* (Chatham, N.J.: Chatham House, 1991), 142.

15. Norton E. Long, "Power and Administration," *Public Administration Review* 9 (Autumn 1949): 257–64. See also his "Bureaucracy and Constitutionalism," *Political Science Review* 46 (September 1952): 814.

16. National Commission on the Public Service, *Leadership for America*, 246.

17. Quoted in Jameson W. Doig and Erwin C. Hargrove, *Leadership and Innovation* (Baltimore: The Johns Hopkins University Press, 1987), 3.

18. Ibid., 7–12.

19. Almost all academic experts are supported by government or foundation grants, yet they are autonomous in determining how they proceed in their work. Far more than colleagues in colleges and professional institutions, well more than half are satisfied with their staff support, salary, and teaching load. Two-thirds are committed to tenure, and a whopping 95 percent endorse the criterion of publish or perish. See Howard R. Bowen and Jack H. Schuster, *American Professors* (New York: Oxford University Press, 1986), 27, and the *Chronicle of Higher Education Almanac*, January 15, 1992, which reports enrollments, endowments, research and development spending, faculty compensation, and degrees awarded. For a further classification of institutions of higher learning, see the technical reports of the Carnegie Foundation for the Advancement of Teaching.

20. For the more prominent senior public figures, see Calvin MacKenzie, ed., *The In-And-Outers* (Baltimore: The Johns Hopkins University Press, 1987).

21. Carol Weiss, "The Uneasy Partnership Endures," in *Social Scientists, Policy and the State*, ed. Stephen Brooks and Alain G. Gagnon (New York: Praeger Publishers, 1990), 109.

22. Bernard Barber, *Effective Social Science: Eight Cases in Economics, Political Science and Sociology* (New York: Russell Sage Foundation, 1987), 62.

23. Ernest A. Lynton and Sandra E. Elman, *New Priorities for the University* (San Francisco: Jossey-Bass, Inc., 1987), 11.

24. Seymour Martin Lipset and Everett Ladd, Jr., "The Changing Social Origins of American Academics" (mimeograph of paper sponsored by National Institute of Education and Spencer Foundation, 1975), later published as *The Divided Academy: Professors and Politics* (New York: McGraw-Hill Publishing Co., 1975).

25. Alvin W. Gouldner, *The Future of Intellectuals and the Rise of the New Class* (New York: Seabury, 1979), 35.

26. This profile is drawn from a roundtable discussion on political consultancy and governance in *PS: Political Science and Politics* 22, 1 (March 1989): 11–29. The commentators were Mark P. Petracca, Larry Sabato, Benjamin Ginsberg, Walter DeVries, and Celinda Lake. For an earlier analysis, see Sabato, *The Rise of Political Consultants: New Ways of Winning Elections* (New York: Basic Books, 1981). Walter DeVries provides the basis for figures cited in his *PS* commentary.

27. See *PS: Political Science and Politics*, 11–29.

28. DeVries and Petracca, in *PS*.

29. DeVries in ibid., 23.

30. Louis Hartz, *The Liberal Tradition in America* (New York: Harcourt Brace, 1955), 50–51.

31. Gouldner, *Future of Intellectuals*, 37. With Soviet-style Communism in collapse almost everywhere, the only metaphysical dogma now advanced is the rise of a "New Class," discovered and proclaimed principally among intellectuals. The New Class is committed to discourse and introspection, possessed of "cultural capital" by the intellectuals' own admission and poised to be "the judges and regulators of the normative structure of contemporary societies." To date, this call to modern-day philosopher-kings has found little response or recognition anywhere in the

political process. Its appeal is puny alongside the strident, self-satisfied praise of unfettered capitalism, the marketplace, and the genius of the entrepreneur.

32. Lewis A. Dexter, "Court Politics: Presidential Staff Relations as a Special Case of a General Phenomenon," *Administration and Society* 9, 3 (November 1977): 267–68.

33. Ibid., 269.

34. Ibid., 280.

35. Matthew Holden, Jr., "The Twenty-Person Government: A Discussion Paper on Iran, Contras, and the Executive" (Paper presented at the Meeting of the Committee on the Constitutional System, Washington, D.C., December 5, 1986), 3.

36. Ibid., 4.

2. The Glory Years Begin

1. Theodore H. White, "The Action Intellectuals," *Life*, June 9, 1967. Parts 2 and 3 of the series appeared in the June 16 and 23 issues.

2. Alvin W. Gouldner, *The Future of Intellectuals and the Rise of the New Class* (New York: Seabury, 1979), chap. 1.

3. William J. Barber, "The United States Economists in a Pluralistic Polity," *History of Political Economy* 13, 3 (Fall 1981): 521.

4. Harold Seidman and Robert Gilmore, *Politics, Position: Power from the Positive to the Regulatory State* (New York: Oxford University Press, 1986) is an authoritative account of how theoretical concepts of public administration have shaped federal government structure since World War II.

5. The origins, substance, and evolution of the behavioral sciences and their distinction from "behaviorism" is well treated in the essay by Bernard Berelson in *The International Encyclopedia of the Social Sciences*, ed. David L. Sills (New York: Macmillan Co., 1968), 2:41–45.

6. The presidential addresses of the American Political Science Association are published annually in the quarterly *American Political Science Review*. Redford's appeared in 55, 4 (December 1961): 755–62.

7. Ranney's address appeared in *American Political Science Review* 70, 4 (December 1976): 140–48.

8. William Foote Whyte, "Social Inventions for Solving Human Problems," *American Sociological Review* 47, 2 (February 1982): 1–13.

9. Special Commission of the National Science Foundation, *The Behavioral and Social Sciences: Outlook and Needs* (Washington, D.C.: U.S. Government Printing Office, 1969), 16, 22.

10. Bauer carried out a comprehensive review of the social sciences in the sixties and forecast much of his future work in Raymond A. Bauer and Kenneth J. Gergen, eds., *The Study of Policy Formation* (New York: Free Press, 1968).

11. Advisory Committee on Government Programs in the Behavioral Sciences, National Research Council, *The Behavioral Sciences and the Federal Government* (Washington, D.C.: NAS, 1968), ix.

12. Ewa Golebiowska, "Social Sciences in the National Academy of Sciences and the National Research Council" (Research paper, Public Affairs Center Advanced Seminar, Wesleyan University, May 1989).

13. White, "Action-Intellectuals," June 23, 1967, 85–86.

14. Herbert Goldhamer, *The Adviser* (New York: Elsevier Science Publishing Co., 1978), 25.

15. Ibid., 27.

16. Joseph A. Califano traces well the rise of the politics of innovation, itself founded on the assumption of rising public resources, in *The Triumph and Tragedy of Lyndon Johnson: The White House Years* (New York: Simon and Schuster, 1991).

17. John Gardner, interview with author, November 17, 1986.

18. White, "Action-Intellectuals," 1:57.

19. Mary O'Furner, *Advocacy and Objectivity* (Lexington: University of Kentucky Press, 1975).

20. Edward T. Silva and Sheila A. Slaughter, *Serving Power: The Making of the Academic Social Science Expert* (Westport, Conn.: Greenwood Press, 1984), 16–17.

21. John Kenneth Galbraith, interview with author, October 8, 1986.

22. Indeed, the contributions of New Deal academic experts are put in perspective not only by such historical predecessors as the Wisconsin School and Hoover's commission but by the scope and intensity of subsequent expert contributions to national policy. A recent and comprehensive account of twentieth-century policy experts, academic and otherwise, is James Allen Smith, *The Idea Brokers: Think Tanks and the Rise of the New Policy Elite* (New York: Free Press, 1991).

23. Ibid., chap. 4.

24. Silva and Slaughter, *Serving Power*, 22.

25. White, "Action-Intellectuals," 1:74.

26. Smith, *Idea Brokers*, chap. 5.

27. Samuel A. Stouffer et al., *The American Soldier* (Princeton, N.J.: Princeton University Press, 1949). This four-volume work represents a near-perfect example of the practical, result-oriented, policy-sensitive orientation of the American social sciences.

28. Theodore Sorensen, interview with author, October 29, 1986. The media judgment of Robert Kennedy was largely negative at that time.

29. Galbraith interview.

30. Lipset and Ladd, "Changing Social Origins of American Academics," 14.

31. Galbraith interview.

32. Peter Edelman, Oral History Transcript, Robert Kennedy Project, JFK Presidential Library, 30–31.

33. Sorensen interview.

34. Ibid.

35. The description of the role of Cambridge academics in the 1960 campaign is drawn from the oral histories and files of the participants at the JFK Library in Dorchester, adjacent to the University of Massachusetts, Boston, campus. Files respecting the Academic Advisory Committee are in Boxes 21, 32–37, and 992. They are augmented by the notes I made and retained at the time as I moved from List B to List A of preferred academics (which turned out to be chiefly important in terms of the number and quality of invitations to the 1961 inaugural), my correspondence of that period, and my recollections. The last I confirmed in the course of the interviews I conducted in 1986 and 1987.

36. Stevenson was particularly severe in editing what I still regard as one of my best drafts on urban policy, which Willard Wirtz persuaded me to write and the remnants of which were delivered in Newark sometime in 1958. I recall that one paragraph of mine, mostly statistics, survived. It diminished my commitment to future Stevenson endeavors more than a little.

37. Academic Advisory Committee Files, specifically the Howe and Cox letters in the Henderson file, JFK Library. The lists of professors (A and B) are also located there.

38. Neustadt to David Truman, 29 June 1960, Neustadt file, Box 1, Academic Advisory Committee Files.

39. Richard Neustadt, interview with author, October 8, 1986.

40. Sorensen interview.

41. Neustadt interview.

42. Mel Elfin, interview with author, November 19, 1986.

43. Ibid.

44. R. Joseph Monsen, Jr., and Mark W. Cannon, *The Makers of Public Policy: American Power Groups and Their Ideologies* (New York: McGraw-Hill, 1965), 212.

45. Ibid., 214.

46. Ibid., 219.

47. The term is from Carl M. Brauer, *Presidential Transitions: Eisenhower through Reagan* (New York: Oxford University Press, 1986), xiv, who contrasts these first ten weeks with the postinaugural six months of a transition when the stamp and style are put on an administration. Brauer's is the most authoritative treatment of the passage of candidates for president to the presidency that has been written. I supplement it with interviews of specific participants and my personal recollections of the transition task forces of Kennedy and Johnson.

48. Neustadt interview.

49. Schlesinger, interview with author, October 26, 1986.

50. Galbraith interview; Brauer, *Presidential Transitions*, 107.

51. Adam Yarmolinsky, interview with author, November 18, 1986. The Shriver group continued to identify persons qualified for permanent presidential appointments, and academics such as McGeorge Bundy, Walt Rostow, and Schlesinger headed for Washington on a more permanent basis. In all, twenty-four members identified in the task forces or the campaign were perceived to possess John Gardner's "two skills in one skull" and were recruited into the administration from the campuses.

52. Richard E. Neustadt, "Presidency and Legislation: The Growth of Central Clearance," *American Political Science Review* 48, 3 (March 1957): 641–71.

53. Schlesinger interview.

54. Sorensen interview.

55. King and Ragsdale, *Elusive Executive*, 66.

56. James Sundquist, interview with author, November 18, 1986.

57. Joseph Pechman, interview with author, November 18, 1986.

58. Summary of transcript of Fort Ritchie, Maryland, meeting, August 1, 1964, JFK Library. The library sponsored an oral history project which brought together Gardner Ackley, Kermit Gordon, Walter Heller, Joseph Pechman, and James Tobin for two days of recollections and reflection.

59. Fort Ritchie transcript.

60. The particulars of this account are drawn from Paul Ylvisaker, interview with author, October 9, 1986. Subsequently, Nicholas Lemann, *The Promised Land* (New York: Alfred A. Knopf, 1991) confirmed and expanded the record. Additional details and sources are found in Isabel Miller, "Experts in the Policy Arena: Their Influence on the War on Poverty," (Senior thesis, based on JFK Library archives, Wesleyan University, June 1986).

61. This three-year, nine-volume study, including twenty-year projections of key economic indices for the New York region, represented an intellectual breakthrough by which Vernon and his associates made the study of urban areas academically respectable in the social sciences. The studies were published by Harvard University Press from 1959 to 1961, under the general editorship of Max Hall.

62. Ylvisaker interview.

3. Flood Tide

1. Harry McPherson, interview with author, November 18, 1986.

2. White House Confidential Files, Box 31, LBJ Library and Museum, Austin, Texas [hereafter cited as LBJ Library].

3. Emmette S. Redford and Richard T. McCulley, *White House Operations: The Johnson Presidency* (Austin: University of Texas Press, 1986), Chap. 5.

4. White House Confidential Files, Box 362, LBJ Library.

5. Redford and McCulley, *White House Operations*, chap. 5. See also U.S. Government, National Archives, "Records of Temporary Committees, Commissions and Boards," Record Group 220, revised August 14, 1985.

6. Memoranda to author's files, July–December 1968.

7. White House Confidential Files, Boxes 285 and 286, LBJ Library.

8. Ibid., Box 286. See also letter from Califano to Nelson Polsby, December 15, 1968.

9. Galbraith interview.

10. Neustadt interview.

11. Ylvisaker interview and author's file memoranda.

12. McPherson interview.

13. Daniel Patrick Moynihan, *Maximum Feasible Misunderstanding* (New York: Free Press, 1970).

14. Lemann, *Promised Land*, Chap. 3, especially 164–70 and 186–88. See also White House Confidential Files, Box 4, LBJ Library.

15. David Walker, "The Nature and Systemic Impact of Creative Federalism," in *The Great Society and Its Legacy*, ed. Marshall Kaplan and Peggy Cuciti (Durham, N.C.: Duke University Press, 1986). See also Califano, *Triumph and Tragedy of Lyndon Johnson*, 76–80.

16. Ylvisaker interview.

17. Miller, "Experts in the Policy Arena," 91.

18. Ibid.

19. Bill Moyers, interview with author, April 11, 1986.

20. White House Confidential Files, Box 4, LBJ Library.

21. Harold Seidman, interview with author, September 8, 1986.

22. Moyers interview.

23. Francis Keppel, interview with author, October 9, 1986.

24. LBJ White House Confidential Files. Box 361, LBJ Library; Califano memorandum.

25. Moyers interview.

26. John Gardner, interview with author, November 17, 1986.

27. For a further discussion of this task force, see my book based on the Radner Lectures, *The Necessary Majority: Middle America and the Urban Crisis* (New York: Columbia University Press, 1972), Chap. 6.

28. Keppel interview.

29. Norman C. Thomas and Harold L. Wolman, "Policy Formulation in the Institutionalized Presidency: "The Johnson Task Forces," in *The Presidential Advisory System*, ed. Thomas E. Cronin and Sanford D. Greenberg (New York: Harper & Row, 1969), 140. See also Jennifer Neel, "Task Forcing in the Great Society" (Senior thesis, Wesleyan University, 1986), 21–26.

30. Harold Howe, interview with author, October 9, 1986.

31. Gardner interview.

32. King and Ragsdale, *Elusive Executive*, 73.

33. White House Confidential Files, Box 4, LBJ Library.

34. Califano, *Triumph and Tragedy of Lyndon Johnson*, Chap. 1.

35. White House Confidential Files, Box 362, LBJ Library.

36. Joseph Califano, oral history, June 30, 1973. LBJ Library.

37. White House Confidential Files, Boxes 285 and 286, LBJ Library; see also, generally, Box 35.

38. White House Confidential Files, Box 362, LBJ Library.

39. John Macy, interview with author, November 10, 1983.

40. Wood, *Necessary Majority*, 43; author's file memoranda.

41. Harry McPherson, *A Political Education* (Boston: Little, Brown, and Co., 1972), 297–98.

42. The most authoritative analysis on Model Cities remains Bernard J. Frieden and Marshall Kaplan, *The Politics of Neglect: Urban Aid from Model Cities to Revenue Sharing* (Cambridge: M.I.T. Press, 1975), and updated in Kaplan and Cuciti, eds., *The Great Society and Its Legacy*. Most recently, see my essay, "Model Cities: What Went Wrong—The Program or Its Critics?," in *Neighbourhood Policy and Programmes: Past and Present*, ed. Naomi Carmon (London: Macmillan Press, 1990).

43. Rufus Browning, Dale Rogers Marshall, and David H. Tabb, *Protest Is Not Enough* (Berkeley: University of California Press, 1984), 236, 207.

44. Califano, *Triumph and Tragedy of Lyndon Johnson*, 135.

45. White House Confidential Files, Box 362, LBJ Library.

46. Califano oral history, June 20, 1973.

47. Neel, "Task Forcing," 48.

48. William Bundy, "Lyndon B. Johnson, a Texan in Washington" (Remarks presented at fifth annual presidential conference, Hofstra University, April 11, 1986).

49. Neel, "Task Forcing," 49–55. See also Report of the Task Force on Education, June 30, 1967, Summary of Principal Recommendations, LBJ Library.

50. Ibid., 55.

51. Ylvisaker interview.

52. Seidman interview.

53. Neel, "Task Forcing," 58.

54. Redford and McCulley, *White House Operations*, 96.

55. Walker, "Nature and Systematic Impact of Creative Federalism," 199–200.

56. Ibid., 198–99.

57. Redford and McCulley, *White House Operations*, 96.

58. Lester Salamon, "The Presidency and Domestic Policy Formulation," in *The Illusion of Presidential Government*, ed. Hugh Heclo and Lester M. Salamon (Boulder, Colo.: Westview, 1981).

59. Robert Wood, "The Great Society in 1984: Relic or Reality," in *Great Society*, ed. Kaplan and Cuciti, 17.

60. Spritely rebuttals to the literature of failure are found in Sara Levitan and Robert Taggart, *The Promise of Greatness* (Cambridge: Harvard University Press, 1976); Henry J. Aaron, *Politics and the Professors: The Great Society in Perspective* (Washington, D.C.: Brookings Institution, 1978), and, more recently, John E. Schwarz, *America's Hidden Success: A Reassessment of Public Policy from Kennedy to Reagan*, rev. ed. (New York: Norton, 1988) and Malcolm L. Goggin et al., *Implementation Theory and Practice: Toward a Third Generation* (Glenview, Ill.: Scott, Foresman, 1990).

61. Donald Matthews et al. to Califano, June 18, 1968, copy in my personal files, provided by the authors.

62. Wood, "The Great Society in 1984," 18.

4. Cracks in the System

1. Henry Kissinger, *The White House Years* (Boston: Little, Brown, and Co., 1979), 4.

2. Martin Anderson, interview with author, August 30, 1990.

3. James David Barber, *Presidential Character: Predicting Performance in the White House* (Englewood Cliffs, N.J.: Prentice-Hall, 1972), 373–74. John Kessel has observed, "Nixon could work with intellectuals . . . such was the quality of his mind, but he was so suspicious that they had to be intellectuals he trusted." Kessel to author, October 24, 1991.

4. Elfin interview (author's emphasis).

5. Ibid.

6. McPherson interview.

7. Ben W. Heineman, Sr., interview with author, October 12, 1979. Then CEO of North-Western Railroad, Heineman was an influential and trusted corporate supporter of Johnson's, having served as chair of the White House Conference on Civil Rights and on the Model Cities Task Force.

8. Anderson interview.

9. Martin Anderson campaign research files, 1968. Aside from presidential libraries, Anderson has the most complete and authoritative files for the presidential elections of 1968, 1976, and 1980 of which I am aware.

10. Anderson interview.

11. Frank Lindsay, interview with author, April 4, 1989.

12. These memos are in Lindsay's personal files.

13. President-elect Nixon, press release, December 2, 1968, Hotel Pierre, New York, N.Y., Lindsay's personal files.

14. Anderson files.

15. Heineman interview.

16. Lindsay interview. More generally, see Carl M. Brauer, *Presidential Transitions: Eisenhower through Reagan* (New York: Oxford University Press, 1986), Chap. 3, on the Nixon transition and the interplay of personalities in that period. The Ash group did not formally report until 1970, but its major recommendations were conveyed earlier.

17. Ibid., and Richard P. Nathan, interview with author, October 27, 1986. Nathan's book, *The Administrative Presidency* (New York: Wiley, 1983) is the authoritative account of how Nixon sought to oversee and discipline the administrative elite.

18. Anderson and Nathan interviews.

19. Lester Salamon, "The Presidency and Domestic Policy Formulation," in *The Illusion of Presidential Government*, ed. Hugh Heclo and Lester Salamon (Boulder, Colo.: Westview, 1981), 184–85. For a more general analysis, see Lester G. Seligman and Cary R. Covington, *The Coalition Presidency* (Chicago: Dorsey, 1989), Chap. 6.

20. Seidman interview; see also Heclo and Salamon, eds., *Illusion of Presidential Government*, 13.

21. Nathan interview. For the membership lists of Nixon task forces, see the Ehrlichman, Clapp, and Colson files, Nixon Presidential Materials Project, Alexandria, Va.

22. Seidman interview.

23. Anderson interview and files.

24. Roswell Perkins, interview with author, September 9, 1989. As a young Eisenhower appointee (assistant secretary of HEW at the age of twenty-seven), Perkins met Rockefeller in the early fifties and thereafter was a central figure in the Rockefeller brain trust until 1967–1968. He served as counsel and established political and policy task forces in 1959 and 1964. His knowledge of the Rockefeller-academic relationship is a superb and largely unrecorded account. It was confirmed by Richard Nathan and long-term Rockefeller associate Robert Armstrong, currently president of the Henry R. Luce Foundation, in several conversations during my association with the Luce Foundation.

25. Robert H. Connery and Gerald Benjamin, *Rockefeller of New York* (Ithaca, N.Y.: Cornell University Press, 1979), 128.

26. The Rockefeller Panel Reports, *Prospect for America* (New York: Doubleday, 1961).

27. *Critical Choices for Americans* (Lexington, Mass.: Lexington Books, 1976). Each of the six panels issued separate reports. Perkins's account of the informal processes of choosing the membership of these endeavors and "seeing the reports through" reinforces Nathan's and Robert Armstrong's recollections. They converge to provide a classic portrait of "action intellectuals" paired with major private-sector executives and lawyers.

28. Their influence seems to persevere; see *The Cuomo Commission Report: A New American Formula for a Strong Economy*, Lewis B. Kaden, chairman, and Lee

Smith, director (New York: Simon and Schuster, 1988). Here the mix of commission members is tilted more to the private sector.

29. Nathan interview.

30. In my last week as secretary of HUD, secretary-designate George Romney asked in a very pleasant transition conversation if I would consider continuing in my former position as undersecretary. Because my tenure at M.I.T. was already in jeopardy after three years of absence, I prudently declined.

31. Clapp to file, memorandum, August 14, 1969, records a conversation with Henry Loomis; Clapp to Lucy Winchester and Dwight Ink, memorandum, April 1 and March 13, 1970, respectively, describes changes to task forces and criteria for membership selection. White House Confidential Files, Clapp Box 5, Nixon Project, National Archives.

32. The Anderson and Nathan interviews are especially precise in identifying the extent of influence of the major task forces, particularly on the welfare issue, which would hold center stage domestically in the early years of the Nixon administration. The Lindsay papers and interview provide further confirmation.

33. Keppel interview. Anderson and Nathan interviews provide confirmation on the process. For specifics, see Clapp file, Nixon Project.

34. White House Confidential Files, Clapp File, Box 5, Nixon Project. See also Box 8, File 1. Interesting notes on the criteria established in the key memorandum were "to put knowledgeable people up front . . . pay the members $100 . . . it is helpful to university people."

35. Clapp file (including Loomis memo and undated *Guidelines for Task Force*), Nixon Project.

36. There is some discrepancy in the materials in the Clapp and Colson files, Nixon Project, and the present recollection of Martin Anderson as to the development of the guidelines and the degree of public dissemination. Printed copies of the task force reports are on file in the Nixon Project archives, and I have two copies given to me by former task force academic members. It is clearly established that the task force "shows" were run by Burns and Anderson with Clapp and Loomis serving in administrative capacities.

37. Anderson interview.

38. Ibid.

39. The complex substance of the Nixon welfare plan, as with most presidential welfare plans since the New Deal, is not susceptible to quick summaries. Seligman and Covington, *Coalition Presidency*, offer a short summary of the policy positions within the administration; see 19–20. Anderson provides a more extensive account in his book *Welfare: The Political Economy of Welfare Reform in the United States* (Stanford, Calif.: Hoover Institution Press, 1978), 81–85. Politically, Anderson paints an aggressive Moynihan "bold attack" and a Burns-Anderson counterattack.

40. Nathan interview.

41. Brauer, *Presidential Transitions*, 140.

42. Kessel interview.

43. Brauer, *Presidential Transitions*, 140.

44. Kessel interview.

45. Ibid.

46. Nathan interview.

47. Ibid.; see also Nathan, *Administrative Presidency.*

48. Kessel to author, October 30, 1991, attributes the idea of the "super department" to Harold Christian Krogh.

49. Robert Wood, "The Great Society in 1984: Relic or Reality," in *The Great Society and Its Legacy,* ed. Marshall Kaplan and Peggy Cuciti (Durham, N.C.: Duke University Press, 1986), 20.

50. For a concise post-Watergate reckoning of the status of the presidency in the mid-1970s, see John Hart, *The Presidential Branch* (New York: Pergamon Press, 1987), 177.

51. For a detailed account of the appointment and the subsequent White House staff conflicts, see Robert L. Hartmann, *Palace Politics: An Inside Account of the Ford Years* (New York: McGraw-Hill, 1980). Hartmann's analysis is supplemented by the Kessel interview and Roger Porter, interview with author, October 24, 1986. Porter's book, *Presidential Decision Making: The Economic Policy Board* (Cambridge: Cambridge University Press, 1980) is a scholarly analysis of Ford economic policy-making and more restrained than Hartmann's in the treatment of personalities. It is largely confirmation of Rockefeller vice-presidency experience.

52. Hartmann, *Palace Politics,* 280. For extended discussion of Rockefeller-Rumsfeld relationship, see 304–15.

53. Ibid., 425.

54. Ibid., 312.

55. Porter, *Presidential Decision Making,* 174–252.

56. John Osborne, *The White House Watch: The Ford Years* (Washington: New Republic, 1977), 236, 248.

57. Porter, *Presidential Decision Making,* 35. Porter worked with Martin Anderson in the Reagan White House in 1981–1982 and returned to the Bush White House in 1988.

58. Hartmann, Palace Politics, 365–69, confirmed by Kessel.

59. The role of the Science Advisor and the Office of Science and Technology had been substantially downgraded by Nixon.

60. Osborne, *White House Watch,* 248.

61. Ibid., 249.

62. Porter interview.

63. Nathan Glazer, interview with author, October 29, 1986. For board and commission members, see National Archives, *Presidential Commission, Records of Temporary Committees Commissions and Boards.* Once again, John Kessel's correspondence provided valuable insights on Goldwin, "a Straussian" who linked the White House with "a much more conservative network of which he was a part."

64. Glazer interview.

65. Ibid.

66. Kessel correspondence.

67. My own return to M.I.T. in 1969 had been marred by the Vietnam resistance in the Harvard "bust" and the M.I.T. "March on the Labs" in 1969. By the mid-1970s, the focus of neoconservative critiques was on domestic programs and their ineffectiveness as well as on the growing perplexities of my colleagues in economics.

68. "Social Science: The Public Disenchantment; A Symposium," *The American Scholar* (Summer 1976). The contributors included sociologists James S. Cole-

man, Mario Janowitz, and Daniel P. Moynihan; economists Harry G. Johnson, Robert Lekachman, and Thomas Sowell; author Martin May; and Harold Orlans of the National Academy of Public Administration Foundation. Their attack on the New Frontier and the Great Society was emphatic, if not always persuasive. See in particular 336–49.

69. As a review and response to these critiques, see my article, "Academe Sings the Blues," *Daedalus* (Winter 1975). A general account of the growing neoconservative influence is found in Sidney Blumenthal, *The Rise of the Counter Establishment* (New York: Times, 1986).

70. Edward Banfield, *The Unheavenly City Revisited* (Prospect Heights, Ill.: Waveland Press, 1991). In this reissue of his 1970 *Unheavenly City,* Banfield states that his original conclusions "were accurate"; see 61. For a response, see my *The Necessary Majority: Middle America and the Urban Crisis* (New York: Columbia University Press, 1972).

71. Ibid., 23. Banfield still prefers Negro as the correct designation for black Americans or African Americans.

72. Moynihan in "Social Science: The Public Disenchantment," 350.

73. For the general thesis, see D. P. Moynihan, *The Politics of a Guaranteed Income: The Nixon Administration, The Family Assistance Plan* (New York: Random House, 1973).

74. Wood, "The Great Society in 1984," 18.

5. The System Disassembles

1. Arnold Meltsner's *Policy Analysis in the Bureaucracy* (Berkeley: University of California Press, 1976) focuses authoritatively on the rise of "in-house" experts. The literature on federal budgeting system analysis, in particular the writings of Aaron Wildavsky, Allen Schick, Charles T. Hitch, and Alain C. Enthoven, explores the contributions and limitations of PPBS from different perspectives, but collectively it documents persuasively PPBS's continuing impact.

2. For an account of developments in the 1970s, see John W. Ellwood, "A Morphology of Graduate Programs for the Public Service" (Report Commissioned by the Mellon Foundation, 1981). By that time, the National Association of Schools of Public Affairs and Administration listed 215 programs and had issued regular reports since 1973. I carried out further analyses of the substance of and variations among the programs in a study for Dartmouth College in February 1982, when the Nelson A. Rockefeller Center was established there.

3. For a further discussion, see my "The Disassembling of American Education," *Daedalus* 109, 3 (Summer 1980).

4. Lloyd Cutler, interview with author, November 20, 1989. Cutler's estimates are confirmed by calculations Andrew Nakahata carried out in the Wesleyan Presidential Expert Project (hereafter cited as Wesleyan Project), personal files May 17, 1989.

5. Abram Chayes, Harvard Law School, interview with author, October 24, 1975. Chayes had agreed to form a Cambridge advisory committee for Carter (as he had helped Archibald Cox do for Kennedy) following a visit with then-candidate Carter in my offices at the University of Massachusetts.

6. See "Social Science: The Public Disenchantment," *The American Scholar* (Summer 1976).

7. Sorensen interview.

8. Stuart Eizenstat, interview with author, November 20, 1989.

9. Eizenstat Exit Interview, October 10, 1981, Carter Presidential Library Archives (hereafter cited as Carter Library).

10. Ann Crittenden, "Jimmy Carter's Economic Team," *New York Times*, July 18, 1976.

11. Ibid. Klein expanded on his perception of Carter in an interview with A. Nakahata, May 4, 1989, Wesleyan Project.

12. Ibid., confirmed by Eizenstat interview.

13. Cutler interview.

14. Lawrence H. Shoup, *The Carter Presidency and Beyond: Power and Politics in the 1980s*, foreword by Richard A. Falk (Palo Alto, Calif.: Ramparts Press, 1980) 7, 15, 16. Martin Anderson commented to the author that "many conservatives did not care much for it either."

15. Cutler interview.

16. Hedley Donovan, exit interview, August 14, 1980, Carter Library. Trilateral Commission file in general provides further detail on the Carter association.

17. Shoup, *The Carter Presidency and Beyond*, 55.

18. Huntington's trilateral paper foreshadowed his *American Politics: The Promise of Disharmony* (Cambridge: Belknap Press of Harvard University Press, 1981).

19. Carl M. Brauer, *Presidential Transitions: Eisenhower through Reagan* (New York: Oxford University Press, 1986), 175, and Eizenstat interview. See also Leslie Gelb, "A Team of Young Experts Aids Carter on Foreign Policy Plans," *New York Times*, August 18, 1976.

20. Nakahata-Lawrence Klein interview, May 4, 1989, Wesleyan Project.

21. Nakahata-Bosworth interview, May 8, 1989, Wesleyan Project.

22. Brauer, *Presidential Transitions*, 180.

23. Gleb, "Team of Young Experts."

24. Ibid.; see also Brauer, *Presidential Transitions*, 180.

25. Brauer, *Presidential Transitions*, 18; see also Elizabeth Drew, *American Journal: The Events of 1976* (New York: Random House, 1977), 480–82.

26. Eizenstat interview.

27. Brauer, *Presidential Transitions*, 181.

28. Ibid., 182.

29. *U.S. News and World Report*, November 15, 1976, 45.

30. *U.S. News and World Report*, January 10, 1977, 14–15.

31. Shoup, *The Carter Presidency and Beyond*, 104. See also Zbigniew Brzezinski, *Power and Principle* (New York: Farrar, Straus and Giroux, Inc., 1983), 289.

32. Eizenstat interview.

33. Hedrick Smith, "A Neatly Balanced Cabinet," *New York Times*, December 24, 1976.

34. Eizenstat interview.

35. Ibid.

36. Erwin C. Hargrove, *Jimmy Carter as President: Leadership and the Politics of the Public Good* (Baton Rouge: Louisiana State University Press, 1988), 38–39.

37. Hargrove, *Jimmy Carter as President*, 40.

38. Charles O. Jones, *The Trusteeship Presidency: Jimmy Carter and the United States Congress* (Baton Rouge: Louisiana State University Press, 1988), 86.

39. Ibid., 92.

40. Ibid., 90.

41. Hargrove, *Jimmy Carter as President*, 41.

42. Eizenstat interview. Eizenstat makes explicit reference to the increased department capacity in policy analysis and his reliance on the "new" policy techniques emerging from the policy schools. James L. Sundquist elaborates on the pattern then emerging in his now classic reprint, *Research Brokerage: The Weak Link* (Washington, D.C.: Brookings Institution, 1978).

43. Nakahata-Bosworth interview, Wesleyan Project.

44. James Fallows, "The Passionless Presidency," *Atlantic Monthly*, May 1979, 40, 42.

45. Ibid., 42.

46. Hargrove, *Jimmy Carter as President*, 45.

47. Ibid., 170.

48. Cutler and Eizenstat interviews.

49. Jones, *Trusteeship Presidency*, 176.

50. White House Central file, Box MC-16, File 1, 3–38, Carter Library.

51. Jones, *Trusteeship Presidency*, 177, confirmed and elaborated upon in Eizenstat interview.

52. White House Central File, Box MC-16, Carter Library.

53. Hargrove, *Jimmy Carter as President*, 175.

54. Alvin Gouldner's *The Future of Intellectuals and the Rise of the New Class* (New York: Seabury, 1979) coined the term "new class." See also "Social Science: The Public Disenchantment: A Symposium," *The American Scholar* (Summer 1976).

55. Alan K. Campbell, interview with author, November 18, 1989.

56. Jones, *Trusteeship Presidency*, 160.

57. Campbell interview. Summary descriptions in the works of Jones, Hargrove, and Fesler and Kettle support this account, but the specifics are from Campbell's interview.

58. Peter Edelman, interview with author, July 29, 1990, and author's files on Vice President's Task Force on Youth Employment.

59. Ibid.

60. Ibid.

61. Ibid.

62. Jones, *Trusteeship Presidency*, 201.

63. Ibid., 211.

64. Edelman interview.

65. Hargrove, *Jimmy Carter as President*, 13–16.

66. Fallows, "Passionless Presidency," *Atlantic Monthly*, June 1979, 76.

67. Hargrove, *Jimmy Carter as President*, 189.

68. Jones, *Trusteeship Presidency*, 82–84.

69. Fallows, "Passionless Presidency," 1:38.

70. Ibid., 36–37.

6. Takeover

1. Barrett Seaman, *Time*, November 1990, 30.

2. David Stockman, *The Triumph of Politics: How the Reagan Revolution Failed* (New York: Harper and Row, 1986), 135.

3. John L. Palmer and Isabel V. Sawhill, *The Reagan Record* (Cambridge: Ballinger, 1984), 2.

4. Garry Wills, *Reagan's America: Innocents at Home* (Garden City, N.Y.: Doubleday, 1987), 4.

5. Larry Berman, ed., *Looking Back on the Reagan Presidency* (Baltimore: Johns Hopkins University Press, 1990), 4, 7.

6. Quoted in "Ideology and Economic Policy" in Berman, *Looking Back on the Reagan Presidency*, 124–25.

7. Anderson interview. I also rely on Anderson's files relating to the 1976 and 1980 campaigns in my account. They are supplemented more formally by two of Anderson's books, the expanded and updated edition of *Revolution: The Reagan Legacy* (Stanford, Calif.: Hoover Institution Press, 1990) and *Welfare: The Political Economy of Welfare Reform in the United States* (Stanford, Calif.: Hoover Institution Press, 1978). I am especially indebted to Anderson for making his files available and providing an extensive critique of an earlier draft of this book. More general analyses are found in Berman, *Looking Back on the Reagan Presidency*, Palmer and Sawhill, *Reagan Record*, and Stockman, *Triumph of Politics*.

8. Anderson interview and files. The quotation is from a July 16, 1978, "talking points" memorandum Anderson used to brief top staff people in the 1980 campaign.

9. Ibid.

10. Ibid.

11. Anderson to Reagan, August 17, 1978, Anderson Files.

12. Reagan for President Committee, news release, Sunday morning, April 20, 1980.

13. Reagan-Bush Committee news release, October 23, 1980, Anderson Files.

14. Anderson, *Revolution*, 166.

15. Ibid., 168.

16. Ibid., 170–71.

17. Martin Feldstein, "The Retreat From Keynesian Economics," *The Public Interest* (Summer 1981): 92–105.

18. Anderson, *Revolution*, 114–21.

19. Ibid., 164.

20. Ibid., 262–64.

21. Ibid., 225–26.

22. Harold Lasswell, *Politics: Who Gets What, When, How* (Cleveland: Maridan, 1964), 13.

23. Stockman, *Triumph of Politics*, 55.

24. Anderson, *Revolution*, 157–61.

25. Ibid., 160; Anderson to author, August 31, 1991.

26. Stockman, *Triumph of Politics*, 272.

27. Anderson, *Revolution*, 163.

28. Weatherford and McDonnell in Berman, *Looking Back on the Reagan Presidency*, 135.

29. Stockman, *Triumph of Politics*, 400.

30. Ibid., 378.

31. Weatherford and McDonnell in Berman, *Looking Back on the Reagan Presidency*, 145.

32. Anderson, *Revolution*, 120.

33. Ibid., 181.

34. Advisory Commission on Intergovernmental Relations, *Summary Report* (Washington, D.C.: U.S. Government Printing Office, 1980), 1.

35. Ibid., 5.

36. ACIR, "Executive Summary," in *Summary Report*.

37. Ibid., 13.

38. George Peterson, "Federalism and the States," Palmer and Sawhill, *Reagan Record*, 219, is the source of the Reagan proposals and reforms described in succeeding paragraphs; see especially 227–34.

39. Ibid., 220.

40. Ibid., 230.

41. Ibid., 228.

42. Richard P. Nathan et al., *Reagan and the States* (Princeton: Princeton University Press, 1987), 6.

43. Ibid.

44. Committee on National Urban Policy, *Urban Change and Poverty* (Washington, D.C.: National Research Council, 1990), 127–63.

45. Peterson, "Federalism and the States," 224.

46. Ibid., 226.

47. Ibid., 258.

48. Paul Ylvisaker, "Introduction," *Urban Policy in a Changing Federal System* (Washington, D.C.: National Academy Press, 1985), 5.

49. President's Commission for a National Agenda for the Eighties, Panel on Policies and Prospects for Metropolitan and Non-Metropolitan America, *Report* (Washington, D.C.: U.S. Government Printing Office, 1980), 99.

50. I trace the neoconservative treatment of President Johnson's urban programs more completely in *The Necessary Majority: Middle America and the Urban Crisis* (New York: Columbia University Press, 1972).

51. Michael J. Rich, "Learning to Live with Less: Federal Aid for Housing and Community Development in the 1980s," *Urban Politics Newsletter* (Summer 1986): 14.

52. These ideas are part of a more extensive analysis of national urban policy in my address to the twentieth annual meeting of the Urban Affairs Association, April 19, 1990, "Present before Creation: Lessons From the Paleozoic Age of Urban Affairs," and later published in the *Journal of Urban Affairs* 13. 1 (1991): 111–17.

53. In 1989, as Bush's secretary of housing and urban development, Kemp would try again. The account of his efforts is in his own testimony before the Senate and House Committees on Small Business from 1987 through 1989. The summary of the enterprise zone program, its history, and its present status are also drawn from the published hearings of that period. See particularly the testimony of Stuart M.

Butler, Robert Woodson, and Kemp in Senate Committee on Small Business, *Hearings*, 101st Cong., 1st sess., June 21 and September 21, 1989.

54. U.S. General Accounting Office, *Enterprise Zones: Lessons From the Maryland Experience, Executive Summary*, December 1988.

55. Senate Committee on Small Business, Hearings, 203.

56. The President's Commission on an Agenda for the Eighties reports—Carter's swan song—were "downbeat," concluding that the United States was overextended in its policy commitments relative to its resources and that the next decade should be one of retrenchment or at best consolidation of past gains. At the end of what had been a dreary decade in domestic affairs, it provided a thoroughly respectable bipartisan base, shaped heavily by the academic members of the commission, for the Reagan administration's subsequent sharp reductions in federal programs and federal taxation. The mood the reports reinforced was to "hunker down."

7. The New Order

1. John Kessel to author, November 24, 1991. See also my "Academe Sings the Blues," *Daedalus* 105, 2 (Winter 1975), and "The Disassembling of American Education," *Daedalus* 109, 3 (Summer 1980): 4.

2. As a consistent conservative philosopher, Allan Bloom, in *The Closing of the American Mind* (New York: Simon and Schuster, 1987), has recounted his experience and sense of outrage at the time of the Cornell riots and protests; see especially 315–19 and 347–48. The treatment of Edward Banfield, a neoconservative at Harvard and the University of Pennsylvania, was also shameful.

3. For a review of Coleman's changing views during this period, see my "Disassembling of American Education" and "Academe Sings the Blues." Diane Ravitch, in *The Troubled Crusade: American Education, 1945–80* (New York: Basic Books, 1983), 179–80, and Christine Rossell in *The Carrots or the Stick* (Philadelphia: Temple University Press, 1990), 65–71, provide further evaluations from quite different perspectives.

4. Bernard J. Frieden and Marshall Kaplan, *The Politics of Neglect: Urban Aid from Model Cities to Revenue Sharing* (Cambridge: M.I.T. Press, 1975), 234.

5. For a description and evaluation of the early impact of Banfield and Moynihan's analyses, see my *The Necessary Majority: Middle America and the Urban Crisis* (New York: Columbia University Press, 1972), Chap. 2.

6. James Allen Smith, *The Idea Brokers: Think Tanks and the Rise of the New Policy Elite* (New York: Free Press, 1991), 149. The classic paper on the predisposition of evaluation research to find program "failures" rather than "successes" is Peter Rossi, "Issues in the Evaluation of Human Services Delivery," *Evaluation Quarterly* 2, 4 (November 1978). A "failure" finding almost always gains more publicity and career notoriety than an evaluation of genuine accomplishment. There are now appearing, however, more positive evaluations. See Martin A. Levin and Barbara Ferman, *The Political Hand* (New York: Pergamon Press, 1985).

7. John Kessel to author, November 24, 1991. His evaluation is succinct: "While there was a shrinking number of academic jobs, there were many more jobs available to those who have a policy bent . . . I would put research universities at one end

of the continuum and full-time politicos/bureaucrats on the other. . . . In between I would see three "middle man" groupings that act as translators between academia and government . . . public policy schools, think tanks, and "the MA/ABD/Ph.D.s who take government jobs and follow policy careers."

8. Lance deHaven-Smith, *Philosophical Critiques of Policy Analysis: Lindblom, Habermas, and the Great Society* (Gainesville: University of Florida Press, 1988), ix–xii.

9. Ibid., 126.

10. Smith, *Idea Brokers*, 22.

11. Quoted in deHaven Smith, *Philosophical Critiques of Policy Analysis*, 87. See his Chapter 6 for a general discussion of Habermas's "critical reason."

12. John Searle, "The Storm over the University," *The New York Review of Books*, December 6, 1990, 34.

13. Ibid., 36.

14. Ibid., 38.

15. Lerner, *Evidence and Influence* (Glencoe, Ill.: The Free Press, 1958), 7.

16. Reischauer to author, May 16, 1985. Reischauer comments on the declining use of the academic: "My hypothesis is that the experts [the White House] now turn[s] to have become random choices determined more by previous friendships than by competence or real expertise . . . As time goes on, however, they become less useful because they aren't 'up to speed' on the day to day problems faced by the White House staff and therefore tend to recommend policy changes that don't reflect the staff's view of reality or the politically possible."

17. Kenneth Fox, letter to author, November 22, 1989.

18. Smith, *Idea Brokers*, xiii, xiv.

19. R. Kent Weaver, "The Changing World of Think Tanks," *PS* 22, 3 (September 1989): 563–64.

20. Martin Anderson, *Revolution: The Reagan Legacy* (Stanford, Calif.: Hoover Institution Press, 1990), 3.

21. My Wesleyan colleague David Titus, who translated portions of Takanori's 1990 book for me, reports that Takanori is a banker and energy executive stationed for some years in New York City and an "international journalist" who has written books on AT&T and NTT.

22. Smith, *Idea Brokers*, vi.

23. Weaver, "Changing World of Think Tanks," 565.

24. The Meyerson contribution is recorded in my notes as chair of the 1964 urban task force. For further elaboration, see my *The Necessary Majority*, in which I outline the context of the task force's work.

25. Urban Institute, *Annual Report*, 1990, 3.

26. Weaver, "Changing World of Think Tanks," 567.

27. Smith, *Idea Brokers*, 236–39. That Smith begins his book with Jonathan Swift's Gulliver on the Isle of Balnibarbi and ends it with the Wizard and the Scarecrow of Emerald City is a commendable and important insight.

28. Weaver, "Changing World of Think Tanks," 573.

29. Fox to author, November 22, 1989.

30. Weaver, "Changing World of Think Tanks," 577.

INDEX

Aaron, Henry J., 170, 188 n.60
Academic Advisory Committee of 1959, 6, 46–54
Academic experts. *See* Policy experts
Academic institutions
  antagonism toward social sciences in, 166–69
  critical debate within, 165–66
  socioeconomic developments and, 162–64
ACIR. *See* Advisory Commission on Intergovernmental Relations
Ackley, Gardner, 74, 185 n.58
"Action-intellectuals," 39, 41, 42, 113, 135. *See also* Policy experts
Adamany, David, 181 n.7
Adams, John, 12, 35
Adams, Sherman, 107
Advisory Commission on Intergovernmental Relations (ACIR), 151–52
Agree, George E., 181 n.7
Alcorn, Meade, 54, 96, 115
Alexander, Herbert E., 181 n.7
Allen, James, 77
Allen, Richard V., 89, 92, 141
Allison, Graham, 120
Alsop, Joseph, 53
American Association of Enterprise Zones, 159
Anderson, Martin, 22, 91–92, 93, 94, 99–102, 104, 188 n.2, 190 n.32, 195 n.7
  mentioned, 98, 110
  Reagan administration and, 140–43, 145, 146, 148n, 149, 150
Antipoverty programs. *See also* Urban policy
  Johnson and, 72–73
  Kennedy and, 64–66, 71–72
Applegate, Douglas, 12

Areeda, Phillip, 92, 93
Armstrong, Robert, 189 n.24
Arnold, Hap, 172
Arnold, Thurman, 44
Arrow, Kenneth, 121
Ash Council, 91, 94, 95, 103
Asher, Herbert, 179 n.1, 181 n.7
Askew, Reubin, 12
Atwater, Lee, 27

Babbitt, Bruce, 12
Bailey, Steven, 100
Baker, James, 31
Banfield, Edward C., 41, 100, 111, 112–13, 197 n.2
  mentioned, 118, 157, 165
Barber, Bernard, 22–23
Barber, James David, 12–13, 180 n.2
Barber, William, 34
Barton, Dennis A., 179 n.1
Bator, Francis, 74
Bauer, Raymond A., 37
Beer, Samuel, 51
Bell, Carolyn, 119
Bell, David, 58
Bell, Jeffrey, 141
Benjamin, Gerald, 189 n.25
Benson, Lucy, 124
Berelson, Bernard, 183 n.5
Berle, Adolf A., Jr., 44
Berman, Larry, 140
Bernstein, Marvin, 75
Bloom, Allan, 167, 197 n.2
"Blue smoke." *See* Rhetoric
Blumenthal, Michael, 120, 124
Blumenthal, Sidney, 29, 48n, 192 n.69
Bohen, Fred, 78
Bonello, Frank J., 148n
Boone, Richard, 64, 72, 73
Boorstin, Daniel, 98

Bosworth, Barry, 119, 122, 127
Bourne, Peter, 119
Bowen, Howard R., 182 n.19
Bowles, Chester, 54
Boyer, Ernest, 98
Bram, Dyke, 63
Brandeis, Louis, 44
Brauer, Carl M., 57, 59, 102–3, 121,
    122–23, 185 n.47, 189 n.16
Brookings Institution, 171
Brooks, Stephen, 182 n.21
Brouder, Joseph, 119
Brown, Douglas, 100
Brown, Harold, 120, 124
Brown, Jerry, 118
Browning, Rufus, 81
Brzezinski, Zbigniew, 7, 118, 120, 121,
    124
Buchanan, James, 150, 162
Buchanan, Patrick, 92, 106
Bundy, McGeorge, 7, 185 n.51
Bundy, William, 82
Bureaucrats. See Professional admin-
    istrators
Burns, Arthur
    dispute with Moynihan, 6, 101–5
    mentioned, 144, 149, 162
    Nixon administration and, 90, 93,
        98, 99–102
Burns, James MacGregor, 49, 138,
    179 n.1
Bush, George, 6, 12, 21, 26, 149, 151,
    160
Butler, Paul, 115
Butler, Stuart, 158
Butz, Earl, 110

Caddell, Patrick, 27, 28, 130
Califano, Joseph
    Johnson's task forces and, 70, 71,
        78–84, 85, 86, 95
    mentioned, 31, 69, 101, 125, 127,
        136, 141
    Nixon transition and, 90
    The Triumph and Tragedy of Lyn-
        don Johnson, 184 n.16, 186 n.15
Cambridge intellectuals. See also Neo-
    conservative critique
    Carter and, 118
    Johnson and, 70–71, 75
    Kennedy and, 46–54, 57–59
    Nixon and, 91–93
    Reagan and, 142
Campaign for election, 5
    Carter and, 117–24
    Kennedy and, 46–54

    Nixon and, 54–55, 91–93
    Reagan and, 140–43
Campbell, Alan, 22, 131–32, 134
Candili, Henry, 65
Cannon, James L., 119
Cannon, Mark, 54, 55
Cannon, William, 65, 72, 76, 83
CAP. See Community Action Program
Capitalism, 28–29, 140, 174–75. See
    also Ideology
Capron, William, 65, 72
Carmon, Naomi, 187 n.42
Carp, Burt, 124
Carpenter, Elizabeth, 81
Carter, Jimmy
    campaign advisers, 117–21
    Camp David summit of July 1979,
        129–30
    civil service reform program and,
        130–32, 134–35
    domestic policy staff of, 124–30
    economic policy and, 144–45
    effectiveness of, 134, 135–38
    gatekeepers and, 31
    Jordon-Watson affair and, 121–24
    "malaise" speech of, 129–30
    mentioned, 6, 21, 145
    policy development process under,
        127–29, 135–38
    rhetoric vs. ideas and, 32
    source of ideas for, 5
    urban policy under, 156–57
    Youth Employment program and,
        132–35
Cater, Douglass, 31, 74, 78, 82
Cattrell, Leonard, 72
Cavanaugh, Jerome, 79
CEA. See Council of Economic Ad-
    visors
Center for Strategic and International
    Studies, 173
Chayes, Abram, 51, 54, 119, 192 n.5
Chayes, Antonia, 79
Cheney, Richard B., 17, 110
Christopher, Warren, 124
Civil service reform
    Carter and, 131–32, 134–35
    Nixon and, 105
    Reagan's New Federalism and, 151–
        56
Clapp, Charles, 99, 100–102
Clark, Joseph, 52, 60
Clark, Kenneth, 64
Clark, Richard, 63
Cleveland, Harland, 98
Clifford, Clark, 56, 59, 129

Cloward, Richard, 63, 64
Cohen, Wilbur, 77
Cohen, William, 100
Coleman, James S., 112, 165, 191 n.68
Commission on Civil Disorder (Kerner Commission), 69
Committee for Economic Development, 171
Committee on Social Trends, 40, 43
Common, John, 43
Community Action Program (CAP), 65–66, 72, 73, 165
Connery, Robert H., 189 n.25
Cooper, Richard, 119, 120, 124
Cottrell, Leonard, 64
Council of Economic Advisors (CEA), 34, 45, 125
Covington, Cary R., 179 n.1, 189 n.19, 190 n.39
Cox, Archibald, 50, 51, 52, 54, 60, 121, 122
Cranston, Alan, 12
Critical Choices for Americans project, 97, 141
Crittenden, Ann, 193 n.10
Cronin, Thomas E., 87, 179 n.1, 187 n.29
Cronkite, Walter, 129
Cuciti, Peggy, 191 n.49
Curtis, Gerald, 120
Cutler, Lloyd, 120, 129, 136, 192 n.4

Dahl, Robert, 98, 180 n.4
Daley, Richard M., 55
Dean, Alan, 20
Deaver, Michael, 28
DeHaven-Smith, Lance, 166–67
Derrida, Jacques, 168
Derthick, Martha, 55
Deutch, John, 119
DeVries, Walter, 27, 28, 182 n.26
Dewey, John, 163, 172
Dexter, Lewis, 29–30, 31
Dillon, Douglas, 61
Dirksen, Everett, 54
Doig, Jameson W., 18–19, 182 n.17
Dole, Robert, 12, 13
Domestic Policy Council, 6
  in Carter administration, 124–30
  in Nixon administration, 102, 103–4, 106–9
Donovan, Hedley, 193 n.16
Doolittle, Fred, 154
Doty, Paul, 121
Douglas, Paul, 69
Downs, Anthony, 100, 170

Draft, abolition of, 102
"Dreamboats." *See* Ideology
Drew, Elizabeth, 181 n.7
Dugan, Ralph, 57
Duhl, Leonard, 79
Dukakis, Michael, 12, 47, 118
Duke, David, 12
Dunlop, John, 100, 106, 110, 115
DuPont, Pete, 12
Dusenberg, Jim, 51

Eckstein, Otto, 145
Economic policy
  Keynesian economic influence and, 34, 35–36, 130–31, 144–45
  supply-side economics and, 147–51, 160
Economic Policy Board, 107–8
Economic Policy Coordinating Committee, 143–44, 146, 159–60
Economists. *See also* Council of Economic Advisors; Keynesian economics; Supply-side economics
  Kennedy and, 60–62
  Reagan and, 143–47
  Wisconsin school, 43
Edelman, Peter, 47–48, 132–35, 184 n.32
Education policy
  academic debate over, 165
  Johnson administration and, 75, 76–77, 83
  neoconservative critique and, 112
Ehrlichman, John
  Domestic Policy Council, 102, 103, 106
  mentioned, 31, 94, 95, 99, 123, 125, 127, 136
Eisenhower, Dwight D.
  administrative reforms and, 34
  Goals for America commission, 97
  initiatives and, 9
  mentioned, 156
  policy experts and, 41n
  presidential programs and, 58, 59
Eisenhower, Milton, 41n, 55
Eizenstat, Stuart
  Carter campaign and, 118–19, 121, 122, 123
  domestic policy under Carter and, 124–30, 131, 136, 194 n.42
Elazar, Daniel, 151
Elfin, Mel, 53, 96
Elites. *See* Intervening elites; Policy experts; Politicians; Professional administrators

Ellwood, John W., 192 n.2
Elman, Sandra, 24
Elsberg, Daniel, 110
Energy Resources Council, 107–8
Enterprise zones, 158–59
Enthoven, Alain C., 192 n.1
"Entrepreneurial" public executives,
    18–20
Environmental policy
    in Johnson administration, 75, 76
Erikson, Erik, 181 n.8
Etheridge, Lloyd S., 13, 14, 181 n.8

Falk, Richard A., 119, 180 n.5
Fallows, James, 128, 136, 137
Family Assistance Program, 6. See also
    Moynihan, dispute with Burns
Federal deficit, 149–50, 160
Feldman, Meyer, 74
Feldstein, Martin, 111, 144, 150, 162
Ferman, Barbara, 197 n.6
Fesler, James W., 16, 181 n.14
Finletter, Thomas, 46
Fleishman, Joel, 119
Flemming, Arthur, 55
Ford, Gerald
    academic experts and, 21, 110–14
    events of administration of, 105–6
    Rockefeller and, 106–9
    sources of ideas of, 109–10
Ford Foundation, 34–35, 63
Foucault, Michel, 87, 168
Fox, Ken, 170, 173
Frank, Jerome, 44
Frankel, Charles, 98
Freeman, Orville, 57
Freund, Paul, 70
Frieden, Bernard J., 80, 100, 165,
    187 n.42
Friedman, Milton, 22, 102, 111, 143,
    144–45, 149, 162
Fuller, Lon, 55

Gagnon, Alain G., 182 n.21
Gaither, James, 78–79
Galbraith, John Kenneth, 22, 30–31
    Johnson and, 70
    Kennedy and, 60, 61
    mentioned, 65, 115, 129, 162
    New Deal and, 43–44
    primary campaign of 1959 and, 46,
        47, 50, 52
    transition period influence of, 57
Gardner, John, 40–41, 45, 75, 76, 77,
    87, 136, 185 n.51
Gardner, Richard, 120, 121
Garment, Leonard, 89, 91–92

Garth, David, 27
Gatekeepers, 4, 29–32, 40
Gelb, Leslie, 193 n.19
Gephart, Richard, 12
Gergen, Kenneth J., 183 n.10
Gilmore, Robert, 183 n.4
Ginsberg, Benjamin, 27–28, 182 n.26
Ginsberg, Eli, 22, 129
Girtzman, Milt, 119
Glazer, Nathan, 22, 76, 100, 110–11,
    118, 157
Glenn, John, 12, 15
Glenn, Tom, 133
Goggin, Malcolm L., 188 n.60
Goldberg, Arthur, 61, 133
Goldhamer, Herbert, 39–40
Goldman, Eric, 70–71, 75
Goldwater, Barry, 55, 96
Goldwin, Robert, 110, 111, 191 n.63
Golebiowska, Ewa, 183 n.12
Goodman, Robert, 27
Goodwin, Richard, 5, 52, 61, 68, 70, 74
    mentioned, 100, 121, 136
Gorbachev, Mikhail, 171
Gordon, Kermit, 60, 61, 74, 79
Gordon, Lincoln, 98
Gore, Albert, 12
Gorman, Michael, 63
Gouldner, Alvin W., 33, 87, 182 n.25,
    194 n.54
Governance, influence of dominant
    elites on, 5, 115. See also specific
    presidents
Gramsci, Antonio, 168
Great Society programs. See also
    Johnson, Lyndon; Neoconservative
    critique
    antipoverty war and, 71–73
    Califano task forces and, 78–84
    evaluation of task forces and, 84–88
    Johnson's Ann Arbor speech and, 68,
        74, 75
    lasting impact of, 174
    Moyers task forces and, 74–78
    Nixon and, 105
    Urban Institute and, 172
Green, Edith, 62
Green, Phillip, 63
Greenberg, Sanford D., 187 n.29
Greenspan, Alan, 92, 110, 141, 144
Greenstein, Fred, 12–13, 180 n.2

Haar, Charles, 75, 76, 79, 80, 84, 119
Habermas, Jurgen, 87, 166, 167
Hackett, David, 62, 63–64, 65, 71, 72
Haig, Alexander, 12
Haldeman, H. R., 31, 94, 99

Hall, Max, 186 n.61
Hall, Peter, 158
Halleck, Charles, 54
Halperin, Samuel, 77
Hanks, Nancy, 19, 97, 98
Hannah, John, 55
Hargrove, Erwin C., 18–19, 125, 126, 127, 128, 130, 135, 136, 179 n.1, 182 n.17
Harlow, Bryce, 98
Harrington, Michael, 31, 65
Harris, C. Lowell, 143
Harris, Seymour, 47, 144
Hart, Gary, 12, 13
Hart, John, 191 n.50
Hartmann, Robert L., 106, 107, 191 n.51
Hartz, Louis, 28
Hauge, Gabriel, 54
Hayes, Frederick, 64, 73
Head Start program, 86
Heard, Alexander, 181 n.7
Heclo, Hugh, 108, 179 n.1, 188 n.58, 189 n.19
Heineman, Ben W., Sr., 79, 91, 94, 125, 188 n.7
Heineman Report, 91, 94
Heller, Walter, 57, 61, 65, 66, 74, 129, 144
Henderson, Deidre, 49–52, 54
Heritage Foundation, 171, 173
Herrenstein, Richard, 112
Hess, Stephen, 90, 95
Hirsch, E. D., Jr., 167
Hitch, Charles T., 192 n.1
Hofstadter, Richard, 70
Holden, Matthew, Jr., 30, 31
Hollins, Ernest, 12
Hoover, Herbert, 32, 40, 43
Hoover, J. Edgar, 17
Hoover Institution, 171
Hornig, Don, 74
Howard, John, 51
Howe, Harold, 187 n.30
Howe, Mark deWolfe, 50, 170
Humanism, class-based, 166–69
Humphrey, Hubert H., 50, 51, 56, 61, 98, 118
Hunter, David, 63
Huntington, Samuel, 51, 120, 121

Ideologues, 28–29
Ideology ("dreamboats"), 4, 174–75, 176
    Reagan policies and, 140, 147–51, 154–56, 159–61
Image makers, 26–28

Ink, Dwight, 20, 101, 190 n.31
Interagency task forces, 69, 79, 127, 132, 133
Intervening elites. See also Policy experts; Politicians; Professional administrators; Think tanks
    concerns about influence of, 87
    relationships among, 90, 115–17, 145–46
    theory of, 10–11
    types of, 3

Jackson, Henry, 56, 119
Jackson, Jesse, 12
Jacoby, Russell, 25
James, William, 163, 172
Janowitz, Mario, 192 n.68
Jencks, Christopher, 111, 112
Jennings, M. Kent, 181 n.8
Jenson, Arthur, 112
Johnson, Andrew, 109
Johnson, Harry G., 192 n.68
Johnson, Howard, 164
Johnson, Lady Bird, 14, 76, 81
Johnson, Lyndon
    academic experts and, 21, 37, 40, 53, 67–87
    antipoverty program, 66, 72–73
    Congress and, 60
    "creative federalism" of, 152
    education policy and, 75, 76–77, 83
    gatekeepers and, 31
    mentioned, 6, 20, 90, 106
    policy development process and, 137
    rhetoric vs. ideas and, 32
    as Senate majority leader, 9, 46
    source of ideas for, 5
    urban policy and, 75, 76, 79–81, 82–83
Jones, Charles O., 125–26, 127, 131–32, 136
Jones, Roger, 20
Jordan, Hamilton, 121–24, 126, 131
Juvenile Delinquency and Youth Offenses Control Act of 1961, 62–64

Kaden, Lewis B., 189 n.28
Kaiser, Edgar, 79
Kaplan, Marshall, 165, 187 n.42, 191 n.49
Kaysen, Carl, 51, 121
Kelly, Peter, 171
Kemp, Jack, 12, 148, 149, 158, 196 n.53
Kennedy, Edward, 47, 133
Kennedy, Jacqueline, 56

Kennedy, John F.
    antipoverty program of, 40, 64–66
    appeal to intellectuals, 55
    assassination of, 66, 70, 74, 114
    campaign advisers and, 46–54
    Congress and, 60
    gatekeepers and, 31
    mentioned, 6, 12, 68, 77, 145
    source of ideas for, 5, 6
    transition period advisers and, 56–
        59
    use of policy experts, 21, 59–66, 67
Kennedy, Joseph (civil engineer), 76
Kennedy, Robert, 47, 60, 62, 71, 72,
    114, 131, 133
Kennedy, Rosemary, 62
Keppel, Frank, 77, 100, 187 n.23
Kernell, Samuel, 180 n.3
Kerner Commission (Commission on
    Civil Disorder), 69
Kerr, Clark, 162
Kessel, John H., 21n, 41n, 103, 163,
    179 n.1, 181 n.9, 188 n.3,
    191 n.48, 197 n.7
Kettl, Donald F., 16, 181 n.14
Keynesian economics, 34, 35–36, 130–
    31, 144–45
Keyserling, Leon, 61
Khrushchev, Nikita, 51
Killian, James, 41n, 45, 55
King, Gary, 84, 179 n.3, 187 n.32
King, Martin Luther, Jr., 72, 114
Kingdon, John W., 15, 181 n.12
Kirkland, Lane, 129
Kissinger, Henry
    Ford administration and, 106, 109
    mentioned, 7, 49, 94, 96, 98, 103,
        110
    Nixon administration and, 89, 90,
        92, 93, 104
    Prospect for America project and, 97
Kistiakowsky, George, 41n, 55
Klein, Lawrence, 122, 124, 125, 129,
    145
Knowledge ("reality time"), 4
Koenig, Louis, 179 n.1
Kozak, Andrew F., 148n
Kraft, Joe, 52
Kravitz, Sanford, 64, 73
Kristol, Irving, 86, 111, 118, 157
Krogh, Harold Christian, 191 n.48

Ladd, Everett, Jr., 182 n.24
Laffer, Arthur, 143, 148, 149
Lake, Celinda, 182 n.26
Lampman, Robert, 65

Lance, Bert, 126, 131, 135, 136, 137
Land, Edwin, 70, 77
Landis, James, 44
LaRouche, Lyndon, 12
Lasswell, Harold, 12, 14, 23n, 147,
    181 n.8
Latham, Earl, 49, 50
Lawrence, William, 64
Lekachman, Robert, 192 n.68
Lemann, Nicholas, 72, 186 n.60
Lerner, Daniel, 23n, 168, 175
Levi, Edward, 110
Levin, Martin A., 197 n.6
Levinson, Lawrence, 78
Levitan, Sara, 188 n.60
Lewis, Ann, 27
Lilienthal, David, 19
Lindblom, Charles, 148n, 166
Lindsay, Franklin A., 92, 93
Linowitz, Sol, 129
Lipset, Seymour Martin, 46, 182 n.24
Literary criticism, 167–68
Long, Norton E., 181 n.15
Loomis, Harry, 99, 101
Luce, Henry, 53
Lynn, James, 110
Lynton, Ernest, 24

McCracken, Paul, 99, 102, 103, 144,
    146
McCulley, Richard T., 68, 84–85, 95
McDonald, Dwight, 65
McDonnell, Lorraine, 140, 149
McGovern, George, 12, 28, 117
McIntyre, James, 126
MacKenzie, Calvin, 182 n.20
McNamara, Robert, 40, 78, 115–16
McPherson, Harry, 31, 67, 70, 71, 80,
    82, 83, 90
Macy, John, 20, 187 n.39
Manatos, Mike, 82
Manning, Bayless, 98
March, James, 18
Marland, Sidney, 77
Marshall, Alfred, 145
Marshall, Dale Rogers, 81
Marshall, F. Ray, 127
Martilla, John, 27
Martin, John Barlow, 46
Mason, Edward, 22
Matthews, Donald, 87
Matthews, F. David, 110
"Maximum Feasible Participation," 65–
    66, 72, 73
May, Ernest, 92
May, Martin, 192 n.68

Mead, Margaret, 70
Meadow, Dennis, 163
Media, 26–28, 39, 53–54, 122–23
Meese, Edwin, 31
Meltsner, Arnold, 116
Merriam, Robert, 41n
Meyers, John, 51
Meyerson, Martin, 76, 100, 172
Miles, Rufus, 5
Miller, Isabel, 73, 186 n.60
Milliken, Max, 98
Mitchell, William C., 180 n.6
Mobilization for Youth (MFY), 63–64
Model Cities program, 79–81, 82–83, 165
Moley, Raymond C., 44
Mondale, Walter, 12, 47, 122, 130, 133
Monsen, Joseph, 54, 55
Moos, Malcolm, 41n, 54
Morton, Thurston, 55
Moyers, Bill, 31, 67, 70, 71, 74–78, 79, 136
Moynihan, Daniel Patrick
    dispute with Burns, 6, 101–5
    Ford and, 111
    Johnson and, 71
    mentioned, 22, 91, 110, 192 n.68
    neoconservative critique and, 72, 112, 113, 118, 157, 165
    Nixon administration and, 89, 90, 98, 100, 101–2, 104
Multiple advocacy strategy, 108–9
Muth, Richard, 143

Nakahata, Andrew, 192 n.4
Napolitan, Joe, 27
Nathan, Richard, 22, 98, 102, 154, 189 n.17, 190 n.32
National Academy of Science (NAS), 38–39
National Commission on Urban Problems, 69
National Institutes of Health (NIH), 37, 45
National Research Council, 36–37
National Science Foundation, 36–37, 45
National Security Council, 125
Natural scientists, 7, 33–34, 38–39
Neel, Jennifer, 82, 84, 187 n.29
Nelson, Richard, 70
Neoconservative critique, 29, 80, 86, 111–14, 131, 152, 163
Neustadt, Richard, 180 n.3
    Johnson and, 70
    Kennedy and, 50–51, 52, 56, 58

mentioned, 22, 59, 86, 180 n.3
Nixon administration and, 92
New Deal, 43–44
New Federalism, 151–56, 160
New Frontier, 37, 71–72, 177. See also Kennedy, John F.
Niemi, Richard G., 181 n.8
NIH. See National Institutes of Health
Niles, Roger, 27
Nimetz, Matthew, 78
Nisbet, Robert, 112
Nixon, Richard M.
    academic support for, 55
    advisers in 1960 election, 54–55
    economic policy and, 145
    gatekeepers and, 31
    mentioned, 6, 41, 126
    "New Federalism" of, 152
    policy process under, 102–5, 116
    prominent appointments by, 89–90
    relationship with appointees, 93–95
    rhetoric vs. ideas and, 32
    Rockefeller experts and, 95–99
    source of ideas for, 5, 6
    task forces under, 99–102
    transition period and, 89–93
    urban policy and, 81, 157
Nofziger, Lyn, 28, 141
Nourse, Edwin C., 34

O'Brien, Larry, 27
O'Furner, Mary, 43
Ohlin, Lloyd, 63, 64, 73
Okun, Arthur, 52, 119, 129, 144
Oppenheimer, Robert, 45
Orlans, Harold, 192 n.68
Osborne, John, 109, 191 n.56
Outriders, 3–4, 26–29, 31
Owen, Henry, 118, 121
Owen, Wilfred, 120

Palmer, John, 139
Patterson, Orlando, 111
Pechman, Joseph, 61, 170
Percy, Charles, 54, 132
Perkins, Roswell, 189 n.24
Personal staff. See Gatekeepers
Peterson, George, 153, 154, 155
Petracca, Mark P., 27, 182 n.26
Pfiffner, James P., 180 n.3
Pifer, Alan, 100
Planning-Programming-Budgeting System (PPBS), 85, 115–16
Pluralist theory, 9–10
Policy analysis field, 116–17, 166–67

Policy experts. *See also* Think tanks
  characteristics of, 20–26
  decline in influence of, 124–30,
    170n
  future of, 174–78
  pre-sixties influence of, 42–46
  Reagan administration and, 140–47
  sixties success of, 33–42
Political appointees
  Carter administration and, 128
  Nixon administration and, 93–95,
    105
  professional administrators and, 18
Political philosophers, 28–29. *See also*
  Capitalism
Political scientists, 34–36
Politicians, 11–15. *See also* Political
  appointees
Polsters. *See* Image makers
Pomper, Philip, 4, 6, 176
Porter, Roger, 108, 110
Powell, Adam Clayton, 62
Power, linguistic interpretation of,
  167–68
PPBS. *See* Planning-Programming-
  Budgeting System
Preservation of natural beauty policy,
  75, 76
Presidential commissions
  in Ford administration, 110
  in Johnson administration, 69
  in Nixon administration, 102
Presidential initiative, 5–6, 8–9. See
  also *specific presidents*
Presidential politics, stages of, 5. *See
  also* Campaign for election; Gover-
  nance; *specific presidents*; Transi-
  tion period
Price, Raymond, 92
Professional administrators
  characteristics of, 15–20
  Nixon administration and, 93–95,
    104–5
  relations with outside experts, 90
Progressivism, 42–43
Project Camelot Affair, 37–38
Prospect for America project, 97
Prothro, James, 87
Psychologists, 36
Pye, Lucian, 51

Rafshoon, Gerald, 130
Rafsky, William, 80
Ragsdale, Lyn, 84, 179 n.3, 187 n.32
Rand Corporation, 171–72
Ranney, Austin, 35, 42

Rapkin, Chester, 80
Rathgens, George, 121
Ravitch, Diane, 197 n.3
Rayburn, Sam, 6, 46
Reachtenburg, William E., 179 n.1
Reagan, Ronald
  academic experts and, 6–7, 21, 22,
    88, 140–47, 160, 162, 164
  career administrators and, 18
  deficit reduction and, 149–50
  early consensus on, 139–40
  economic policy and, 147–51
  gatekeepers and, 31
  ideology and, 29, 140, 147–51, 154–
    56, 159–61
  initiatives and, 8
  New Federalism and, 152–56
  rhetoricians and, 28, 32, 140
"Reality time," 4
Redford, Emmette S., 35, 68, 71, 84–
  85, 95
Reedy, George, 78
Reese, Matt, 27
Regan, Donald, 31, 146
Reischauer, Edward, 120
Reischauer, Robert D., 169
Republican Committee on Program and
  Progress, 54
Reuther, Walter, 79
Rhetoric ("blue smoke"), 4, 175–76.
  See also Image makers
Rhoads, James B., 179 n.1
Ribicoff, Abraham, 80, 132
Rich, Michael J., 196 n.51
Richardson, Eliot, 18, 124
Rickover, Admiral Hyman, 17, 19
Riesman, David, 70, 77, 110
Rivlin, Alice, 99, 170
Robertson, Pat, 12
Roche, John, 71
Rockefeller, David, 10, 98, 119, 120,
  121
Rockefeller, Laurance, 76
Rockefeller, Nelson
  Ford administration and, 105, 106–
    9, 114
  mentioned, 89, 93, 120, 131
  Nixon campaign advisers and, 95–99
  use of experts by, 95–99, 121
Roelofs, H. Mark, 3
Romney, George, 190 n.30
Ronan, William, 97
Roosevelt, Franklin D., 8, 43–44, 46,
  68, 134, 145
Roosevelt, Theodore, 43
Rossell, Christine, 197 n.3

Rossi, Peter, 197 n.6
Rossiter, Clinton, 180 n.1
Rostow, Elspeth, 98
Rostow, Eugene, 98
Rostow, Walt, 7, 51, 52, 98, 185 n.51
Rowan, Harry, 110
Rowe, James, 44
Rumsfeld, Donald, 106–7, 108, 110
Rusk, Dean, 31

Sabato, Larry, 182 n.26
Salamon, Lester, 85–86, 189 n.19
Saltonstall, Leverett, 99
Samuelson, Paul, 22, 60, 144, 148n, 149, 162
Sasso, John, 27
Sawhill, Isabel, 139
Sawhill, John, 129
Sayre, Wallace, 98
Schelling, Thomas, 98
Schick, Allen, 192 n.1
Schlesinger, Arthur M., Jr.
    countercyclical clock and, 161
    Kennedy and, 52, 56–57
    mentioned, 31, 70, 71, 115, 180 n.1
    Stevenson and, 46, 47, 50
Schlesinger, James, 110, 127
Schottland, Charles, 51
Schultz, Charles, 74, 78, 119, 124, 144
Schuster, Jack H., 182 n.19
Schwartz, David, 180 n.6
Schwartz, John E., 188 n.60
Science, repudiation of, 167–69
Scientists. See Natural scientists; Policy experts; Social scientists
Scranton, William, 164
Seaman, Barrett, 139
Searle, John, 167, 168
Sears, John, 27, 92, 141
Seidman, Harold, 20, 84, 95, 183 n.4, 186 n.21
Seidman, Phillip, 119
Seligman, Lester G., 179 n.1, 189 n.19, 190 n.39
Semple, Robert, 102
Shalala, Donna, 119
Shoup, Lawrence H., 119–20, 180 n.5
Shriver, Eunice, 62
Shriver, Sargent, 57, 72, 73, 119
Shultz, George, 22, 98, 103, 115, 162
    Ford administration and, 106
    Nixon administration and, 90
    Reagan administration and, 141, 143–44, 146, 149
Silva, Edward T., 43
Simon, Herbert A., 23n

Simon, Paul, 12
Simonton, Dean Keith, 180 n.2, 181 n.8
Slaughter, Sheila A., 43
Smith, Hedrick, 124
Smith, Howard, 62
Smith, James Allen, 165, 167, 170–71, 172–73, 184 n.22
Smith, Lee, 190 n.28
Smithies, Arthur, 51
Smock, Raymond W., 179 n.1
"Social indicators," 37
Social scientists
    antagonism toward, within academia, 166–69
    as intervening elite vs. revolutionaries, 168–69
    political debate without, 174–75
    sixties success of, 33–42
    skepticism and, 38–39, 165, 172–73, 176
    socioeconomic developments and, 162–64
    think tanks and, 169–74
Sociologists, 36
Solomon, Ezra, 143
Solow, Robert, 149, 162
Sommers, Albert, 119, 129
Sorauf, Frank, 181 n.7
Sorensen, Theodore, 31, 136, 141, 170
    Carter and, 121
    Kennedy and, 46, 48, 49–52, 57, 59, 118, 121, 122
Sowell, Thomas, 192 n.68
Spencer, Herbert, 112
Spring, William, 133
Squier, Robert, 27
Staats, Elmer, 20, 74
Stans, Maurice, 92
Starr, Joseph Albert, 119
Stein, Al, 119
Stein, Herbert, 146
Stevenson, Adlai, 46–54, 56, 60, 115, 185 n.36
Stockman, David, 139, 140, 149, 150, 157
Stouffer, Samuel, 45
Strauss, Robert, 131
Sundquist, James, 52, 60, 99, 100, 180 n.1, 194 n.42
Supply-side economics, 147–51, 160
Swartz, Thomas R., 148n

Tabb, David, 81
Taggart, Robert, 188 n.60
Takanori, Mizuno, 171

Talk, types of, 4
Task forces
   Carter and, 121, 122, 125
   insider vs. outsider groups and, 68–69, 79
   Johnson and, 67–69, 73–78, 82–88
   Kennedy and, 57–59
   Nixon and, 99–102, 103–5
   Reagan and, 141–44
   Rockefeller and, 96–98
Teeters, Robert, 27
Teller, Edward, 98
Think tanks, 7, 169–74
Thomas, Norman, 77
Thurow, Lester, 22, 119
Titus, David, 198 n.21
Tobin, James, 61
Traficant, James, 12
Transition period, 5
   Carter and, 122–24
   Kennedy and, 56–59
   Nixon and, 93, 96–99
   Reagan and, 146–47
Trent, Darrell, 92, 142–43
Trilateral Commission, 10, 98, 119–21, 122, 124
Truman, David, 8, 51, 180 n.1
Truman, Harry S., 34, 58, 59, 93, 94, 106, 127
Tugwell, Rexford G., 44

Udall, Morris, 119
Urban Institute, 171–72, 173
Urban policy. See also Antipoverty programs
   academic debate over, 165
   Carter and, 132–35, 156–57
   Johnson administration and, 75, 76, 79–81, 82–83
   neoconservative critique and, 112–13
   Nixon and, 81, 157
   Reagan and, 154, 156–59, 160

Vance, Cyrus, 124
Van Dyke, Ted, 27
Vernon, Raymond, 63, 100

Vietnam War, 82–83, 163
Volker, Paul, 15, 144, 149

Walker, David, 85, 186 n.15
Walras, Leon, 145
Wanniski, Jude, 148–49
Watson, Jack, 120, 122–24
Watson, Marvin, 81
Weatherford, Stephen, 140, 149
Weaver, Kent, 171, 173–74
Weaver, Robert, 110
Webb, James, 19
Weber, Max, 24, 29
Weidenbaum, Murray, 144, 162
Weiss, Carol, 22
Welfare reform, 101, 102–5. See also Antipoverty programs
White, Cliff, 27
White, Lee, 74
White, Theodore H., 33, 39, 44–45, 46, 48n, 135
White House staff. See Gatekeepers
Whitman, Marina V., 129
Whyte, William Foote, 36
Wiesner, Jerome, 129
Wildavsky, Aaron, 180 n.1, 192 n.1
Wills, Gary, 139–40
Wilson, Carroll, 98, 120
Wilson, James Q., 91, 100, 180 n.4
Wilson, Woodrow, 43
Winchester, Lucy, 190 n.31
Wirthlin, Richard, 27
Wirtz, Willard, 185 n.36
Wolanin, Thomas R., 179 n.1
Wolman, Harold, 77, 165
Wood, Robert, 7, 75, 76, 79–81, 83
Woodson, Robert, 197 n.53
Wooten, James, 123
World War II era, 44–45

Yarmolinsky, Adam, 56, 185 n.51
Ylvisaker, Paul, 63, 64, 71, 79, 83, 100, 155–56, 186 n.60
Young, Whitney, 79
Youth Employment program, 132–35

Zacharias, Jerrold, 77
Zink, Steven D., 179 n.1